THE
IRISH
IN
AMERICA

THE IRISH IN AMERICA

EDITED BY **MICHAEL COFFEY** ✳ WITH TEXT BY **TERRY GOLWAY**

HYPERION
NEW YORK

Library of Congress Cataloging-in-Publication Data

The Irish in America / edited by Michael Coffey ; with text by Terry Golway. —1st ed.
        p.   cm.
     Includes bibliographical references.
     ISBN 0-0768-6344-7
     I. Irish Americans—History. I. Coffey, Michael. II. Golway, Terry.

E184.161684 1997   97–21907
973'.049162—dc21   CIP

Design and Production by Claudyne Bianco Bedell

THIS BOOK IS DEDICATED TO OUR PARENTS

✿

Tom and Mary Golway

John and Eleanor Coffey

CONTENTS

*

This is an Irish book in more than subject matter: It's Irish in soul. It makes you proud, and it makes you cry. It makes you smile and tap your foot to the deep, remembered beat of the music and the poetry—and it makes you look backward and forward at the same time. It breaks your heart and lifts your heart.

To open it and read the story of my great-great grandparents, Patrick Kennedy and Bridget Murphy, reminds me of the hard sea and the hard roads my own family traveled from the potato blight to East Boston and beyond. Leaving the Famine land, the Irish came to a promised land, almost the only place they could go and still live. But people can't eat promises—and the reality had to be pulled out of a new urban soil of struggle, deprivation, and sorrow. Here you will read how Patrick Kennedy died, exhausted and stricken with cholera, at the age of thirty-five. His wife carried on—and worked on—and raised their five children. To me, their greatness is more than a matter of genealogy; it symbolizes the daring of a desperate generation that left the land they loved so they and their families could survive and hope again.

Frank McCourt tells us how the Irish still at home always remember the Great Famine, but Irish Americans have not written much about the struggle of their own since they came here. Perhaps the reason is that, at least measured on history's grand scale, the Irish in America rose so fast and then so far. But we can't forget what came before; it teaches us that poverty is something to be redeemed, not tolerated. That's the lesson we surely need to learn anew at a time when the poor are out of fashion and written off. Today, their names aren't Kennedy or Murphy, but the truth of our own past calls us to care and to act.

Of course, there's politics, which in urban America became nearly a synonym for being Irish. Many doors might have been closed to the Irish when they first came, from the Union League to Wall Street. Ultimately, our people forced those doors open, too; but first there was the vote. Terry Golway shows us how the Irish Americans built power precinct by precinct. Thomas Mallon rejoices that many at last became Republicans. (He notes a leading indicator: in 1964, in his Irish town in New

York, voters generally went for Barry Goldwater for president, but, out of tribal pride, pulled the lever for Robert Kennedy for the Senate. Tom, thanks for the help on the way out.)

Robert Shrum traces the Irish journey to the presidency, and Peggy Noonan tells us more about Ronald Reagan, for whom she wrote memorable and very Irish speeches. She recounts slipping one of the favorite poems of her Irish aunt Mary Jane, who'd spent her life in America as a domestic, into Reagan's speech on his return from the anniversary of D-day and a trip around the world. She says Mary Jane would have loved it. I only wonder if President Reagan knew.

There's so much in this book, as rich as the Irish experience itself: Pete Hamill explaining the Americanization of the Irish through the prism of his own life, and Golway revealing the way the Irish changed America. In the performing arts, the marquees have blazoned the names of Eugene O'Neill and Helen Hayes—at first O'Neill didn't want her in one of *his* plays. There was Katie "Scarlett" O'Hara in *Gone With the Wind*—but played by an Englishwoman with a Southern accent. Authentically, there were George M. Cohan, Grace Kelly, and Gene Kelly, a sky full of Irish stars and a more earthbound legion including the likes of Malachy McCourt, who tells his story here with power, eloquence, and a rich lacing of humor. Today, there's an Irish explosion in film and on stage and we hear the clashing chorus of Irish sounds in U2's rock and *Riverdance*, the latest manifestation of an Irish music that has sounded across America for a hundred and a half years. In literature there have been F. Scott Fitzgerald, James T. Farrell, John O'Hara, and Bill Shannon, who criticized O'Hara—and now Frank McCourt and his *Angela's Ashes*. In commentary, we have Jimmy Breslin and Pete Hamill, Mary McGrory, Maureen Dowd, Michael Kelly, and, to my own more than occasional regret, William F. Buckley Jr.

So various are the Irish viewpoints that at one point an Irishwoman, Elizabeth Gurley Flynn, was leading the American Communist Party, while the first Irish Catholic president, John Fitzgerald Kennedy, was swearing the nation's resolve to win "the long twilight struggle" against communism.

This book traces the green thread, emerald bright, in the American fabric, its many hues, its political contradictions, its hurts, joys, and contributions. If you're Irish you have to read this book; if you read it, you will want to be Irish.

Finally, I have to note that while I don't subscribe to all of Denis Leary's humor, he does remind us of one truly eternal truth: Cabbage, which would have been steak in the Famine, is something most of our kids—and maybe most of us—won't eat. We have come a long way.

—REP. JOSEPH P. KENNEDY II

America is an immigrant country. In size, in scale, in the diversity of its peoples, no other land can challenge its claim as the ultimate melting pot. Half a millennia ago there were Native Americans here, perhaps two million spread across the vast continent. Since that time the population has increased more than a hundredfold. Waves of Dutch, English, Spanish, and French were the earliest colonizers; there were Scots and Irish and Germans and Italians in their wake looking for work or fortune or freedom; Africans came in large numbers, though not always of their own volition; there have been influxes of Jews from Europe, Hungarians, Poles, many fleeing oppressive regimes or abominable pogroms; more recently, immigrants from Latin America, the Far East, and the Caribbean have come for both political and economic reasons. All have contributed to the enrichment of our collective culture, subtly changing the way America looks and sounds and thinks of itself.

But of all these immigrations, none has been longer, more sustained, or more storied than that of a people who came from a small island, hardly larger than the state of South Carolina, that has sat precariously on the western flank of Great Britain since time immemorial: Ireland.

As the pages that follow will remind readers, the Irish came early—but was St. Brendan the first, or was it Belfast's William Ayers aboard ship with Columbus? The mists of history own that answer. But what history does incontrovertibly show is that Irish immigration to America reached unprecedented rates shortly after the potato blight *Phytopthora infestans* ruined its first crop in the Irish fields in 1845. It was an enormous and sudden stream of hungry and frightened Irish, most of them Roman Catholics, many of them farmers, a good proportion of them native speakers of Irish, who came. And kept coming. Slowly, the struggles of those early Famine immigrants, their children, and their children's children made America a more inviting place for the Irish to come to, and for others as well, but it was not easy.

This book intends to tell that story, to render the character and soul of the Irish people who came to America, and to do so by looking at the institutions and folkways they brought with them, as well as the ones they invented here on the fly. For it is the institutions—the bricks and mortar of the scrabbling immigrant life—and the traditions—the songs, the airs, the popular myths and myth-ical figures—that really carry a people's sense of who they are from generation to generation.

Terry Golway provides the encompassing historical narrative within which our story of the Irish in America unfolds, limning not only the brute facts of the Famine years, but detailing the kind of America the Irish came to and what they did and how. For the most part they founded churches and schools and orphanages; they built neighborhoods of influence in parishes and political precincts; they cleaned homes and tended children; they built canals and unions and fought wars; they sang and danced to whatever beat the paying public fancied; they wrote books and poems; they boxed and played ball and charmed Hollywood. And from fairly early on, they ran for office. By 1961, on a cold January day in Washington, D.C., more than just Irish Americans welcomed an Irish Catholic great-grandson of a Famine immigrant as he took the oath of office as President of the United States.

That was not the end of the story, for the story of a people should never end. The Irish in America are now an American story; their success in escaping servitude, in overcoming discrimination, in ascending to power in both the public and private sectors, has given them different perspectives and different priorities. We tell that chapter, too. And to complicate and challenge the popular notion that the Irish in America are now contented homeowners manicuring their lawns in the suburbs and besporting the green but once a year, a new wave of young Irish are reaching these shores—bright, intelligent, ambitious, with a spirit freshened by a liberalization in Ireland itself, and determined not to fall prey to some old demons.

It is a remarkably varied tale to tell, and we have been graced with a variety of authentic voices to help tell it in their own words. When your mind's ear hears the Limerick accent of Frank McCourt and his brother Malachy, the Bronx assurances of Dennis Smith, the lyrical flights of Pete Hamill, the precisely measured observations of Tom Mallon or Peter Quinn, the warm reveries of Peggy Noonan and Mary Higgins Clark or the gruff wisdom of Jason Robards talking about Eugene O'Neill, you will recognize, we hope, the sound and the spirit of the Irish, living and breathing in America.

—MICHAEL COFFEY
JUNE 16, 1997

ACKNOWLEDGMENTS

＊

We would like to thank several people whose advice and insights throughout this project have been invaluable: Peter Quinn, for his encyclopedic knowledge of things Irish-American; Greg Delanty for his assistance in culling poems and songs for the book; Chris Cahill for facilitating access to the holdings of the American Irish Historical Society; Bob Scally and Angela Carter for their bibliographical assistance; Dermot McEvoy for his unerring memory for names of Irish Democrats anywhere, any time; and Tom Dillon for his suggestions on approaches to the work of Eugene O'Neill and John Ford. We would also like to thank the filmmaker Tom Lennon for the inspirational glimpses he allowed of his work-in-progress on the Irish immigration to America.

The advice and encouraging words, early on, from Marylouise Oates, Ed Burns, Joan Ganz Cooney and Liz Smith, as well our agent, John Wright, were instrumental in getting this project off the ground, for which we are grateful.

The vision of designer Claudyne Bedell gave this book its final, handsome look; photo researcher Deborah Bull worked tirelessly to run down obscure photographs and engravings; Navorn Johnson walked us nimbly through production traffic; and Jennifer Lang made many of the administrative tasks less than excruciating. We thank them.

We would also like to thank the contributors to this volume, who, without exception, came through for us in timely fashion.

We must also mention those people behind the scenes who gave us the time and space to devote to the project; namely, our wives and partners, Eileen Duggan and Jenny Doctorow, whose forbearance during months of late night toil made this book possible; and our "day-job" employers, *The New York Observer*'s Arthur Carter and Peter Kaplan, who granted a much-needed leave to Terry Golway, and the staff at *Publishers Weekly*, which left Michael Coffey alone at the fax machine while he anxiously awaited copy.

Finally, we'd like to thank our editor at Hyperion, Maureen O'Brien, whose insistent good cheer and smart counsel gave this book the direction, focus, and momentum it needed.

—TERRY GOLWAY AND MICHAEL COFFEY

THE
IRISH
IN
AMERICA

CHAPTER 1

THE GREAT FAMINE

BETWEEN HUNGER AND

THE WHITE HOUSE

THE ROADS and lanes of Ireland were choked with the poor and the hungry when Patrick Kennedy, the twenty-six-year-old son of a farming family in County Wexford, decided to join the Irish exodus to America. The year was 1849, the worst year of the most fearsome hunger Ireland had ever known, the worst year in the greatest human catastrophe of nineteenth-century Europe—the Great Irish Famine. For generations, the Irish poor had depended on the potato, rich in nutrition and easy to grow, for their daily existence. To be sure, they grew other crops, and even now, as Patrick Kennedy paid his respects to the parish priest and left the village of Dunganstown to begin his journey to the New World, Ireland's green fields were abundant with barley and oats and wheat. Livestock grazed peacefully, growing fat and content as the slaughterhouse beckoned.

Where potatoes once grew, however, all was ruin. A mysterious blight had appeared after a wet summer in 1845, and newspapers reported with barely concealed fear that the disease had laid waste to potato beds literally overnight. "In one instance the [farmer] had been digging potatoes—the finest he had ever seen—from a particular field . . . up to Monday last; and on digging in the same ridge on Tuesday he found the tubers blasted, and unfit for the use of man or beast," the Dublin-based *Freeman's Journal* reported. In those few words, the worst nightmares of the Irish people were about to come true.

Famine death and immigration reduced Ireland's population from 8.1 million in 1840 to 6.5 million ten years later; normal rates of growth should have brought the population to 9 million. Today the population, including Northern Ireland, is about 5 million.

The newspaper referred to the blight as a "cholera" for lack of a better name. In fact, the blight was a fungus brought to Ireland from America via the Continent. Years later, the fungus was diagnosed and given a formal scholarly name, *Phytopthora infestans*.

The land Patrick Kennedy, was about to leave had become a mass grave. By the time the Famine was over and the potato restored to health, a million people were dead and another million were scattered across the seas. In the west of Ireland, where the hunger did its worst damage, the stark beauty of the region known as Connemara was scarred with derelict cottages and abandoned villages. The *Times* of London noted with unseemly glee that "an Irishman in Connemara will soon be as rare a sight as a Red Indian on the shores of Manhattan."

It seemed for a time that the newspaper's ghoulish prediction might become a reality. In the years immediately following the end of starvation in Ireland, another million people boarded vessels that took them elsewhere, so that between 1845 and 1860, nearly two million Irish immigrants—a quarter of the Irish nation—were flung onto the shores of America. Bishop John Hughes of New York, an Irish immigrant who took great pleasure in upsetting the city's native-born ascendancy, called the tidal wave at his doorstep the "scattered debris of the Irish nation."

Among the later immigrants were Edward and Mary O'Neill from County Kilkenny, survivors of the hunger but driven from Ireland all the same. James O'Neill was the youngest of their little party of immigrants, old enough to have acquired an Irish accent that he would later expunge but young enough to adapt to his new life and new home. His father, however, never adjusted to life in America, so different from the life he had known in Ireland. Eventually, in his despair, Edward O'Neill abandoned Mary and their eight children and returned to his native land, condemning the family to a life of grinding poverty in America. The episode scarred young James for life, and no doubt contributed to the obsession with security that marked his later career as an actor—a profession that rewarded him with the applause and affection, however fleeting, that his father had so conspicuously denied him. James started his own family, and in time his children, too—most particularly a son named Eugene— would bear witness to the damage that hunger, abandonment, and poverty had caused.

For the descendants of Patrick Kennedy, a different fate lay in store: the ascension of one of Patrick's great-grandsons to the highest office in the land of America. But back then, in the middle of the nineteenth century, in the middle of a dispiriting tragedy on a blighted North Atlantic island, the thoughts of young James O'Neill, of Patrick Kennedy, of hundreds of thousands of starving Irish men and women, could not have ranged much further than a vision of food and some small smidgen of opportunity in a place they did not know and that did not know them.

*

In 1845, before Irish history was changed forever, 3 million of Ireland's 8 million people depended on the potato for their daily existence. They ate potatoes with every meal, pounds of potatoes every day. In the poorest regions of the country, in the west and southwest, there simply was no other food because everything else was used to pay the rent. Ireland was a country of landless peasants and farm laborers who worked fields they did not own and raised crops they could not eat. Midsummer was a time of hunger every year, for it was during those long weeks that the previous harvest's supply of potatoes ran out and the new harvest was not quite ready to be eaten. When the potato failed, the poor of Ireland starved. And from 1845 to 1851, the crop failed repeatedly, disastrously, and fatally.

Meanwhile, the bounty of Ireland—the barley and the oats and the wheat and the livestock—was transported on the same roads that brought the starving poor to Ireland's seaports, once places of color and excitement but now as gray and brooding as the Irish sky. In accordance with the belief, held with religious fervor among Ireland's rulers in Great Britain, that there could be no interference with the workings of free trade and the free market, the food grown in Ireland's fields was designated for export. The British journalist and historian Robert Kee compiled a list of food shipped out of Cork on a single day, November 18, 1848: 147 bales of bacon, 120 casks and 135 barrels of pork, 5 casks of hams, 300 bags of flour, 300 head of cattle, 239 sheep, and 542 boxes of eggs.

Years later, when they were safely across the water in America, Ireland's exiles would tell their children born in New York and Boston and Chicago and San Francisco of the sight of food convoys under armed guard making their way past hollow-eyed men, women, and children whose mouths were green from eating grass. Such stories were the foundation upon which the American Irish built their narrative of forced exile and heartrending loss. Their critique of America, of life itself, was rooted in the blasted potato fields of their ancestral homeland. So was their determination to do what they could to make Ireland master of its own land.

The potato originated in the Andes Mountains of Peru and was introduced to Ireland in the sixteenth century by the English in one variety only, which proved to be very susceptible to fungus. *Phytopthora infestans*, at the time an unknown fungus, struck the Irish fields in 1845, turning the leaves black. The potatoes that did result at first seemed healthy enough, but in storage the starch rapidly decayed into a kind of sugar, producing a putrid, inedible meat. By 1846, the blight had reduced the potato crop to 20 percent of its pre-Famine yield.

During the horror of Black '47, a large family from County Cork decided to emigrate to the United States through Canada. The Fords of Ballinascarty, with grandmother, two sets of parents, and eleven children in their party, left starving Ireland and traveled directly to Quebec. En route, one of the party, Thomasina Ford, died, a common occurrence on vessels that were nicknamed, with chilling aptness, "coffin ships." Passengers were crammed below decks in steerage compartments, where foul privies and spoiled food made conditions unbearable. Passengers were allowed on deck, where they could breathe the fresh air for short periods only when the weather was fair and the sailing smooth. Otherwise, their home was in dark, fetid steerage. Thomasina was one of thousands of Irish people who never made it to the promised land. She left behind her husband John to care for their seven children, the eldest of whom was William, aged twenty-one. The Fords left Canada and moved on to Michigan, settling near Dearborn. William eventually married and found a farm in the vicinity, and there, in 1863, his eldest son, Henry, was born, a youngster who proved particularly adept in the family farm's machine shop. At right, Henry Ford in one of his early horseless carriages.

The departure of the Irish from their stricken land was a mass migration on an epic scale, and in the villages and towns of Ireland a way of life, a communal culture, and an ancient language were wiped out. At the same time, the arrival of the Famine Irish in America transformed the young republic so profoundly that the flight of the hungry from Ireland became a milepost in U.S. history. The Famine Irish immigrants were the original huddled masses. They came not with dreams and plans, but with the modest goal of staying alive. Most were unskilled and poorly educated, a rural people whom the established Americans soon came to regard as dangerous aliens. "Our Celtic fellow citizens are almost as remote from us in temperament and constitution as the Chinese," wrote George Templeton Strong, a New York lawyer, politician, and diarist. By "us," he meant the Anglo-Dutch merchants and politicians who ruled America's cities before the Civil War.

Strong's distaste for the immigrants was obvious, but his observation, however skewed, was correct. The Famine Irish immigrants *were* different. They were impoverished, and with their poverty came disease, especially cholera, which soon became linked inextricably with the Irish in their crowded tenements and basements. In addition, the Famine Irish were almost uniformly Roman Catholic, and America in the middle of the nineteenth century was an overwhelmingly Protestant country, a place where Catholic churches already had been put to the torch, where the first of many battles already had taken place between the immigrant and the native-born. Many more would follow.

Still, whatever disappointments and struggles America had in store, nothing was worse than starving Ireland. A Catholic school textbook later summed up in poetic language the desperation of the poor Irish who saw America as their last and only hope: "Come, let us leave the dying land, and fly unto the land of the living." But it was a journey not everyone could or would make. "A woman with a dead child in her arms was begging on the street yesterday," wrote a relief official in Skibbereen, County Cork, where conditions were particularly gruesome. "Nothing can exceed the deplorable state of this place."

Such scenes were commonplace in Ireland by the end of 1846, but they had been a year in the making. Actual starvation had been averted at first, when the British government under Prime Minister Robert Peel moved aggressively to counter the potato failure in 1845. Peel was an old hand on matters Irish; he had been the government's chief secretary in Ireland, which meant that he was responsible for implementing government policy on the island. One of those policies was the introduction of a police force to keep watch over the rebellious Irish, and so even today it is not unusual to hear the police referred to in Ireland as "peelers."

Peel had received an early warning of the potential disaster in Ireland when potatoes on the Continent and in England failed several weeks before the blight was detected in Ireland. While the potato was notoriously fickle, any report of its failure was bound to be greeted with apprehension, for even in England, the poor depended on the potato as a twice-a-day staple. In Ireland, the poor had nothing else, as everyone from prime minister to farm laborer knew. An Irish newspaper referred to the potato as "the poor man's property"—the only property the poor owned. William Gladstone, the future British leader, understood what might happen: "Ireland, Ireland, that cloud in the West, that coming storm," he wrote.

When it came, its winds lashing Britain's political establishment, Peel and his Conservative Party government scrambled to build makeshift shelters. They quickly ordered supplies of American corn shipped to Ireland, where the food was held in depots for eventual sale to the Irish poor. Public works projects, usually consisting of road building, were devised to give employment to men, women, and children, many of them so weak they could barely expend the energy, but all so desperate that they flocked to the projects. More dramatically, Peel proposed a genuinely radical and politically courageous reform. For years, British farmers (and, more to the point, British landowners) had enjoyed government-sanctioned protections in the form of high taxes on imported grain. The so-called Corn Laws were a linchpin of Britain's agricultural economy and indeed its social structure, for the land-owning aristocrats profited immensely from protection against foreign competition, allowing them to charge artificially high prices for their grain. Those landed aristocrats also happened to be the core of Peel's party.

The prime minister, however, decided that the Corn Laws would have to go, that the emergency in Ireland demanded nothing less. Free trade would lower grain prices and encourage shipments to Ireland, where bread and other grain products could take the potato's place.

Peel told his cabinet that the government could no longer in good conscience purchase corn from America for Ireland while a set of laws kept the price of food artificially high. His colleagues

FRANK McCOURT

SCRAPS AND LEFTOVERS: A MEDITATION

Frank McCourt is the author of ANGELA'S ASHES, *which won the Pulitzer Prize for biography*

If you grew up in Ireland you were told about the Famine. It was dinned into you. In the history books there were pictures of huddled families dying of hunger in their hovels, the same families being evicted—by English landlords—and with no place to go but a ditch.

In the 1930s and 1940s old people in Limerick City still whispered of the horrors of that Famine less than 100 years before. They said it was the fault of the English. They said it was a fact that tons of corn were shipped out of the country to feed Her Majesty's armies beyond. There was enough food to go around to feed Ireland ten times over.

The old people said they would never forgive that of the English and they hoped we wouldn't either.

Now the pope himself is talking along the same lines. He's saying there's enough

were appalled. As reports of dreadful, though not yet fatal, conditions in Ireland continued to pour into London, the cabinet debated, revolted, and adjourned; then debated, revolted, and adjourned again without taking action, even as conditions in Ireland worsened. But this was no act of callousness, for what Peel proposed was nothing short of revolutionary. So much of what his colleagues held dear was intertwined with the Corn Laws. Their social, political, and economic dominance was held in place by the artificial prosperity of government-guaranteed profits from the land.

Just before Christmas in 1845, Peel paid the ultimate political price for his courage. With his own cabinet against him, he resigned. Queen Victoria asked the opposition leader, John Russell, to form a Whig government, but he could not do so because his own party, though pledged to reform the Corn Laws, also was divided on the issue. Peel once again became prime minister (even though a parliamentary colleague declared that he ought to die an unnatural death) and found himself forced to work with the Whigs to win reforms—all in the name of saving the Irish poor. He won his battle in June 1846, and shortly thereafter his enemies in both parties combined to oust him once and for all from the prime minister's office. His career was ruined, a casualty of the Irish Famine. Under Peel, nobody died of starvation in Ireland, though many suffered. With the change of administration in London, however, the situation in Ireland would change, too.

food for everyone and that's supposed to squelch the arguments of the pro-choice people, who might claim there's an awful scarcity of vital stuffs in this world, of both love and food.

But the pope's right. Isn't the pope always right? There *is* enough to go around. Surely everyone knows that and isn't it banal even to say it? Hannah Arendt spoke of the banality of evil: had she devised a catalogue of banality she might have included hunger.

*

When you talk of hunger you can't avoid talking of its opposite—excess. All over America there are restaurant signs inviting you inside to eat all you can for less than ten dollars and there are cars, large cars, driving up to disgorge people so obese they can hardly get out the door or in the door.

As an English teacher in various New York City high schools I was often assigned to "cafeteria duty." I was to patrol the students' lunchroom, make sure they behaved themselves, break up fights, tell them to take their trays back and to clean up around their tables.

I watched them eat and drink. I listened to them complain about the food as they dumped their untouched lunches into the garbage. I saw them sneak out of school to various fast-food joints in the neighborhood.

IRISH BOG TROTTERS.

The rural poor of Ireland often were portrayed as ignorant bogtrotters incapable of governing themselves. "The great evil with which we have to contend," wrote Charles Trevelyan, the British treasury official in charge of relief operations in Ireland, is "not the physical evil of the famine, but the moral evil of the selfish, perverse and turbulent character of the people."

It was a film rerun from my army days: the moaning and bitching over food in Camp Kilmer and Fort Dix, New Jersey, and in a soldiers' mess hall in Bavaria.

From GI days to teacher days I stood in awe of the delicate and discriminating palates of American youth. I shook my head when kids in American films had to be coaxed to eat their hamburgers. I wished I could have so loftily rejected real food. In the army, I wished I could have whimpered for Mom's delicious dishes. Instead I just whimpered.

My mother, in our Limerick City slum, had neither food nor dishes. We lived mostly on bread and tea, a solid and a liquid, a balanced diet, and what more do you want?

As soldier or teacher I wanted to yell, "Shut up. Eat your goddamn food. There are millions starving everywhere this very minute." I wanted to ransack the garbage, retrieve discarded food, wrap it, ship it to Africa, India, Mexico.

Wasn't it Michael Harrington who told us, through the powerful voice of John F. Kennedy, that millions of American children go to bed hungry?

✳

In the racial unconscious of the Irish there must be some demon tormenting us over food. Mention Irish cuisine and most Americans will laugh and sputter, "Yeah, corned beef an' cabbage," and we'll have to admit that up until recently we've had an uneasy rela-

In early July 1846, a shipload of American corn was turned away from Ireland on orders of a man Peel had appointed to oversee relief operations in Ireland. Charles Trevelyan was a devoutly religious and hardworking young man in his late thirties, and while he owed his assignment to Peel's patronage, he strongly disagreed with his approach to easing the crisis. In Trevelyan's eyes, the Famine quite literally was a God-sent opportunity to reorder Irish society. With Peel out of office, Trevelyan began to put his own stamp on Britain's response to Ireland's misery. He and the new prime minister, John Russell, were much more compatible.

As the new potato crop neared harvest in late July 1846, all seemed well, and it appeared as though the suffering would soon be at an end. Trevelyan began shutting down relief operations in anticipation of an abundant harvest. Like so many of his peers, Trevelyan believed that government should not meddle with the marketplace, for the market was nothing less than a reflection of God's will. As Trevelyan closed up the food depots, he argued that it was the "only way to prevent people from becoming habitually dependent on government."

Almost overnight, in early August, the promised harvest, the anticipated salvation, was ruined. The potatoes of Ireland turned black and rancid, and the fields smelled of death itself. Disaster had returned, and now the suffering would be fatal thousands of times over. A police official wrote: "A

tionship with food. Our forebears, landing on the eastern seaboard of the United States, hesitated to move inland, where they could have farmed to their hearts' content. Oh, no, they weren't going to be caught again. Look at what the land had done to them in Ireland. They'd stay in the big cities, never again be victims of the treacherous spud. Irishmen worked in construction: the buildings, the canals, the railroads. They were ignorant of food. The Irishman drank—and died early. Irishwomen—Brigids, Marys, Mollys—worked in the great houses of the rich in New York and Boston. They learned to clean and stitch and sew, to pour wine and to cook the best of foods. They lived long lives and left money for their children to go to school and learn how to sell insurance. Historians tell us those servant girls sent money to the Old Country far in excess of what women from other countries sent to *their* countries. Was there enough to go around, then?

In Irish-American literature there isn't much about poverty, never mind hunger. We don't have the Dickens who wrote in his *American Notes* of the horrors of the infamous Five Points, a notorious Irish/African slum near what is now Chinatown in New York (by Irish-slash-African I mean the population of indigent Irish and runaway slaves living in riotous miscegenation). A connoisseur of "poverty" writing could go to James Plunkett's *Strumpet City* or George Orwell's *The Road to Wigan Pier*. Alone among Irish-American writ-

stranger would wonder how these wretched beings find food . . . They sleep in their rags and have pawned their bedding."

Landlords began evicting their tenants, sending families into the countryside with nothing save the rags they wore on their backs. The eviction process was stark in its brutality: An eviction party, usually accompanied by constables, arrived to serve notice and, to underscore the point, pull down the roof of the tenant's cottage. The Irish countryside was filled with scenes of families, desperate and weeping, scrambling to retrieve what they could as the eviction party proceeded with its work. After the cottage was razed, most had nowhere else to go.

And it was only just beginning.

The bureaucrats and politicians in London, charged as they were with seeing to it that the Irish people did not become dependent on government assistance, took a decidedly unemotional view of the suffering. Trevelyan continued with the work he had begun in midsummer, when the potato crop

A poor woman on Achill Island, off the coast of Kerry and part of the Irish-speaking Gaeltacht region, which was hard hit by the Famine.

ers, William Kennedy, in *Ironweed*, evokes the stink and desperation of poverty. Or you could go back to Upton Sinclair's *The Jungle*.

The Famine is over, we're well fed now; we're sniffing and sending back the wine. Here we are on the threshold of a new century looking forward and, since we're Irish, looking back.

"We don't forget, Joxer. We don't forget."

＊

We may have been baptized in the Catholic way with a splash on the forehead but we've received total immersion in Irish history. We learned the songs and the poetry and we are expected to suffer retroactively. We were told then, and we know it now, the Famine was the worst thing ever to happen to the Irish race.

I recently wrote a book in which hunger of the physical type is a major theme but I wanted to show the psychological effects of hunger, how it breaks you, how it hinders any kind of emotional development. You can think of nothing but your belly. You're an animal.

When I was nine my mother got a job in Limerick cleaning a judge's house. That Sunday we had boiled bacon, cabbage, boiled potatoes, and, for dessert, jelly and custard.

had held such promise. He continued to shut down government-run food depots and public works projects, while Britain's chancellor of the exchequer (the equivalent of an American treasury secretary) made the government's intention clear: "It is not the intention at all to import food for the use of the people of Ireland," he said. Public opinion, at least in some circles, was equally unsympathetic. Cecil Woodham-Smith, in the classic study of the famine, *The Great Hunger*, noted that British cartoonists portrayed the Irish not as impoverished, starving victims but as apelike brutes begging for money that they would then spend not on food but on weapons. The *Times* of London, the voice of Britain's establishment, took note of Ireland's pleas for help with a detached, almost resigned, view: "It is possible to have heard the tale of sorrow too often."

At his desk in Dublin, Trevelyan tried to make some sense of the chaos around him. His wife complained that he was working such long hours that his health was sure to fail. Nevertheless, he was a hostage to Victorian

For the next day she saved three boiled potatoes and some jelly and custard and placed them on a windowsill which served as the larder.

Next day I was the first one home. I thought I'd taste the jelly and maybe the custard. I did. I thought I'd have half a potato.

You can imagine the rest. I didn't stop till everything was gone.

I ran away and slept in a hayloft outside Limerick. I could hardly sleep with the worry and the guilt and knew I had to go home. My mother was sitting by the fire as usual. She didn't stir but said, "Frankie, you must have been very hungry to eat everything like that."

"I was," I said.

"You know your brothers were hungry, too," said my mother.

"I suppose they were."

"Well, you're going on ten and growing and I don't think you'd ever do the likes of that again, would you?"

"I wouldn't," said I.

But I would and did in other places and I'm not a bit sorry because there's enough to go around. And there always *was* enough to go around. ❖

OLD SKIBBEREEN

Oh, father dear, I often hear you speak of Erin's Isle,
Her lofty scenes and valleys green, her mountains rude and wild,
They say it is a lovely land wherein a prince might dwell,
Oh, why did you abandon it? The reason to me tell.

Oh, son! I loved my native land with energy and pride,
Till a blight came o'er my crops—my sheep, my cattle died;
My rent and taxes were too high, I could not them redeem,
And that's the cruel reason that I left old Skibbereen.

Oh, well do I remember the bleak December day,
The landlord and the sheriff came to drive us all away;
They set my roof on fire with their cursed English spleen,
And that's another reason that I left old Skibbereen.

Your mother, too, God rest her soul, fell on the snowy ground,
She fainted in her anguish, seeing the desolation round,
She never rose, but passed away from life to mortal dream,
And found a quiet grave, my boy, in dear old Skibbereen.

And you were only two years old and feeble was your frame,
I could not leave you with my friends, you bore your father's name—
I wrapt you in my cotamore at the dead of night unseen,
I heaved a sigh and bade good-bye, to dear old Skibbereen.

—Anonymous

certainties, chief among them that poverty was a sign of God's censure. In the middle of the nineteenth century, Ireland was one of the poorest countries on earth, a place that invariably shocked visitors ranging from Benjamin Franklin to Alexis de Tocqueville. To Trevelyan and like-minded policymakers, that poverty was a sign of something else, something that could be cured only by the application of the stern principles of what was called "political economy."

"The great evil with which we have to contend," he wrote, is "not the physical evil of the famine, but the moral evil of the selfish, perverse and turbulent character of the people." The goal of British policy, then, was not simply to feed people but to transform their character, to make them something other than Irish. For virtuous Victorians, famine and death in Ireland were yet another reflection of Irish morals and values, so unlike those of British politicians.

When the extent of the disastrous failure of 1846 became clear, Trevelyan rather unenthusiastically decided to reopen the government's food depots and start a new round of pointless road building. It was by no means enough. The dying started in October, when the body of a worker was found on the roadside outside Skibbereen. He had been employed on a public works project but had not been paid for eight days. The coroner noted that he had not eaten for "many days."

Nearly a half-million Irish men, women, and children were at work on government projects by Christmas. At the same time, coffins were beginning to become as scarce as potatoes in parts of Ireland, and a new, reusable model was being built, one with a trapdoor on the bottom. It was used to carry a corpse to a

A sketch from the summer of 1850 in Galway that was recently found in an unknown traveler's notebook.

One out of the group on the floor in the Ballinasloe school opened 4 months on 10 N

Oh some of them are too Naked to stand up

grave site, at which point the trap was opened, the corpse deposited, and the coffin returned for further use. In other places, the dead simply were covered up in straw.

Many of the dead didn't die of starvation as such but of the diseases and illnesses associated with lack of food and appalling poverty. One such illness was described simply as "road fever." It was typhus, and it was an insatiable killer.

The place where the first Famine death was recorded soon became so overrun with the dead and dying that even 150 years later, its name is linked with starvation. Skibbereen was the Famine's ground zero, a place of such horror that British relief officials could scarcely believe their eyes. Letters dispatched to London recorded the awful conditions: A man, barely alive, on the roadside with his three dead children lying next to him: dozens of bodies half-consumed by rats; a wraithlike woman, hollow-eyed, standing in a field.

A local official in Skibbereen wrote to the Duke of Wellington about seeing "six famished and ghastly skeletons, to all appearance dead . . . huddled in a corner on some filthy straw, their sole covering what seemed to be ragged horsecloth and their wretched legs hanging about, naked above the knees. I approached in horror and found by a low moaning that they were alive, they were in a fever— four children, a woman and what had once been a man."

Children, of course, were the most tragic of the Famine's victims. Many of them suffered from brittle bones; they were wrinkled and lifeless, looking for all the world like tiny septuagenarians. All these decades later, of course, anyone with a television set is all too familiar with the heartbreaking sight of a child in the throes of starvation. Such sights broke many British hearts when they saw drawings of the disaster or read accounts by courageous journalists from such publications as the *Illustrated London News*. Just as today's television pictures from the Third World have moved the well fed to organize private relief operations, the illustrations that began to appear in British newspapers—a far cry from the political cartoons showing vicious brutes rather than starving children—inspired groups such as the Quakers to set up soup kitchens in Ireland. The Quakers, like the doctors and clergy who worked with the poor, put their own lives at risk. Even the well fed were not immune to the diseases that were killing the Irish poor by the thousands.

To add to the horror, the winter of 1846–47 was cold and bitter, with snow falling at levels never seen before in Ireland. Those who had considered themselves fortunate to find work on government projects began dying by the side of the useless roads they were building. A Catholic priest was horrified by the suffering of those who were working outdoors during the dreadful winter: "The old and decrepit of both sexes . . . were exposed without food or clothing to the piercing cold of winter. Indeed, almost all of these are dead." The priest noted that many people waited weeks to be

RATION CARDS: 1847.
Ration cards used during the great famine
under the Soup-kitchen Act of 1847 which
[...] operation from the Spring of that
[...]til the following September. Adults
[...]titled to a full ration each day - a
[...] allowance - while children under
[...]s of age were given a half ration.
[...]cards came from the collection of
[...]gan, Omagh, and were presented to
[...]chool Museum by Br. D. Hamill.

Soup kitchens helped the Irish get through the bleak summer of 1847. Ration cards were distributed throughout the countryside, but when a new potato crop seemed healthy, the kitchens were shut down. The new crop was not healthy and the situation worsened.

placed in a job, and then "had scarcely time to earn themselves the price of a coffin."

Death was everywhere. The sick and the starving died in their hovels or in ditches; the living stripped the land of anything that might be edible—weeds, berries, even the grass itself. Meanwhile, Trevelyan still complained about the "social evils" of those who were starving to death in the snow. In early 1847, a year that would become known as Black '47 because of its horror, the great Irish parliamentarian Daniel O'Connell rose to address his colleagues in the British House of Commons, the legislative seat of the United Kingdom of Great Britain and Ireland. O'Connell in his prime had been one of the great orators of his day and had helped organize nonviolent protest in Ireland against anti-Catholic laws and practices. Now, however, he was more than seventy years old and only a few months from death. His age, his condition, and his humanity had made him a respected figure in the Commons, so when he began his speech, members hushed and strained to hear a once powerful voice now reduced to a faltering whisper: "Ireland is in your hands, in your power," he said. "If you do not save her, she cannot save herself . . . I predict with the sincerest conviction that a quarter of her population will perish unless you come to her relief."

Finally, the government took its most radical step since the abolition of the Corn Laws: It began giving away food. By the summer of 1847, Trevelyan supervised the most extensive relief mission ever

The mass of Irish people lived off land they did not own, their lives subject to the whim of the landlord. Eviction scenes were common during the Famine, especially after the passage of the Poor Law Extension Act in 1847, which made the landlords, rather than the Crown, responsible for the welfare costs of the impoverished tenantry. To evict was to remove that burden.

undertaken by a modern Western government. The British had abandoned the notion of demanding that the starving Irish be put to work building roads; instead, they simply opened up soup kitchens. The effort was immense—by July 1847, three million people a day were lining up for soup, provided and paid for by the British treasury. Meanwhile, the potato crop of 1847 held out the same promise of the previous summer; in fact, this time it seemed certain that the horror finally had ended.

When the new potato crop came in and seemed healthy, the soup kitchens were closed. Though the harvest appeared to be free of blight, it was small, only about a fifth of the normal yield, because the desperate Irish had eaten the seed potatoes. Trevelyan regarded the small harvest as a blessing, for he believed it would help wean the Irish off the potato. The government's assistance, he feared, had made the Irish people "worse instead of better."

Parliament then passed legislation known as the Poor Law Extension Act of 1847, which allowed local workhouses in Ireland to take in the poor in exchange for their labor. The workhouses

The Irish fled from the countryside to the port cities of Ireland—Cork, Galway, and Dublin—to seek passage to Canada and America. Most of the routes led through the docks of Liverpool, where the Irish were "as numerous as maggots in cheese," noted a disgusted Nathaniel Hawthorne.

ROBERT SCALLY

THROUGH LIVERPOOL: "VISTAS OF WANT AND WOE"

Robert Scally is a professor of history at New York University and director of Ireland House in New York City. He is also author of THE END OF HIDDEN IRELAND.

If there was one experience common to the Irish refugees from the Great Famine, other than hunger, it was the sight of Liverpool. Very few sailed directly from Ireland across the Atlantic—fewer than one in four. The vast majority first sailed east to Liverpool, the greatest seaport of the nineteenth century—leaving Cork City, Dublin, Wexford, and Belfast behind. For these future Americans, the grimy seaport of Liverpool was the last they would see of Europe.

Liverpool was the first gateway to America, directing the flow of hundreds of thousands of Irish to New York, Quebec, New Orleans, Boston, Charleston, Savannah. Its influence extended along a global maritime network of commercial ties and routes that

were grim places—designed that way so nobody became too comfortable—where husbands were separated from their wives and parents from their children. Inside, the inmates performed whatever chores they were assigned in return for government-provided shelter and food.

The legislation contained a fearsome clause: Anyone who owned even a tiny quarter-acre plot was ineligible for assistance unless he or she surrendered the land. For an island where land was destiny, this was a cruel choice. But it was a clear choice as well. Staying on the land, ineligible for assistance, meant certain death. Going to the workhouse at least offered a chance to live. Or so it seemed. In reality, though, workhouses functioned as an assembly line of death. With so many sick people living and working cheek by jowl, disease ran wild. Some workhouses produced more than a hundred corpses a week.

had been in place, and growing, for more than a hundred years by the time the migration reached its peak during the "hungry forties." Slavery and cotton were two of the main reasons for Liverpool's maritime dominance— it had cornered the slave trade before its abolition and then became the main receiver in Europe of the cotton from the Old South, the endless flow of five-hundred-pound bales picked and hauled by slaves to the levees of New Orleans and Charleston.

Black '47 witnessed more Irish than ever pouring from the country, most of them refugees fleeing the hunger as best they could but among them, too, many thousands who had saved for and set their minds on emigrating for years. For the destitute, there was often no choice of destination: They had but money enough to be among the half-million who would immigrate only to Britain with perhaps a hope of one day returning. Or they were among those whose immigration to America was "assisted"; that is, passage was paid for by their landlords, who, under the Poor Law Extension Act, either moved their poor charges off the Crown's soil or paid for the tenant's welfare in Ireland. For those who could muster

Finally, the new legislation also made clear Parliament's impatience with the United Kingdom's eternal Irish problem. From now on, the law declared, the cost of relief operations in Ireland, including the workhouses, would fall on the shoulders of Irish property owners. The United Kingdom of Great Britain and Ireland had been created in 1801 with the idea that the two islands would now be one country. But in Black '47, Parliament decreed that Ireland would have to fend for itself. For those who had nothing to eat, Trevelyan recommended "independent exertion." Ireland, he wrote, "must be left to the operation of natural forces." He retired to write his history of the Famine, and was given a knighthood for his exertions.

The boon harvest of 1847, which seemed so promising and led to the dismantling of the soup kitchens, was false. The potato failed again, and when it did, there was nothing left. The Irish property owners, many of whom were going broke themselves, couldn't pay for relief. But they could make their land a great deal more efficient—they could evict their tenants and their potato fields, and turn the land over to animals. So they did, and mass eviction was added to the long list of horrors.

The Irish who were turned out of hearth and home, or who were dying for lack of food, occasionally turned their wrath on landlords, their agents, and government officials. But the only orga-

the fare, the courage, for the long voyage across the Atlantic, the choice was clear: a new life away from the blight, away from the Brits. And that route went through Liverpool.

*

Ironically, it was into the maw of Liverpool and its massive warehouses that the cargoes of grain, meat, and dairy goods denied to the starving Irish countryside flowed unceasingly from Irish ports. Now the ships were carrying the supercargo of hungry Irish. In the two decades before the Famine, a rising tide of emigrants passed into Liverpool, reaching nearly 100,000 in some years before 1845. In 1847, at least 320,000 Irish men, women, and children poured from the Irish ferries, many of them unable or unwilling to go any further.

It might be said that Liverpool beckoned the torrent of Irish emigrants to its doorstep through its Irish network. There was profit in the emigrants' fares, but thousands of them were also needed in the port itself for hauling cargoes, excavating the roads and railway cuttings, and in extending the great docks. For these tasks they were welcome. But as their numbers grew and their condition worsened, their popular reception became increasingly hostile.

In the story of the Famine emigration, the Liverpool ordeal attracted more attention at the time than London or New York. The scandal of death and suffering on its water-

nized effort at rebellion came in 1848, when a group of middle-class intellectuals, most of them Protestant, took up arms in what amounted to a mere token show of force. Nevertheless, the rebellion of 1848 was enshrined in the minds of Irish nationalists as yet another violent demonstration of Ireland's passion to win independence. The rebel class of '48 included men who would later emigrate and fight in a bloodier and more prolonged battle beginning in 1861, when the United States went to war with itself. There were Irishmen fighting on both sides and sometimes firing at each other.

*

By 1849, the horrendous plight of Ireland was known around the world. In America, relief supplies bound for Ireland were made exempt from tolls on turnpikes and canals. From Oklahoma came a donation of $170 from the Choctaw Indians, a tribe whose own sufferings and poverty were considerable. A remarkable woman from New York, Asenath Hatch Nicholson, traveled to Dublin to minister to the needs of the starving Irish. She wrote a book about her experiences called *Annals of the Famine*, and it remains, with its stark descriptions of the poor, a riveting testimony to Ireland's suffering. When she came face to face with starvation for the first time, she wrote:

front was widely reported in the press and in reports to Parliament from the municipal health authorities. Contemporary writers like Nathaniel Hawthorne and the Brontës depicted some of the horrors to which the Famine emigrés were routinely subjected as they were disgorged from the Irish ferries. Some were outraged by what they witnessed there. But not all observers of Irish misery on the Liverpool docks were moved by the spectacle of human suffering. Hawthorne, who was the American consul in Liverpool at the time, took note of the ragged throngs of Irish huddled around the dock gates, but in him they inspired only disgust: "The people are as numerous as maggots in cheese," he wrote.

Almost alone among the witnesses who wrote of Liverpool at the time, the young Herman Melville declared his outrage at the wanton cruelties the newcomers met in the town. In what is by far the most eloquent account of midcentury Liverpool, Melville described in *Redburn: His First Voyage* the "endless vistas of want and woe staggering arm in arm along these miserable streets."

The desensitized feelings of humanity apparent in Liverpool may have been more extreme than elsewhere at the time, with its volatile mix of Celts, evangelists, and lawlessness. But it was not the end of the callous faces the Irish immigrants would encounter on their long journey to America. ❖

Reader, if you never have seen a starving human being, may you never!
In my childhood I had been [frightened] with stories of ghosts, and had seen actual skeletons; but imagination had come short of the sight of this man . . . emaciated to the last degree.

Those who had thus far survived had suffered through four long years of awful deprivation. They were but walking skeletons. In Kilkenny, Edward and Mary O'Neill tended to the needs of their growing family, with James having arrived in 1846, just as people were beginning to die. The Kennedys of County Wexford similarly managed to keep themselves alive. Luckily for the two families, they lived in the eastern part of the country, where the suffering was not nearly as severe as it was in Skibbereen to the south and County Mayo to the west. Still, it was not as though they were unaffected, for Ireland's very culture was under assault. The communal village life, with its tradition of hospitality and shared sacrifice, was giving way to a rugged individualism of the most extreme sort. Neighbors no longer opened the door for other neighbors, and in the remote Irish-speaking areas of the west and southwest, the language itself—and the sense of identity that came with it—was dying.

Meanwhile, the potatoes continued to fail, and the dying went on, into 1849 and beyond. Queen Victoria visited Dublin in 1849, two years after Charles Trevelyan had retired to write his memoir of the Famine—as if it were over—and she found a city that had just been in the grip of a cholera epidemic that took thousands of lives. Most of the bodies were buried quickly in a corner of Dublin's Glasnevin Cemetery. Great expense was laid out to see to it that the queen traveled and lived in at least a semblance of the style to which she was accustomed. She landed in Cork—a city she described as having a "foreign" look to it—and traveled north to Dublin, where great illuminations were prepared for the royal visit. The city celebrated for four days, and many observers remarked upon the enthusiasm of ordinary people, the very Irish men and women portrayed as apes and barbarians in the British press. There was a surreal aspect to the proceedings, for even in Dublin itself there was great suffering, and just beyond its borders, death continued apace.

Hunger continued to stalk the Irish poor into the new decade, but the worst of it was over by the time Victoria left—meaning that most of those who died were dead by then, and most of those who left were long gone. A census of Ireland in 1851 counted 6.5 million people—there had been 8.1 million people ten years earlier. Given normal rates of growth in the Irish population, Ireland should have had about 9 million people in 1851. How many died, and how many emigrated? The figures vary, but the consensus seems to be about a million dead and more than a million exiles. Ireland was never the same, even when the potato returned to health. It continued to bleed human beings, until, some decades later, the population bottomed out at just over 4 million. Among those who left even after the hunger had done its worst was the O'Neill family. Like tens of thousands of their countrymen, they saw no future in a land that remained on the edge of hunger, a hostage to decisions made on distant shores. America held out the promise of something better, and the flight

Denis Mahon was unfortunate enough to inherit the estate of Strokestown in Roscommon in 1845; before long he was besieged by sick and starving tenants unable to pay rent. He moved to clear people off his land and paid for their passage to America. In 1847 he was assassinated, himself a victim of tragic events.

westward continued through the decades. A century and a half after Black '47, the population of Ireland as a whole was about 5 million. It is the only country in Western Europe that has fewer people in the 1990s than it had in the early 1840s.

*

Hundreds of thousands of his countrymen already had departed by 1849 when Patrick Kennedy made his fateful decision to leave his family and take his chances in America. There is nothing to indicate that he was as bad off as the walking skeletons who haunted the Irish landscape. But the thatched-roof cottage and twenty-five-acre farm he left behind offered nothing save continued misery and poverty, if not hunger. Misfortune, indeed, already had visited the Kennedy household. Patrick's older brother John died at a young age, long before the potato failed. And some years after Patrick's departure, the Kennedy family was added to the long list of Irish poor who were evicted from their cottage and farm, left to fend for themselves against the determination of "natural forces."

Patrick's departure itself was something akin to another death in the family, for those who left Ireland and those they left behind knew they would never see one another again. In an age of sailing ships and backbreaking labor, overseas trips were an unknowable luxury for the great masses of ordinary people, and the Kennedy family was in no way extraordinary. When Patrick bade farewell to his parents, brother, and sister, it was forever. Years later, such leave-takings would become known as "American wakes," nearly as tragic and melancholy—and as final—as an actual death.

Patrick's journey to America required a detour to Liverpool, the bustling British port from which many Irish set sail for the trip across the Atlantic, a trip that could take, in 1849, well over a month. From Liverpool, Patrick could have chosen to go to either the United States or British-ruled Canada. During most of the Famine years, it was cheaper to sail to Canada, and thousands took advantage of the lower price with the intention of immediately pressing on to the United States.

THE EMIGRANT IRISH

Like oil lamps, we put them out back—

*of our houses, of our minds. We had lights
better than, newer than and then*

*a time came, this time and now
we need them. Their dread, makeshift example:*

*they would have thrived on our necessities.
What they survived we could not even live.
By their lights now it is time to
imagine how they stood there, what they stood with,
that their possessions may become our power:*

*Cardboard. Iron. Their hardships parceled in them.
Patience. Fortitude. Long-suffering
in the bruise-colored dusk of the New World.*

And all the old songs. And nothing to lose.

—Eavan Boland

A NEW SONG CALL'D THE

EMEGRANTS FAREWELL TO

DONEGALL

Good people all on you I call give ear to those lines von soon shall

Some had no choice but to sail to Canada first because their land-lords booked them on dilapidated vessels that dared not land in the States, where port inspections became more rigorous as the Famine persisted.

For a short time during the Famine years, Canada was the second-most-popular destination for the Irish, after New York. Because of the horrible conditions aboard those less-regulated ships, there was no ease in suffering once the emigrants lost sight of their famished homeland. To accommodate the vast numbers of Irish who were sailing up the Saint Lawrence River to Quebec City and Montreal, Canadian authorities set up a disembarkation area on an island near Montreal called Grosse Isle. Beginning in May of Black '47, the creaky vessels that managed the crossing intact began to deposit the sick and dying on Grosse Isle. The little island became a hellish nightmare as awful as Ireland itself. Authorities were overwhelmed; sick immigrants were placed in hastily constructed fever sheds, where they soon died. The caregivers themselves came down with fevers and died—nurses, doctors, and clergy. In his book *The Famine Ships*, Edward Laxton notes that forty-four medical personnel died on Grosse Isle, half of them nurses. Statistics culled from ships stopping at the island were scandalous: Laxton noted that one ship, the *Larch*, left Sligo with 440 passengers—108 of them died at sea and 150 were taken off the ship at Grosse Isle, too ill to continue the journey. Another ship, the *Agnes*, carried 427 passengers. Sixty-three died en route. More than 200 died on Grosse Isle. Only 150 passengers were alive when the *Agnes* was cleared to leave Grosse Isle for its final destination.

Officially, about fifty-four hundred Irish men, women, and children perished on Grosse Isle, but the actual figure is much higher, perhaps as high as fifteen thousand. In flight from a Famine at home, many unfortunate Irish had simply arrived at a foreign grave. Years later, the Ancient Order of Hibernians in the United States erected a five-story Celtic cross on the island over the spot where the victims were buried. In both the English and Irish languages, the inscription reads, in part: "Children of the Gael died in their thousands on this island having fled from the laws of the foreign tyrants and an artificial famine . . . Let this monument be a token to their name and honor from the Gaels of America. God Save Ireland."

*

Ships carrying thousands of Famine exiles arrived in Quebec, in part because fares to Canada, a British dominion, were cheap. Grosse Isle, an island in the St. Lawrence River, became a huge hospice and burial ground for passengers who suffered en route to the New World.

Anglo-Irish houses then being built outside the town of Carlow. More than one hundred years later, Thomas Hughes was insistent that I, in my turn, should bear witness to a catastrophe caused by a rapacious landlord system and a callous government in London.

For the first few years of the "minding" I drank in his stories and I can still visualize the people dying in ditches with grass stains on their mouths. He detested a government that could stand by and allow millions to either perish or emigrate and he had a burning disdain for most things English; yet like many Irish to this day, he was ready to doff his cap at the first syllable of a BBC accent. The child noted this paradox and the soon-to-be rebellious adolescent was quick to employ it.

Once I discovered the Beatles, the Old Man's xenophobic tribalism seemed anachronistic at best, destructive at worst. And so I avoided him, locked myself in my room, and turned up the Liverpool volume to chase away the ghosts that haunted the shabbily respectable old house. I can only imagine what he thought of me amidst the scream of guitars—a *seoinin*—a hated West Brit!

As soon as I could, I left for Dublin and eventually the Lower East Side of New York City. I was now long past the Beatles and floated self-consciously on the New Wave—burning green lightning streaks in my hair whilst merrily aping David Bowie. I was adrift in a sea of fashion and disposable music lurching negatively down East Ninth Street.

The Old Man died and I didn't even get back for his funeral. Ireland seemed so far away in those days, besides which I didn't have a green card. The breaks came and went; life was fast and furious. I was signed and dropped by a succession of record companies until one day in the mid-eighties, in a fit of self-disgust, I walked away from the rock-and-roll circus.

I immersed myself in writing plays. But often late at night, while reworking a scene for the umpteenth time, I would hear the Old Man's voice across the years.

He had often talked about his uncle, an agent for Charles Stewart Parnell in the Carlow by-election of 1891. And so, I wrote a play about the Uncrowned King and the divorce case that had split a country. Coincidentally, I found I was already familiar with the music of the period, courtesy of the Old Man and his drawing-room sensibility. The melodies, which I had scorned in adolescence, still stood the test of time. Just strip away the Victorian calcification, add a pounding beat, some new lyrics, a sympathetic bridge or two, and you had a whole new world.

Around that time, I was composing commissioned scores for modern dance. Rebelling against the Philip Glass style of minimalism then in vogue, I began writing "ancient" Gaelic melodies for accordion, flute, fiddle, and voice. Choreographers, however, disliked the idea of seeming to interpret English words. So, I would play back the melodies and record whatever words of pidgin Irish that came to mind, then translate these stream of consciousness diatribes. Talk about whispers from the past! Without even knowing it, I was on my journey back.

One night I walked into a bar called Paddy Reilly's. A folk group called Beyond the Pale was playing its last gig. I sat in, had a blast, and later, at the bar, the leader Chris Byrne and I got to talking about the lack of political content in rock music. I was impressed by his knowledge of street life—as it turned out, he was a New York City cop—but also his commitment to Irish America and its right to a full participation in Irish political affairs.

For my own part, I had long since discarded the particular xenophobic mentality that afflicts so many Irish immigrants. So, we formed a band with the idea of upending the whole Irish-American music scene—this, of course, without yet playing a note. What to call this coming revolution? A familiar voice whispered "Black '47" and a band was named.

I still don't know why there was so much resistance at first; of course, we were loud, proud, full of attitude, and unwilling to take any advice. That first year was heartbreaking, probably more so for Chris. My friends simply refused to come to gigs and I shed most of them easily. Chris's, however, were already entrenched in the Irish bar scene and there was much shaking of heads and wondering what he had come to. But we had our eyes on a prize, and the complaints, firings, and constant derision only made us stronger. Night by night, the music got more cohesive as we struggled to meld together our particular brand of traditional, reggae, hip-hop, and rock.

The Old Man was now a constant presence. I threw myself open to all his influences and the songs streamed out—"James Connolly," "The Big Fellah," "Black '47," "Vinegar Hill"—Irish historical characters and events but seen through the prism of New York City. The band struck a chord—not so much with the young immigrants, as we had expected, but with Irish Americans.

We released a record and it took off in all the old-line Democratic cities. The youth flocked to see us, folk memories of their immigrant forebears awakened. We tried not to spoon-feed them answers—only questions. True, we continue to politick, but we don't seek to shape opinions, only inform them. Still, it is our belief that each generation should seek to solve the problems in the North of Ireland. And at each gig we sow that seed—but through allegory, not dogma. Seven years later, long-dormant Irish America is awakening and flexing its political muscle and we continue to play our small part.

In 1997, Black 47 will take its message back to Ireland for the first time. You can be sure we won't be tipping our caps to our Irish cousins and begging for a place at the table. No, we'll be barging in the front door, loud, proud, and still full of attitude, bringing back a legitimate Irish experience informed by the urban realities of New York City.

Somewhere up in the stars, the Old Man will frown at the noise of it all, but I bet the beginnings of smile will play on his lips as he witnesses the last leg of my journey back. ❖

If Patrick Kennedy's voyage lacked for tragedy, it was not exactly uneventful. While still aboard the *Washington Irving,* he met a young woman named, as luck would have it, Bridget Murphy, who was two years his junior. Like Patrick, she was born in County Wexford. The two exiles with their stereotypical first names personified a unique aspect of Irish immigration: Unlike other ethnic groups, the Irish came to America unmarried. That phenomenon, rooted in the poor prospects accorded all sons save the first-born—who was the heir to the farm—and all daughters no matter when they were born, was less notice-able during the Famine years, when entire families fled rather than starve. After the Famine, however, the shiploads of Irish immigrants were filled with Patrick Kennedys and Bridget Murphys, single men and women prepared to start new lives in America. Only 5 percent of Irish immigrants were children, and of the total number of Irish immigrants during the peak years, single women were the majority, a star-tling contrast to other groups, in which men made up the vast majority of new Americans.

It is hard to imagine a romance blossoming in the wretched conditions of an emigrant ship, but so it did. Shortly after Patrick and Bridget arrived in America, they married and set up their house-hold in the Irish ghetto of East Boston, a place where, it was said, children were born to die. Horribly, most did—60 percent in Boston didn't live to see their sixth birthday. Adults fared little better, for the average Famine immigrant lived no longer than five or six years after stepping foot on American soil. The Irish lived in shanties and basements, breeding grounds of disease and despair. A Boston doctor was visiting a patient lying ill in a bedroom filled with water when a tiny coffin floated by. It contained the body of the patient's child.

Patrick and Bridget settled into their new life amid the crowded, teeming slums to which the Irish were confined. Patrick took up the cooper's trade to feed the family that was soon in coming. Bridget gave birth to four children, three daughters and a son, within eight years. The world into which the Kennedy children were born was appalling. A public health commission investigating conditions in Boston's Irish neighborhoods at the time found immigrants "huddled together like brutes, without regard to sex or age, or sense of decency; grown men and women sleeping together in the same apart-ment, and sometimes wife and husband, brothers and sisters in the same bed." In those circumstances, "self-respect, forethought, all high and noble virtues, soon die out," to be replaced by "sullen indiffer-ence and despair, or disorder, intemperance and utter degradation." Not to mention sickness and pre-mature death. Within months of Patrick and Bridget's arrival, a cholera epidemic swept through the Irish slums of Boston, killing more than five hundred immigrants and their children. The disease took its vic-tims quickly. A nineteen-year-old domestic named Ellen McGann was admitted to a Boston hospital at the height of the epidemic. She had been ill for ten hours; she was dead four hours later.

Conditions in East Boston, of course, hardly were unique. The vast majority of the Irish had settled in the great cities of the American Northeast, spurning the farming life that had so cruelly betrayed them in Ireland. They lived in the cheapest available lodgings. An Irish member of the British Parliament, John Francis Maguire, toured several American cities and wrote that he could not find the words to describe the horrors he saw.

Families, in many cases, were irreparably broken by the Famine immigration experience.

Twenty thousand people, most of them Irish immigrants, lived in cellars in New York, and an Irish colony was taking shape in the recesses of Central Park. In Philadelphia, the Irish built shanty-towns along the banks of the Schuylkill River. In Providence, a doctor noted that the city's immigrants, including many Irish, "are under entirely different sanitary influences from the American population." The result of such harsh conditions was not particularly surprising: The cholera that killed so many in Boston in 1849 did the same in New York, and the statistics measuring misery and deprivation told the same story in every city where the Irish congregated. In New York, where 75 percent of the Famine immigrants found themselves at the end of their transatlantic journey, infant mortality among Irish immigrants approached 80 percent, and many of the surviving children would lose at least one parent while they still were young. Many lost both, and the city teemed with homeless children referred to, in the parlance of the times, as street Arabs. Entire families often were put out on the street, evicted from their homes just as surely as if they had never left Ireland. There was, it seemed, no escaping the landlord.

*

If legend is to be believed, the first Irishman to see the New World's shores was Saint Brendan the Navigator, whose fearless journeys in the fifth century A.D. may have taken him as far west as North America. Whether or not he actually beat Columbus by nearly one thousand years or not, his exploits were remarkable. If, in fact, Saint Brendan's story is more legend than fact, then William Ayers probably was the first Irish person to see the New World. A native of County Galway, he served as a crew member on Christopher Columbus's historic journey across the Atlantic in 1492. Whatever the truth, it is a fact that the Irish were a presence throughout the English-sponsored colonial settlements that began with the founding of Jamestown. Protestant Irish were part of America's initial rugged frontier dwellers, scorning the cities that were home to the Anglo-Irish who fit in so easily with the Yankee ascendancy. In the hollows of Kentucky, where Daniel Boone's Ulster-immigrant family settled, and the rugged terrain of the Blue Ridge Mountains where Tennessean Davey Crockett rose to fame, the Ulster Irish carved out a life far from mainstream colonial America.

It was the Ulster Irish who provided the backbone of the ragged rebel army that took on the forces of the Crown beginning with the first shots at Lexington and Concord in 1775. A British colonial official in America reported back to London that "emigrants from Ireland are our most serious opponents." Irish heroes were plentiful during the war, from Henry Knox, descendant of Ulster Protestant settlers who went on to become the nation's first secretary of war, to Commodore John Barry, a Catholic immigrant who founded the U.S. Navy.

In 1790, the U.S. government's first census found 44,000 Irish immigrants among the new nation's 3 million people and another 150,000 people of Irish ancestry. Half of the total lived south of Pennsylvania. Many historians regard the figures as far too low, which makes another figure all the more striking: At the time, the Catholic hierarchy in America, such as it was in those days, estimated the number of American Catholics of all ethnicities at 35,000. If the Catholic number is correct, it's clear that the dominant Irish experience in Revolutionary America was Protestant.

All told, about a million Irish came to America between 1815 and the Famine, and they did so

James O'Neill, with his sons Eugene (left) and Jamie (center), on the porch in New London, Connecticut. In his old age, James O'Neill would occasionally think back to the poverty of his youth and would break down in tears. It was not the Famine-stricken Ireland of his first few years that haunted him, but the terrible conditions that his family contended with in America after his broken father returned to Ireland. So scarring was James O'Neill's childhood that he rarely spoke of it. One day his son Eugene would write that, "I know little about my father's parents . . . or about his brothers and sisters."

in distinct waves. Early on, many of the immigrants were middle-class Ulster Protestants, but later, as the need for labor outstripped the supply, thousands of unskilled, poor Irish Catholics began to cross, ready to wield a shovel and pick and go to work on America's canal system. By 1838, Catholics were the dominant immigrant group, and by 1840, half of all immigrants were Irish. Their poverty foreshadowed the great multitudes that would wash ashore when the potato fields failed, and the conditions in which they lived offered hints of the horrors to come. Cities throughout the Northeast found themselves host to small shanty settlements referred to as "Irishtowns," a term devoid of affection. Jobs were not hard to come by, but they were dangerous and backbreaking. Canals, reservoirs, turnpikes, and, eventually, railroads were needed if the American republic was to achieve its manifest destiny—a term an Irish-American journalist named John L. O'Sullivan coined in 1845, as pre–Civil War America set its sights westward. Ireland, a nation on the eve of starvation was about to turn its eyes westward, too. But its destiny was uncertain at best.

When Famine struck, the coming of the Kennedys and the O'Neills and millions like them

Once in America, the Irish immigrants did not necessarily settle straight away. Although many congregated in major cities and even went into business, such as the Philadelphia ship-joiner shown here, others, especially Irish Protestants, scorned the seaport cities and headed for the wilderness.

utterly changed the Irish-American narrative. From the Famine onward, the Irish experience in America became, in effect, the Irish Catholic experience. Images of the Irish in the popular imagination, from the rude caricatures that populated the drawings of New York cartoonist Thomas Nast (known better for his searing portraits of Boss Tweed and his depiction of Saint Nicholas as a plump, bearded gent) to Bridget the servant girl, were those of the Catholic Irish, not of Andrew Jackson, whose parents hailed from County Antrim; not the department store magnate A. T. Stewart or the banker Thomas Mellon, Irish-American Protestants all. In the years after the Famine, the notion of Irish Protestants marching in honor of Saint Patrick, as they did during the American Revolution, somehow seemed unthinkable, if not downright unnatural. When the starving Irish began washing up on America's shores, a sidelight in American history—Irish immigration—was transformed into an epic of tragedy, bitterness, triumph, and vindication.

*

One of the most remarkable elections in the history of the Commonwealth of Massachusetts was held in November 1854. The great wave of Famine-inspired immigration was over, but Boston, Lowell, and other Massachusetts cities were now inundated with Irish immigrants. Boston had tried particularly hard to resist the tide, imploring the state government to spend less money on public schools and other services that immigrants used. The city had imposed a head tax on immigrants. Nothing worked. In 1847 alone, at least 30,000 immigrants poured into Boston, which at the time had a population of only 120,000. And, of course, 1847 was not nearly the end of the Famine. By

The log cabin housed these hardy frontiersmen and their families. They could not have guessed that their living quarters would become an icon of the American landscape.

the time Patrick and Bridget Kennedy started their family in East Boston, their Yankee neighbors were in an uproar. Nothing had been done, and so voters went to the polls in 1854 and chose candidates who knew nothing, or at least made that dubious claim.

The Know-Nothing movement in its various forms was, and remains, among the most successful third parties in American history. An outgrowth of a network of local organizations with names like the Order of the Star Spangled Banner and, with more sinister connotations, the Black Snakes and the Rip Saws, the Know-Nothings captured local offices throughout New England, the mid-Atlantic, the South, and the West in the 1850s. While the movement despised blacks and foreigners in general, its specific complaint during and after the Famine immigration was with Catholics. A newspaper mocked the movement by printing a Know-Nothing menu, consisting of Jesuit soup, broiled priest, fried nuns and, for dessert, a rich Irish brogue.

While it lent itself to mockery, the Know-Nothing movement was a powerful force in pre–Civil War politics. Its most spectacular success came in 1854 in Massachusetts, which elected Know-Nothings into every statewide office, including governor. Every state senator was a Know-Nothing, and of the 378 members of the state House of Representatives, 376 were Know-Nothings.

The vast majority of the new legislators were amateur politicians who truly knew nothing of government and politics; their field of expertise was the discontent of their fellow native-born Americans. True to their word, they passed two pieces of anti-immigrant legislation: one barring naturalized citizens from voting until they had lived in the United States for twenty-one years, the other prohibiting immigrants, even those who became citizens, from holding elective office in Massachusetts.

America's port cities presented immigrants with a chaotic glimpse of the hard road ahead. Here, Irish families are greeted at Constitution Wharf in Boston.

Demonstrating that they knew *something*, the legislators voted themselves a pay raise before adjourning.

There is no record of Patrick Kennedy's thoughts on the movement that he and his wife and thousands like them inspired. Very likely he was too busy trying to keep his wife and children fed, clothed, and safe in an atmosphere that was the ruin of many a family. Such an effort required the very sort of American virtues so many saw lacking in the Irish immigrants—thrift, patience, determination, and self-sacrifice.

Patrick and Bridget became parents for the fourth time in January 1858, when their first son was born. They called him by his father's name, Patrick Joseph. Ten months later, Patrick Joseph Kennedy Sr. came down with cholera, the disease of the Irish slums. He died, exhausted, at age thirty-five.

The family managed to survive the blow intact, and the Kennedys joined the crowded ranks of Irish households headed by women. With death and desertion common, Irish women were many a family's anchor. The O'Neills and the Kennedys carried on without their patriarchs.

The young Patrick Joseph Kennedy managed to escape the world that killed his father, putting aside money from a job on the Boston waterfront and eventually setting himself up in the saloon business. From such a world of conviviality it was a short journey into local politics, a field the Irish in America remade in their own image once they had the opportunity.

Patrick Joseph Kennedy and James O'Neill were children of the Great Irish Famine. Their parents had suffered through catastrophe only to live through tragedy. As heirlooms, they received the scars of a generation. James O'Neill lived in terror that the poverty of his childhood might one day come knocking on his door again. Although he went on to win great fame and praise in that most unstable of professions, acting, James O'Neill latched onto a role that offered a regular paycheck and a semblance of security. As the lead in traveling productions of *The Count of Monte Cristo*, O'Neill

(continued on page 39)

MARGO LOCKWOOD

THE TRUE MEANING OF "LACE CURTAIN"

Margo Lockwood is the author of several volumes of poetry, including LEFT-HANDED HAPPINESS, BARE ELEGY, *and* BLACK DOG. *She lives in Brookline, Massachusetts.*

When people mutter "lace-curtain Irish," I am often bothered. Some Irish Americans use it in a self-mocking way, not about themselves, but about their grandparents perhaps, or some distant relative. I used to hear it employed to describe a section of town more wealthy and established, where people owned rather than rented their houses. It may have been an epithet for people who wanted to better themselves or who were aping their betters. They wanted to have lace curtains up, too, but maybe all their furniture was just right out of the alley. There was a pejorative sense that people were putting up a front. Clannish as the Irish Americans may be, they never stint on intraclannish insult.

✥

When I was eight years old, in 1947, we lived on the second floor of a rented three-decker in a neighborhood of Brookline, Massachusetts, called Whiskey Point. My mother bought a proper frame for the starching and

PETER QUINN

FARMERS NO MORE: FROM RURAL IRELAND TO THE TEEMING CITY

Peter Quinn is the author of BANISHED CHILDREN OF EVE, *a novel about the Irish in New York City during the Civil War.*

In 1975, the year after my father died, my mother announced she was planning a trip to Ireland. She wasn't interested, she said, in a guided tour of the if-this-is-Tuesday-this-must-be-Dublin type. She wanted to visit the places in County Cork that her parents had emigrated from in the 1880s.

To describe my mother's decision as unusual is to understate. A steadfast Catholic who wouldn't hesitate to identify herself as Irish, she had never shown the slightest interest in exploring the past. Occasionally she expressed the opposite, going beyond a blanket dismissal of questions her children posed about the family history to active destruction of birth and death records, diaries, newspaper clippings, and the like. "Excess baggage" was her unadorned explanation.

My parents met in 1928, while my mother was a junior in college and my father was working as a civil engineer and attending law school at night. They carried the stamp of the twenties the rest of their lives, or at least of aspects now considered emblematic of the decade. Urbane and stylish, they were wonderful dancers. They loved going to nightclubs and the theater, where they enjoyed everything from the Marx Brothers to Shakespeare. In a photograph from that time, my father bears a resemblance to Jimmy Walker, dapper in a handsome overcoat, derby cocked at a jaunty angle. Like Walker, my father wanted to be a songwriter but was directed willy-nilly by his father into politics.

✳

My mother and father weren't exactly Zelda and Scott. The idea of marrying outside the Catholic fold was a nonstarter. Ivy League schools were beyond the pale. Though they enjoyed an evening's jaunt in the downtown, cosmopolitan world, their home was uptown, on the ethnic terra firma of the Bronx, where my father made his political career. But they were city people to the bone. Content to rent an apartment rather than own a home, they had an enduring sense that whatever its tensions or temptations, New York was the future, a place safe from the ravages of Prohibition, Fundamentalism, and small-town Republicanism.

Inevitably, although it was never spoken about, there must have been a gap between my parents and their parents, tensions, disagreements, disparate expectations. Three of my grandparents were from rural Ireland and had never set foot in a city until they traveled through Cork or Liverpool on their way to America. Even my father's mother, who was American born—the daughter of immigrants who arrived during the Famine—spent her early years on the farm where her father worked, on the outskirts of New York City. Yet whatever their arguments involved, they weren't over the relative merits of cities and farms. If there was the slightest nostalgia on my grandparents' part for the land or for the life they knew as tenant farmers, it was neither passed on nor mentioned.

✳

This amazingly rapid transformation of a substantial portion of the most thoroughly rural people in the British Isles into stereotypical denizens of America's cities—cops, crooks, pols, tough-talking and streetwise, as immortalized on celluloid by Jimmy Cagney and a cadre of supporting mugs such as James Gleason and William Frawley—is a central part of the Irish immigrant saga. There wasn't a trace of the old clod clinging to their spats, no more than to the stylish dresses of Irish maids strolling the park on their day off. As one nineteenth-century observer noted, "These girls had been brought up in the floorless mud cabins covered with thatch, and gone to mass without shoes or stockings very likely, and now enjoy all the more their unaccustomed luxuries."

The transition these immigrants made was often traumatic, and the high rates at which the Irish were sent off to jails and asylums is one measure of the dislocation they endured. But the Irish weren't simply crowded into the cities by poverty or the native population's prevailing hostility toward foreigners, especially of the Paddy variety. Crowding was a part of who they were. The traditional Irish village, or *clachan*, that many came out of bore no resemblance to the classic European model of orderly streets, neat squares, tidy rows of shops and homes. The *clachan* was a clump of cabins that leaned on one another, a physical embodiment of the tight-knit community built on a communal method of land distribution called the Rundale system.

Outsiders often remarked on the intense conviviality of the *clachan*, the incessant emphasis on singing, dancing, and storytelling that wasn't merely part of Irish culture but its living heart, the vessel of its survival. Asenath Nicholson, an American woman who traveled throughout Ireland at the time of the Famine, wrote of one such community that was owned by a well-intentioned landlord determined to introduce the British system of widely spaced cabins, with fields individually tenanted and tilled.

As described by Mrs. Nicholson, the inhabitants resisted the plan because they feared "it would thin out the crowds and break up the clanship too much." When they finally complied and tore down their homes, they did so in a way that asserted the very identity that was being called into question:

> The Rundale system brought new difficulties to these people; it broke up their clusters of huts, and the
> facilities of assembling-nights, to tell and hear long stories; and they must tumble down their cabins,

which were of loose stones; and the owner of a cabin hired a fiddler, which no sooner known, than the joyous Irish are on the spot: each takes a stone or stones upon his back (for women and children are there)—they dance at intervals—the fiddler animates them on while the day-light lasts, and then the night is finished by dancing.

Perhaps no force in human history is more persistent or less appreciated than the tenacious persistence of traits, customs, and attitudes that embody a group's values and beliefs, and that resist almost every effort to uproot or pull them down. The cabins are razed. The people move on and are scattered. But the stones of experience and understanding are carried with them, in their souls and minds, taken to some new place, and reassembled as the foundation of a new life.

Fifty years after Mrs. Nicholson's sojourn in Ireland Jacob Riis, in his famous exposé of the tenement districts of New York, remarked on the seeming inertia that kept many Irish immigrants and their descendants in the slums. In contrast to the Teuton, Riis wrote, who "makes the most of his tenement . . . and as soon as he can save up money enough, he gets out and never crosses the threshold of one again," the Celt appeared attracted by the density and motion of tenement life: "The Irishman's genius runs to public affairs rather than domestic life; wherever he is mustered in force the saloon is the gorgeous center of political activity."

Riis didn't approve of saloons. What reformers did? At best they saw them as a poor man's recreation, a sorry substitute for the parks and libraries the working classes should have access to; at worst, as a tentacle of the parasitic political machines that deceived and exploited the masses. The reformers weren't entirely wrong. Saloons weren't settlement houses. Yet, in the case of the Irish, the dyad of machine politics and the saloon weren't pernicious weeds grown out of the noxious soil of slumdom, which choked the immigrant's ability to rise to something better, but an urban inflorescence of what had long been basic to the people's resistance to the colonizer's attempt to remake them in his own image and likeness.

For the Irish, the saloon was no more restricted to drinking or the business of vote mustering than the parish church was to the worship of God and the salvation of souls. These activities or ambitions weren't entirely absent. But the power of the saloon and church were as cornerstones of the urban *clachan*; as sodalities for the shared performance of the rituals of song, dance, and talk; as labor exchanges and community forums; as intimate spaces in the urban vastness that reduced the bewilderment of the immigrants and allowed them to make sense of their surroundings before they attempted to move any farther into the New World. At the end of the twentieth century, Irish Americans in New York or Chicago or Boston were still identifying their neighborhoods not by cross streets or avenues but by parishes or even pubs.

There is an incident from the "long" strike of 1872 in New York City that is revelatory of the cultural strands spun forward from rural Ireland into an urban web of mutual support and solidarity. At that time, in the closest the city ever came to a general strike, one hundred thousand men left their jobs to demonstrate for the eight-hour day. When the unified resistance of employers seemed to doom the protest to a quick collapse, John Roache, an Irishman who was both a professional singer and an employee of one of the city's largest foundries, organized a dozen men into a singing group. Instead of spreading pamphlets or making speeches, Roache wrote songs about the workers' cause and went with his troupe from saloons to labor halls, rallying the strikers. Though the walkout eventually failed, the resonance of Roache's appeal among the Irish helped sustain a prolonged contest and left behind an organization to carry on the fight.

Mullen's Alley in New York City: a new kind of lane in a new kind of village for the Irish, who nevertheless preferred close quarters over open spaces.

Out west, the Irish who went to the frontier often wrote of the loneliness and disorientation they experienced amid the wide open spaces other settlers seemed to thrive on. For better or for worse, rugged individualism wasn't an Irish characteristic or aspiration. Back east, weighing the success of Tammany Hall, the cultural elite of the day thought it detected among the Irish a natural proclivity to "bread and circuses." The tendency was undoubtedly there, if by "bread" is meant the desire of the laboring classes for work and some measure of security for themselves and their families, and if by "circuses" is implied not idle spectacle but the ceremonies of community—the rituals of clambakes, boat rides, Fourth of July picnics, election parades, etc.—that dispelled the drabness and alienation that so readily envelop the urban poor.

*

When my mother made her trip to Ireland, she brought along her sister, a granddaughter, and myself. We found the village her father came from, a small forlorn crossroads outside Macroom, in what had been an Irish-speaking area until the early twentieth century. "Greatly shrunk in size and spirit from what it must have been a century ago" is how the parish priest described it to us. The old church had burned fifty years before, and with it the parish records. There wasn't even a faded scrawl on a moldering baptismal registry to connect us to these empty, mist-shrouded fields.

My mother and I left the others on the church steps and walked together a short distance down an unpaved road. Nearby was a crumbling concrete barn with a rusted iron roof. There was a radio on. I looked at my mother. I knew she was still deeply grieved by my father's death, and I was afraid the utter absence of any trace of her own father, of a past gone and forever beyond reach, might bring her to tears.

The mist was quickly changing to rain. "We should go back," I said.

"Listen," she said. I heard the quick fluctuations of fiddles coming from the radio, Irish sounds. "My father sang that tune."

She smiled and lifted her coat above her thin ankles and did a small, graceful jig, the soles of her American shoes gently slapping the ground. It was a step I'd never seen her do before. ❖

CHAPTER 2

THE
PARISH

THE BUILDING
OF A COMMUNITY

OLD SAINT Patrick's Cathedral on Mott Street in New York City has none of the glory of its more famous successor, the Saint Patrick's of Fifth Avenue in midtown Manhattan. Old Saint Pat's was dedicated in 1815, a time when New York's Irish Catholic community was modest in number and humble of means, and Saint Patrick's still has a modest and humble look about it. It was not the first Catholic church in New York, for that honor belonged to Saint Peter's on Barclay Street, which opened in 1785. But the designation of New York's second Catholic church as a bona fide *cathedral* spoke to both ambition and foresight. From this building would rise an institution that New Yorkers—and not only Catholics—would one day refer to as "the powerhouse."

What is most striking about Old Saint Patrick's today is not its relative simplicity nor its incongruousness—the neighborhood consists of immigrants who worship gods of other names. No, what is striking about Old Saint Patrick's is as plain and ordinary as a brick wall. Indeed, it *is* a brick wall, for the old church is sealed off from the bustling streets and crowded sidewalks by a scraped and scarred ten-foot barrier, built for prosaic reasons but symbolizing a distinctly Irish Catholic worldview from the early days of the immigrant experience in America.

The wall was built to protect the cathedral from the torches and missiles of anti-Catholic mobs

St. Patrick's Cathedral on Fifth Avenue in New York City, built in the nineteenth century with the pennies of the poor, is now the seat of one of America's richest archdioceses.

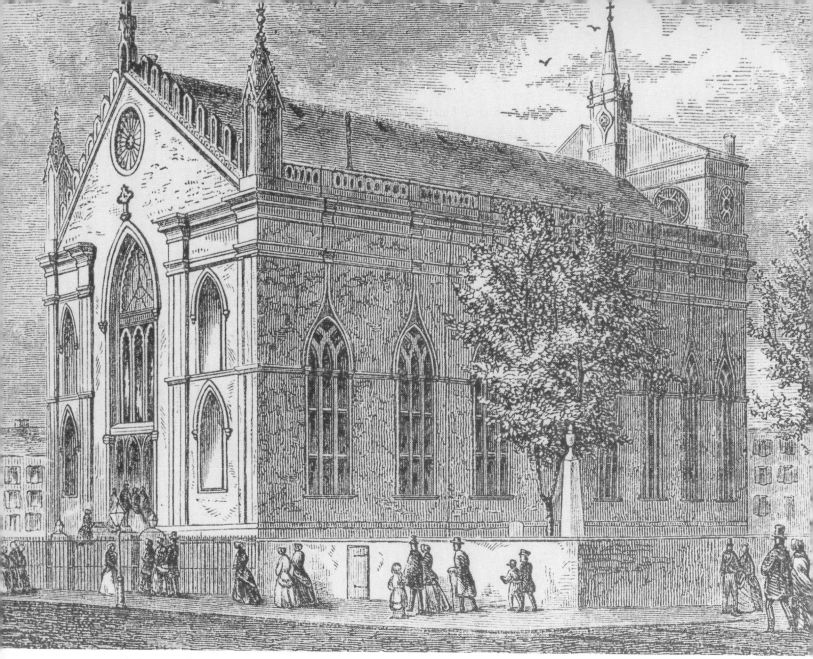

The original St. Patrick's Cathedral in downtown New York, between Mott and Mulberry Streets, was built in 1815 and was protected from the disapproval of hostile neighbors by a stone wall.

that were a regular feature of American urban life in the early nineteenth century. But as the Irish Catholic community began building institutions—such as schools, hospitals, and universities—walls became even more necessary. Not real walls always, but a virtual screen of protection, of power and influence, that became known simply as "the parish."

*

The flight of the Irish from America's cities and the changes brought about by the Second Vatican Council and a more secular, more mobile society have loosened the bonds of the parish, and it is rare today to hear a young Irish Catholic describe his or her neighborhood by the name of its local parish. Still, there are some holdouts, some reminders of a time when Catholics in general and Irish Catholics in particular gave shape and character to American urban life. In Brooklyn, for example, it is not unusual to hear politicians, journalists, and residents refer to a community known only by four letters, OLPH. Located in a neighborhood between the old Brooklyn community of Bay Ridge and the emerging Brooklyn of Sunset Park, the parish of Our Lady of Perpetual Help acts as a bridge of sorts between old-line Italian Catholics and the new Catholic immigrants from Central and South America in their separate neighborhoods. The parish, however, hasn't forgotten its roots: Each year it is the site of a popular Irish music concert, and it has been the setting for various Irish-American commemorations.

For more than a century, the parish was as central to the organization of urban life in heavily Catholic cities as any government institution. The parish was the place no hostile culture and no offensive custom could penetrate. The sons and daughters of immigrant parents met under the auspices of the parish, and those who married often did so in the building where they had been baptized. The pace of parish life was set by the liturgical calendar—individual months were dedicated to certain devotions (the Sacred Heart, Saint Joseph), Saturday evenings were set aside for confessions, and an assortment of Holy Days and First Fridays called parishioners to additional worship. The local fish market was crowded with neighbors every Friday morning. Families with the variety of problems that afflicted the poor and the alienated turned to the parish priest, whose training for such social work was uneven at best. The parish was a world of common values and shared rituals.

When Mr. Dooley, the fictional Irish-American saloonkeeper with an unmistakable accent created by Chicago journalist Finley Peter Dunne, lamented the impositions of keeping true to the Good Friday fast, he struck a chord that resonated in parishes near and far:

> I suppose, Mr. McKinna, that ye'd think nothing iv tuckin' in a slab iv beef on Good Friday, like any prowtestant, but f'r me an' th' likes iv me 'tis different. If I was to ate meat this blessed day I'd go th' way Hinnissy's goat wint that thried to di-gest th' hoop-skirt. I'd choke to death.

For immigrant Irish Catholics thrown into the cauldron of American city life in the nineteenth century—as Mr. Dooley said, "f'r me an' th' likes iv me"—the parish was a reminder of the world they had left behind. In describing that intimate and familiar world back home in Ireland, one immigrant recalled with nostalgia his nightly routine in the village of his birth. After work, he wrote, "I could then go to a fair, a wake or a dance, or I would spend the winter nights in a neighbor's house, cracking jokes by the turf fire. If I had . . . but a sore head I would have a neighbor . . . that would run to see me." Not every immigrant's memories were so nostalgic—some left so embittered and so betrayed that they never looked back. Like the lovers in the ballad "Farewell to Enniskillen," they wished only to leave the hunger, oppression, and even the small world of the village. Once settled in a world free of constraints, "they think no more of Ireland, nor Enniskillen town."

Still, even the most enthusiastic immigrant found what was literally a new world, one for which

From the outset charmed
by the soft, quick speech
of those men and women,
Theresa's friends—and the church

she went to, the "other,"
not the white plain Baptist
I tried to learn God in.
Or, later, in Boston the legend

of "being Irish," the lore, the magic,
the violence, the comfortable
or uncomfortable drunkenness.
But most, that endlessly present talking,

as Mr. Connealy's, the ironmonger,
sat so patient in Cronin's Bar,
and told me sad, emotional stories
with the quiet air of an elder

does talk to a younger man.
Then, when at last I was twenty-one,
my mother finally told me
indeed the name Creeley was Irish—

and the heavens opened, birds sang,
and the trees and the ladies spoke
with wondrous voices. The power of the glory
of poetry—was at last mine.

—ROBERT CREELEY

---

most were unprepared. The parish served to ease the transition from the Irish farm to the American city. It has been suggested, most eloquently by the sociologist William McCready, that the American urban parish was, and remains, a replica of a rural Irish village. Central to the parish, or village, was the church itself. More than a house of worship, although it surely was that, the church was the institution to which the parish community turned for recreation, education, counseling, guidance, arbitration, and even financial support. The parish, like the village, established a sense of place, or, some would say, an unnecessary set of borders. It was a place where immigrants from the villages of West Cork and the stony fields of Connemara could hear voices with a familiar cadence—or at least as familiar as a West Cork accent would sound to a native of Galway.

The American Church always has been an immigrant institution. In 1850, Church officials reckoned that of the 1.6 million Catholics in America, no more than 20 percent were native-born. But it was the Irish, in their overwhelming numbers and their devotion to a Church that historically provided them not only with spiritual solace but an identity, who defined American Catholicism and who provided the bulk of its leaders—of 464 American bishops appointed from the American Revolution to the New Deal, 58 percent were sons of Irish fathers. That figure does not include the sons of Irish mothers who married non-Irish men, nor does it include second-, third-, and fourth-generation Irish.

The Irish, then, helped invent the parish as a quasi-political unit, a network of like-minded people, a community unto itself, enclosed by a wall designed to keep out hostile forces and preserve the faith and devotion of those within.

*

Like so many other aspects of Irish-American life, the relationship between immigrant and parish changed with the coming of the Famine immigrants. Until the late 1840s and early 1850s, Irish Catholics in America were not particularly churchgoing. Weekly mass attendance before the Famine has been estimated at about 40 percent, a number that doesn't suggest images of a devout and pious people. No doubt mass

(continued on page 55)

ELLEN SKERRETT

"BRICKS AND MORTAR": CORNERSTONES OF THE IRISH PRESENCE

Skerrett is a professor of history at the University of Illinois and is the editor of AT THE CROSSROADS:
OLD SAINT PATRICK'S AND THE CHICAGO IRISH

Rising above and beyond the humble surrounding neighborhood, Chicago's Old St. Patrick's called parishioners to worship in a beautiful setting.

No other dimension of the Irish-American experience has been more important—or more misunderstood—than church-building. Throughout the nineteenth century in cities and towns across the country, immigrant Irish Catholics devoted scarce resources to building imposing churches. Financed with the nickels and dimes of poor people, these structures became visible symbols that the Irish were creating a place for themselves in America. But far from being applauded for constructing sacred spaces that dominated urban and rural landscapes, Irish Catholics were routinely criticized for wasting money. Considering the large number of Irish men and women in prison and on the relief rolls of major American cities from the 1830s through the 1890s, wouldn't it have made more sense, the argument went, to build orphanages and reformatories rather than ornate edifices with imported stained-glass windows, statues, and altars?

Contrary to the conventional wisdom of the day, church-building had long-term positive consequences for Irish immigrants and their American-born children and grandchildren. Creating beautiful houses of worship was not an activity for the fainthearted. It demanded commitment, cooperation, vision, and significant sums of money. The challenge was enormous, as Catholics in Charleston, South Carolina, knew all too well. In 1833 they lived in a diocese that was "perhaps . . . the poorest in Christendom," whose houses of worship did "not merit the name of churches." In view of their status as impoverished outsiders in a Protestant-dominated country, it is not surprising that Irish immigrants found strength in brick-and-mortar Catholicism. Whether they lived in the South, West, or urban North, they used church-building to proclaim their identity, create community, and leave their imprint on the landscape.

When Saint Mary's, the "mother parish" of the Carolinas, was destroyed by fire in 1838, the predominantly Irish congregation seized the opportunity to build an elegant Greek Revival church that stands today at 89 Haskell Street. Against a rising tide of nativism, their choice of design was calculated to focus positive public attention on the city's Catholic minority. And it worked! In adopting the most popular style of architecture in America, Saint Mary's parishioners placed themselves on an equal footing with older Protestant congregations, literally putting their church on the map. Charleston's Irish Catholics—like their northern cousins—knew that church-building was as much about competition as it was about worship.

Saint Patrick's Cathedral on Mott Street in New York City symbolized the hopes and dreams of the Irish when it was dedicated in 1815. The first church in the United States built in honor of Ireland's patron saint, it set the standard in Catholic parishes across the nation. The Chicago Irish, in short order, were building their own Saint Patrick's for their "mother parish," but they faced formidable obstacles beyond a lack of money: The neighborhood near the Chicago River was a working-class district, and its unpaved streets were breeding grounds for cholera and typhoid. This was compounded by a new disaster. According to the *Illustrated London News*, the Great Famine halted construction and the unfinished houses of worship stood as "melancholy monument[s] of pride and poverty." Church-building took on new layers of meaning for Famine refugees who arrived in the United States during an era characterized by anti-immigrant and anti-Catholic nativism.

At the time Chicago's Irish were building their Romanesque church—another Saint Patrick's—at Adams and Desplaines Streets, for example, newspapers portrayed them as impoverished aliens, unable to perform their duties as Americans because of their mindless loyalty to church leaders. "Who does not know," thundered the *Chicago Tribune* in 1855, "that the most depraved, debased, worthless and irredeemable drunkards and sots which curse the community, are Irish Catholics?" The completion of Saint Patrick's Church in 1856 did more than provide larger worship quarters for the city's Irish. It challenged deeply entrenched stereotypes about Catholics and provided incontrovertible proof that Chicago's Irish had created a place of beauty in their lives and in their neighborhood. In time, even the *Tribune* changed its view, conceding that churches such as Saint Patrick's contributed to the growth and stability of the city.

✢

The elegant St. Mary's Church on Haskell Street in Charleston, South Carolina, replaced the original St. Mary's, which was destroyed by fire in 1838. Its Greek Revival style drew great attention to the "minority" church, and put it on equal footing with the revered Protestant congregations in the South.

Like their contemporaries in New York and Chicago, the Irish who settled in San Francisco after the gold rush of 1849 also became enthusiastic supporters of brick-and-mortar Catholicism. Competition between denominations reached fever pitch as Protestants, Catholics, and Jews all sought to put their imprint on the Bay City. Indeed, exactly one week after Congregationalists dedicated First Church at the southwest corner of Dupont and California in 1853, Irish Catholics laid the cornerstone of their new Gothic cathedral just across the street! Designed by architects William Craine and Thomas England (a native of Bandon, County Cork) on land donated by John Sullivan, Saint Mary's constituted a powerful symbol of faith in the future of the Catholic Church, to be sure, but also in the Irish and their city. Acclaimed as "one of the architectural beauties of San Francisco," the new Saint Mary's was the most expensive house of worship built at midcentury. Undaunted by its eighty-five-thousand-dollar price tag, Irish Catholics contributed generously through pew rentals, parish fairs, and concerts, including the first production in California of Mozart's Twelfth Grand Mass.

The success of Irish church-building was not lost on Protestant clergymen. Perhaps the highest praise came from the Reverend F. E. Jewell of San Francisco's Howard Street Methodist Church. He commented on the dramatic contrast between the sewers where Irish immigrants worked on weekdays and the churches in which they worshipped on Sunday "surrounded with objects of beauty and with the incense of worship, and these things are as much for [them] as for the richest [men] in the parish."

With its impressive network of parishes, schools, hospitals, and charitable institutions, the Catholic Church in San Francisco quickly eclipsed other denominations in terms of size and scale. Just how much sacred space mattered became evident in the aftermath of the 1906 earthquake. More than twenty-five thousand buildings in a five-square-mile area were destroyed, leaving two hundred thousand people homeless. Determined to save the western section of the city, the fire department made its last stand at the new Saint Mary's Cathedral on Van Ness and O'Farrell Streets. For three days fire threatened the huge brick edifice (nicknamed "Chicago Gothic" because it had been designed by the Windy City's most prominent Irish architects, James J. Egan and Charles H. Prindeville). But thanks to the heroic efforts of two priests who "bravely climbed the spire and at the risk of their lives extinguished the flames," Saint Mary's was spared—along with the rest of San Francisco. When thousands of men, women, and children gathered to give thanks on the shattered steps of their Gothic cathedral on Sunday, April 22, 1906, they had only to look at "the blackened waste just across the street" to see how close their city had come to perishing.

*

Although Irish Catholic churches became landmarks in cities and towns across the nation, nowhere were the results more spectacular than at the second Saint Patrick's Cathedral in New York. Described in guidebooks as "the largest and most beautiful church edifice in America," Saint Patrick's was ranked on a par with "the cathedrals of Rheims, Amiens and Cologne, on the Continent; and the naves of York, Westminster and Exeter in England." It was no accident that Archbishop John Hughes hired James Renwick, the foremost Gothic architect in the United States, to draw up plans for the new structure on Fifth Avenue. In keeping with its status as the largest Irish city in America, New York would have a Catholic cathedral built to endure "as long as any human work can last." In a front-page story in 1858, the *New York Times* lavished praise on this monumental undertaking, predicting that Saint Patrick's "will have no parallel on this continent." According to the *Times,* on the morning of the cornerstone laying, "The Celtic element . . . descended on Fiftieth-street in a body of one hundred thousand strong" and an "unbroken line of carriages" lined Broadway and Sixth Avenue.

The *Times* further provided its readers with detailed descriptions of the colorful vestments worn by presiding officials and it commented favorably on "the precision with which everything was regulated—the dignified and reverent harmony which marked the participants individually and collectively." Of special interest to the *Times* was Bishop Patrick John Ryan's spirited defense of church-building in a two-hour sermon delivered "without notes or assistance of any kind." To the charge that Saint Patrick's "had been mainly built by the pennies of the poor," Bishop Ryan responded: "Most sacred and appropriate offering!"

*

While New York's Gothic cathedral remains the most famous symbol of Irish America, the mother parish of the Chicago Irish provides a classic illustration of the enduring power of sacred space. Between 1912 and 1922, Thomas A. O'Shaughnessy transformed the interior of Chicago's oldest public building into a masterpiece of Celtic Revival art. As a young man visiting the 1893 Columbian Exposition in Chicago, O'Shaughnessy had admired reproductions of such ancient Irish treasures as the Ardagh Chalice, the Bell of Patrick, and the Cross

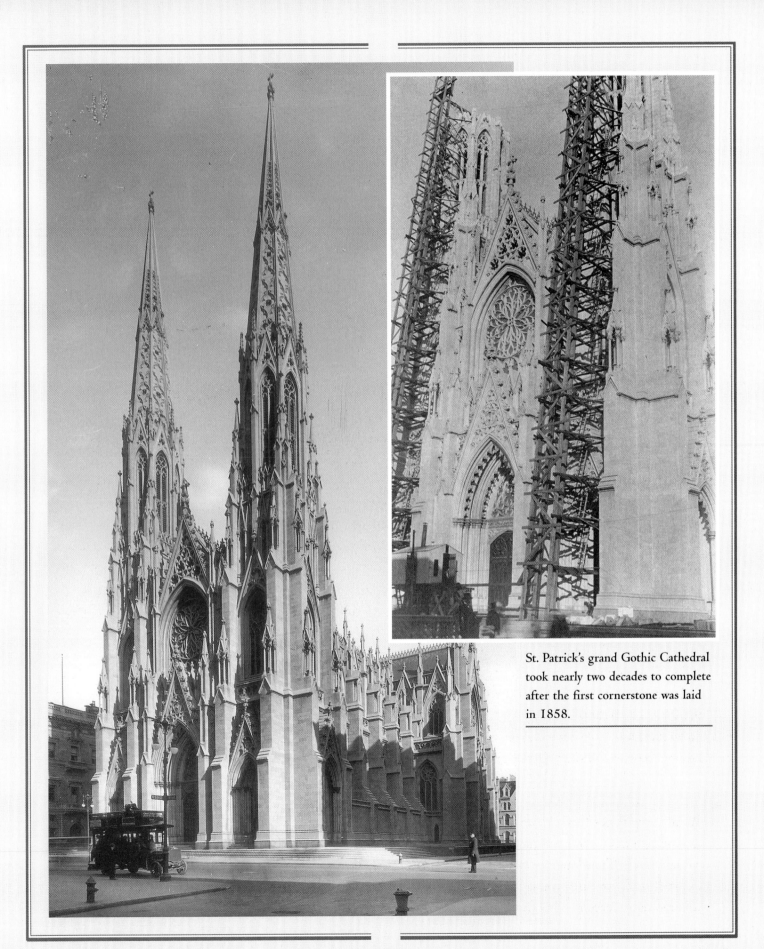

St. Patrick's grand Gothic Cathedral took nearly two decades to complete after the first cornerstone was laid in 1858.

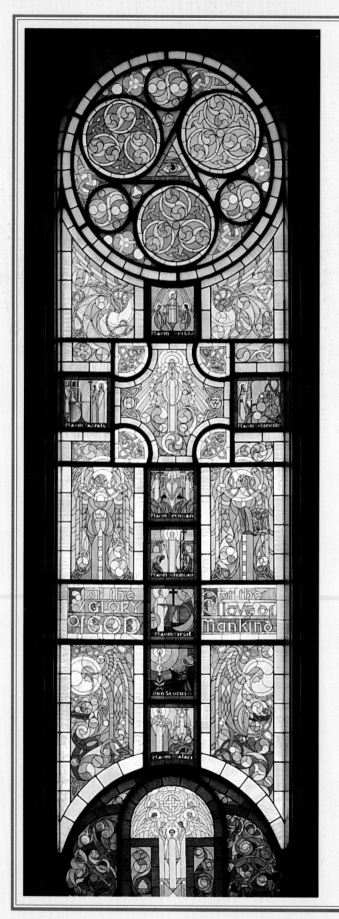

of Cong. But it was the ninth-century illuminated manuscript on display at Trinity College in Dublin that fired his imagination. O'Shaughnessy was one of the last persons allowed to sketch from the *Book of Kells* in 1900, an experience that had long-lasting consequences for his art and for Saint Patrick's in Chicago.

On the walls and ceiling of the old Romanesque church on Adams and Desplaines Streets, O'Shaughnessy created intricate braided crosses and interlaced patterns that ended in abstract characters such as dragons and birds' beaks. The results were breathtaking. Nothing like these Celtic designs had ever appeared in an American Irish Catholic church before. Equally compelling were his luminescent stained-glass windows that depicted the great saints of Ireland as well as such heroes as Brian Boru and Terence MacSwiney, the Lord Mayor of Cork, who starved himself to death in London's Brixton prison in 1920 as a martyr for Irish freedom.

Reconnecting the Chicago Irish with their Celtic past through stained glass and stencils was an act of genius as much as faith, and thanks to a recent multimillion-dollar restoration, Thomas O'Shaughnessy's vision for Old Saint Patrick's continues to challenge accepted notions of sacred art and Irish identity. In few American parishes have the bricks and mortar mattered so much. ❖

Cardinal James Gibbons of Baltimore was a staunch defender of labor unions. He was born in Baltimore and raised in Ireland, but he returned to the United States as a young man.

attendance would have been higher were there more churches, more parishes, and more priests. But the Catholic Church in America before the Famine was low in numbers, money, and priest power. There were ten churches to serve New York's ninety thousand Catholics in 1840, while Philadelphia had twelve parishes and Boston had nine in 1850. The head of the Church in New York, Archbishop John Hughes, an immigrant from County Tyrone who started life in America as a gardener, complained that "the insufficient number of churches has been . . . an immense drawback on the progress of religion."

The Famine immigrants and those who came afterward provided, in spite of their terrible poverty, the means and numbers for an astonishing expansion of parish life in America. The number of parishes in Philadelphia doubled between 1850 and 1860. Growth was somewhat slower, but still astonishing in New York, where the number of parishes doubled between 1845 and 1863, and in Boston, which saw 100 percent growth between 1850 and 1870. Many of the new congregants who escaped starvation in Ireland believed that their suffering was a judgment from on high, an analysis that Charles Trevelyan, who was in charge of Britain's relief operations, hoped the Irish Catholic clergy communicated to their hungry and dying congregations. The "poor people," he wrote, should not be "deprived of knowing that they are suffering from an affliction of God's providence."

In post-Famine Ireland itself, with a rural society and its customs and traditions wiped out, the Catholic Church was all the poor Irish had left, and from the suffering and hunger rose what historian Emmet Larkin called a "devotional revolution." Mass attendance tripled in the post-Famine period. Vocations to the priesthood and convent also grew, and from those ranks would come the Irish priests and nuns who would dominate the American parish. (More than fifteen hundred priests were dispatched to America from a single Dublin seminary in the late nineteenth century.) In place of the decimated institutions of village life, the post-Famine Irish parish offered all manner of societies, groups, and rituals intended to inspire a richer (and more disciplined) faith as well as providing a highly social people with a chance to share one another's company. The political bonds between the Church and Irish Catholics became tighter still, with the Church providing the central organizing

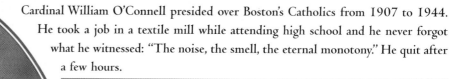

Cardinal William O'Connell presided over Boston's Catholics from 1907 to 1944. He took a job in a textile mill while attending high school and he never forgot what he witnessed: "The noise, the smell, the eternal monotony." He quit after a few hours.

principles of everyday life, including the most intimate. The clergy kept a close watch over relations between men and women, and voices were raised to protest coeducational schools and unsupervised dancing. When the post-Famine Irish Catholics left home for America, as they continued to do in great numbers, they brought with them their renewed devotion, their religious societies, and their parish-based sense of place and morals.

*

The Irish influence over the American Church's development was profound. Other Catholic immigrant groups brought their own traditions, but they were defenseless in the face of overwhelming numbers from Ireland on both sides of the altar. The German-American parish, for example, featured input from lay people unheard of in an Irish parish, and Italian-American pastors were less likely to emphasize weekly attendance at mass. The American Church as a whole, however, took on the stricter, more authoritarian character of the Irish parish as Ireland's exiles landed on the shores of New York, Boston, Philadelphia, and elsewhere. The Catholic population of America increased by a million (from 660,000 to 1.6 million) between 1840 and 1850, and the bulk of these new American Catholics were the Famine Irish, who brought with them a distinct identity based on their religion, an abiding affection for the clergy who shared their sufferings, and a faith they had held on to even in the face of severe discrimination and bigotry. From that moment, everything about the American Church, from its insistence on a separate Catholic identity to the regulation of parishioners' sexual morals to the emphasis on clerical hierarchy, smacked of inherent Irishness. And it was no wonder. Thirteen of America's first seventeen cardinals boasted Irish roots, and the Irish dominated the Church rank and file of parish priests, to the occasional chagrin of German, French, and Italian Catholics who sometimes requested, or demanded, their own national parishes with their own priests, thus accomplishing a segregation within the already segregated Catholic community. (For example, the small number of Lithuanians and Poles in Irish South Boston had their own parishes.)

Irish domination was as true of the convent as it was of the rectory. Historian Suellen Hoy of the University of Notre Dame notes that several thousand nuns left Ireland for America in two distinct waves during the nineteenth century. A Dublin educator named Sister Mary Eustace Eaton, who ran a school for girls from the city's working classes, single-handedly sent four hundred Irish nuns to America in the late nineteenth century. They and many others crossed the Atlantic in response to pleas from Irish-American bishops who found themselves with hospitals to staff, schools to run, and social problems to address. Many of these women

Thomas Nast, the famous cartoonist of the nineteenth century, expressed the feelings of Nativists who believed Catholic immigrants were subverting American institutions. Here, Nast draws bishops as alligators attacking defenseless America. The Vatican looms in the background, with a flag displaying a harp.

were among the most enthusiastic of immigrants, for Irish society offered them little save poverty and grinding routine.

Whether at the altar, in the schools, or in the pews, the Irish presence in the American Catholic Church was ubiquitous. Orders of nuns from Ireland sent young women as far afield as gold-rush-era California. The Christian Brothers of Ireland established Manhattan College in New York, La Salle University in Philadelphia, and Saint Mary's in California, in addition to producing textbooks for use in American Catholic schools. The Irish came to dominate about half of Chicago's parishes by the turn of the century, despite widespread immigration to the Windy City by Catholic Poles and Lithuanians. In fact, Irish priests were everywhere Catholics were to be found in America. So omnipresent was the Irish priest that he gained for himself a place in American popular culture, a distinction that brought with it decidedly mixed blessings.

In nineteenth-century America, there was no separating the Irish-Catholic immigrants from their clergy. Nativists invariably described Irish-Catholic culture as "priest-ridden," a subculture susceptible to antidemocratic and anti-American plots hatched in the Vatican and executed by bishops and pastors. Samuel Morse, inventor of the telegraph and one of the country's leading nativists, complained that Catholic immigrants obeyed "their priests as demigods." The cartoonist Thomas Nast offered a graphic illustration of nativist fears in a cartoon that showed a wave of bishop-alligators landing on American shores to ravage decent Americans. Priests were seen, not entirely without evidence, as the shadow leaders of immigrant Catholics, and, as both priest and immigrant Catholic were perceived to be Irish, the anti-Catholicism that already was a feature of American life in the mid-nineteenth century easily translated into anti-Irish bias.

But by 1944, when Bing Crosby donned a Roman collar and a Saint Louis Browns' cap for his role as the breezy Irish-American priest Father O'Malley in *Going My Way*, America had made a peace of sorts with priest, parish, and parishioner. Irish Catholics were running most of the nation's important cities, and one, Al Smith, had even been nominated for president, with no apparent diminution of American liberties. The film ratified the position of the Irish relative to the American Church, that is, the two were indistinguishable, at least in the public imagination. In *Going My Way*, all three priest characters are Irish, with a real-life Irish immigrant, Barry Fitzgerald, playing second fiddle to Crosby in the role of the aging pastor, Father Fitzgibbon. Fitzgerald's stage Irish accent was made for Hollywood, but his acting skills were more impressive. He was, after all, an Irish Protestant, as a generation of Irish Catholics pointed out with some amazement, and perhaps even a bit of horror.

While *Going My Way* is hard to beat for pure schmaltz, or should we say blarney, it remains the definitively romantic view of the Irish Catholic parish in the middle of twentieth-century America, when the second and third generations were dominant, and immigrants were those with gray hair and stooped posture. Saint Dominic's (Father O'Malley's parish) was intensely urban, filled with social problems (youth gangs, a hint of prostitution) that required priestly intervention, and populated with people who made it their business to know one another's business. Father Fitzgibbon knew that the local Irish cop hadn't been to church in ten years, and the neighborhood busybody, Mrs. Quimp (probably a widow, for her husband never is seen, and such parishes were populated with women whose men died young and exhausted) saw to it that the priests were kept informed of social, cultural, and political developments taking place on the streets and in the tenement flats. Saint Dominic's was the center of its parishioners' lives, and a trip outside its boundaries (to see a ball game) is about all the excitement for which anybody could ask. Why, *Going My Way* had it all, from sainted mothers to an abiding reverence for the beverage referred to in Gaelic as *usquebagh* or, as English-speakers say, whiskey.

Saint Dominic's, of course, was a Hollywood confection, but as a glimpse of a world unknown to the majority of pre—World War II Americans, it served a useful purpose. At the time of *Going My Way*, Catholics still were outside mainstream American culture, their customs and rituals a mystery to most Americans. Filled with sentiment and all-around Americanism, even with the occasional ethnic

The specter of eviction, as seen by Hollywood: Genial Father O'Malley (Bing Crosby) intercedes when the landlord's son tries to throw out the broom-wielding Mrs. Quimp in *Going My Way.*

reference thrown in, the film portrayed the Irish Catholic parish as benevolent, utterly nonthreatening, and, in the end, an important socializing force in American urban life. That was a far cry from the popular image of priests, parish, and parishioners that a young Father Fitzgibbon might have confronted at the beginning of his fictional career.

A more realistic, if less affectionate, view of the Irish parish was offered in the fiction of the Chicago author James T. Farrell, whose Studs Lonigan trilogy ranks as one of the great works of Irish-American writing. Studs lived in Saint Patrick's parish, based on Farrell's own Chicago parish of

Catholic schools staffed by nuns educated the children of immigrants and preserved their sense of separateness.

MAUREEN FITZGERALD

SAVING THE CHILDREN: IRISH-CATHOLIC NUNS

Fitzgerald teaches history at the University of Arizona. Her essay is adapted from a work in progress titled Brigit's Profession: Irish Catholic Nuns, Resistance, and the Origins of New York's Welfare System.

When historians speak of Irish-American political power in the nineteenth century, they seldom speak of nuns. And yet if one looks at the accomplishments of these women of the Catholic Church in insuring that the children of the poor Irish could be raised as Irish, and Irish Catholics at that, one could hardly discount their role. For it was through their efforts that the fabric of Irish immigrant life, already torn by Famine circumstance and a cold reception in their new land, was kept in one piece. And surely, many of the gains thereafter, whether in politics, in the workplace, in the society generally, are attributable to the generations of Irish-American children saved by the concerted activities of Irish Catholic nuns.

Saint Anselm's, and his life was filled not with poverty but with a spiritual emptiness and an ignorance born of small minds. The Catholic nationalism of Bishop John Hughes and other Irish-American prelates served an important purpose in a world in which the parish literally was embattled. But later, when the sons and daughters of immigrant generations were raising their own children, the parish walls no longer served as protection but became an obstacle to understanding the larger society into which the Irish were moving. The parish and Irish Catholic separatism inspired a skewed, if not paranoid, view of the outside world. The New York Irish, for example, nearly disrupted ceremonies commemorating the opening of the Brooklyn Bridge in 1883 because the date coincided with Queen Victoria's birthday. Some Irish refused to believe the date was a coincidence, and concluded that the Anglo-Protestant aristocracy was using the bridge ceremony as cover for a tribute to Britain's queen. (Never mind that New York had elected its first Irish Catholic mayor, William Grace, two years before.)

Warned about the motives and even the beliefs of those outside the parish walls, some Irish Catholics were ill-prepared for the day when the walls came tumbling down.

*

This story begins in midcentury, with the Famine immigration. The hundreds of thousands of Famine survivors who landed in New York City were not only terribly poor, sick, and traumatized, but also represented for middle-class Americans the first large-scale influx of profoundly impoverished people into American cities. Reformers, consisting mostly of the native-born and Protestant elite accustomed to running the affairs of the city, considered poverty to be a mark of moral failings. Individuals who did not work hard, save money, and discipline themselves properly became poor and stayed poor. Their children, theoretically innocent of their parents' fallen nature, were particularly at risk. As early as 1853, legal mechanisms enabling Protestant reformers to remove children from poor parents were officially in place.

The truancy law, for example, allowed for any citizen or police officer to arrest a child who was on the streets during school hours. If parents were found, however, they could retain custody by promising to keep the child in school. If they were not found, or if a child was arrested a second time, the child would be committed for the entire length of his or her childhood to a Protestant institution, such as the Children's Aid Society. Children, once taken from parents, were to be placed out in a "Christian home." The practice of sending urban poor children out to rural Protestant homes in the Midwest—a process often referred to as "riding the orphan train"—rested on the belief

that the American Protestant nuclear family, guided by the maternal devotion of the American woman, was the only proper setting for child-rearing in the American republic. No placing-out society run by Protestants in New York would agree to the option of placing a Catholic child in a Catholic home until after the turn of the century. This Protestant "home" and family were to serve as the setting, and Protestant women as the redemptive agents, in poor immigrant children's reform, and "the family is God's reformatory" became the rallying cry of the Protestant "child-savers" throughout the century. By the mid-1870s, Catholics estimated the number of children who were taken from parents and shipped to the Midwest to be ten thousand per year from New York City alone.

✵

Irish Catholic nuns were themselves Famine immigrants for the most part. The Sisters of Mercy, for instance, came to New York from Dublin in 1848, and for the next twenty years funneled most of their charitable resources to single women needing health care, jobs, job training, and protection from sexual assault in the domestic servant positions they took up upon landing at the port of New York. This charity was paid for largely by the work of the female immigrants themselves, and by periodic donations from church collections. Other orders, such as the Sisters of Charity and Sisters of the Good Shepherd,

Irish nuns provided thousands of poor orphans with food, shelter, and an education. Their efforts were the salvation of many Irish-American children.

all comprised largely of Irish and Irish-American women, struggled through the Civil War to provide only the most basic services for the poor, as they received no public funding to do so, and the depths of poverty among the Catholic population only grew over time.

✿

Catholic nuns did not participate much in the many debates of the day about the origins of poverty or the meaning of charity, nor did they publish a lot of material laying out the principles guiding their charitable work. Instead, they went to work, and their work was swift and decisive.

The Sisters of Charity in New York's Roman Catholic Orphan Asylum wrote to their board of managers in March 1874, stating, "[t]he accounts that we hear of Catholic orphans sent West . . . urge us to make great exertions in order to take a hundred or so more under our care." Although they complained of current overcrowding, they assured the board that help would follow their resolve: "The sisters unite in desiring this; and for the accomplishing of it, many of our particular friends will come forward to assist." Other convents began taking in children to sleep on schoolroom floors, in tents outside their convents, and in makeshift buildings of any sort.

In 1875, the New York State legislature passed the Children's Law, intended by lead-

The parochialism of the parish has inspired the wrath of an assortment of Irish-American writers, whose accounts of psychological suffocation and pathological hypocrisy match anything Sinclair Lewis wrote about his fictional small town of Gopher Prairie in the novel *Main Street*. Jimmy Breslin, in his clear-eyed novel *Table Money*, described an Alcoholics Anonymous meeting at the fictional parish of Saint Stanislaus in Queens, to which Owney Morrison, Irish-American sandhog, has been dispatched as his marriage falls apart: "This was . . . something new for the parish, which had run successful anti-crime meetings and drug education nights, but never had considered that there was any great problem with alcohol, except the possible shortage of it at a major function," Breslin wrote. The first alcoholic to introduce himself was the parish priest, Father Joe.

In their fiction, writers like Farrell and Breslin demand that we come to grips with the realities of post-immigration parish life. To the extent that parish life has changed, that alcoholism and racial prejudice and all manner of intensely personal sins are openly discussed rather than ignored or dismissed as fantasy, the writers have won the argument. But it is a pyrrhic victory at best, for the Saint Patrick's of Farrell's trilogy, and the Saint Dominic's of Father O'Malley, have gone the way of trolley cars, drugstore soda fountains, and choirs of reformed youth gangs (as if the latter ever existed anyway). While the Irish in America remain a bulwark of Catholicism, the urban parish and the

---

ing Protestant reformers to expand the placing-out system and guarantee payment to maintain the children until they were placed out. As a counteractive move, the Catholic Union, a male lobbying group, won support for an amendment stipulating that children be cared for in institutions *of their own religious background*. The nuns in New York City immediately recognized what passage of this law meant: massive funding for children's maintenance. And the nuns were quick and aggressive in securing it. The Sisters of Mercy, for instance, had been struggling financially to support 150 girls, ages three to fifteen, in a building that could accommodate 350. Upon passage of the law, their mother superior quickly informed the superintendent of the poor that the Institution of Mercy would "take charge of any number of little girls at whatever rate the Government proposed."

The Institution of Mercy began to receive children committed through the courts in huge numbers, receiving 559 such children in 1878 alone. The Sisters of Mercy then converted a building outside the city to house boys. In 1870, the Sisters of Mercy had been near bankruptcy, supporting charities on less than ten thousand dollars per year. In the single year 1880, they received more than seventy-seven thousand dollars from the city, and annual budgets thereafter were comparable.

The example of the Sisters of Mercy's expansion was followed by other Catholic institutions throughout the city. Between 1875 and 1880, four of the Catholic children's

Church itself are no longer distinctly Irish as they were in Studs Lonigan's time, and the notion of aggressive separatism has become linked to such cultural relics as the Latin Mass, Tammany Hall, and cold-water flats. The Irish in America could build no walls against the spread of popular culture and mass consumerism, which proved far more effective threats to faith and tradition than American Protestantism. Nor could the Irish—despite the efforts of many a father and mother—prevent the expansion of intermarriage, with all its cultural and religious implications.

A few generations ago, a mixed marriage meant the union of an Irish Catholic and an Italian or Polish Catholic (and such occasions often were the cause of severe disappointment, if not outrage, on both sides of the aisle). Now, however, intermarriage between Irish Catholic and Protestant, or Irish Catholic and Jew, has become commonplace, so much so that there are thousands of American children of Irish ancestry who can embrace both the orange of Protestantism and the green of Catholicism, or who can claim as part of their cultural inheritance both David Ben-Gurion and Eamon de Valera. And recent census figures revealed that of the 44 million Americans who claim Irish ancestry, fully half are Protestant. There was a time when many Irish Protestants tried as best they could to be thought of as something other than Irish.

Even the thickest walls are no match for such human complexities.

institutions expanded to take in those committed as destitute by the courts. In addition, five completely new Catholic institutions were founded to care for children who earlier might have been sent away to unknown Protestant homes via the so-called orphan trains.

Many native-born activists were soon to protest the rapid expansion of Catholic charitable institutions, contending that they had subverted the principles underlying "child-saving" in several ways. Worse yet, instead of a system controlled almost exclusively by Protestant native-borns and geared toward assimilating Catholic children into the native-born, Protestant culture, this system encouraged religious pluralism and the promotion of a distinct Catholic subculture. While native-borns as a group considered this a dangerous promotion of "sectarianism" and merging of church and state, Catholics defended it as just the opposite—the separation of Protestant control over the state and a triumphant victory for the religious rights of minorities.

By 1885, Catholic nuns were rearing 80 percent of New York City's state-dependent children; they received millions of dollars annually from the city's public funds to do so. The situation in New York, in fact, was often cited by Protestant elite and middle-class reformers as an example of how dangerous immigrant city political machines could be. Tammany Hall, it was charged, was responsible for this too-charitable system.

Although the reformers had their moments in the 1890s in their campaign to loosen

The parish, as it evolved under the leadership of Irish Catholic clerics, was based on a simple premise: The faith of new immigrants must be preserved and protected. So the parish and its larger jurisdiction, the diocese, provided generations of Irish immigrants, their children, and their grandchildren with a network of schools, hospitals, orphanages, asylums, and specialized institutions that duplicated services already available, but offered them in a Catholic setting, away from the hostile motives of Protestant social reformers.

This vast array of Catholic institutions was built quite literally from the pennies of poverty-stricken congregations whose generosity in the face of deprivation was astonishing. With a network in place to attend to the spiritual, educational, and physical needs of parishioners, the parish's place as an alternative community was realized. Not long after the American Civil War, just twenty years after the Famine Irish overwhelmed the American Church in numbers and in needs, many parishes and dioceses offered, literally, cradle-to-grave services. There was no need to go anywhere else, especially when the world outside was so unfriendly. It was this network of church, school, hospital, and other social service institutions that kept the Irish Catholic community together in the face of dislocation and poverty.

Tammany's grip, they were never able to dismantle the institutions governing the welfare of children. The system engineered by the Catholic nuns and protected by legislation had become synonymous with public welfare. The 1894 State Constitutional Convention concluded that the state's implicit sanctioning of this system for two decades had in effect established the poor's right to public aid for their children. More than a hundred years later, that long-held right is a matter of public debate. Those who seek to curtail or eliminate public assistance argue that private charities, rather than the government, are most suited to care for the poor. In fact, the right to public aid enshrined in New York's constitution in 1894 is under attack and may well be eliminated if the state's voters approve a ballot measure calling for a new constitutional convention sometime before the turn of the century.

Ironically enough, the system that the Irish nuns built and nurtured—once scorned by the elites—is being held out as a model of self-help and private assistance. Few seem to realize that the nuns were funded with government money and, indeed, worked with Tammany Hall to achieve a measure of social justice for the sake of the immigrant poor and their children. ❖

The parish was the very antithesis of assimilation and a countersymbol to the melting-pot metaphor. "Unable to participate in the normal . . . affairs of the community, the Irish felt obliged to erect a society within a society, to act together in their own way," wrote Oscar Handlin, author of the book *Boston's Immigrants*. Thomas O'Connor, author of *South Boston, My Home Town*, added a significant detail to Handlin's observation: The dominant American culture was more than happy to let Irish Catholics build their own society within a society. In that way, it was thought, the Irish could get along in America—separate, though decidedly not equal.

So, a form of Irish-American separatism, as defined by the Catholic parish community, was both a reaction to violent hostility from anti-Catholic nativists and a logical extension of the society the immigrant Irish left behind. In Ireland, the Church and its priests served as a badge of identity and common purpose in a land where the majority population was oppressed and discriminated against on the basis of its religious affiliation. In that sense, the Catholic Church in Ireland was intensely political, closely identified with Irish yearnings to be rid of Britain and its religion-based aristocracy. Like Poland under Communist rule in the twentieth century, Ireland since the Reformation intertwined its national spirit with the faith of its majority population.

British critics are fond of referring to modern Ireland as a theocracy because of the critical role that Catholic dogma plays in Irish law—until recently, divorce was illegal in the Irish Republic, the only Western European country in which that was so. Abortion remains under government ban, and very likely will remain so for some time to come. Such charges of theocracy often sound amusing, coming as they do from residents of a kingdom whose monarch is both head of state and head of the established Church of England. Indeed, by law members of the royal family are presented with tickets out of the line of succession if they marry a Roman Catholic.

Yet there is no denying that Ireland's government often has given the appearance of being an extension of the Catholic Church. While the bonds holding church and state together are, in fact, showing signs of strain in Ireland, their very existence, and the Irish imprint on the American Catholic Church, is a legacy of a colonial system in which religion, not ethnicity or nationality, was the deciding factor in determining who would have power and who would have power inflicted upon them.

*

There is a story, no doubt the product of some Irish wit's imagination, about a commercial airline pilot who, upon touching down in Northern Ireland, instructed his passengers to set their watches back three hundred years. The joke, of course, is a reference to the ancient religious divisions in Ireland, now expressed formally in the partition of the island into a twenty-six-county Catholic-dominated republic and a six-county Protestant-ruled province of Britain. Such a remark would have the satisfying, if temporary, result of uniting in anger Northern Ireland's Catholics and Protestants. In fact, though, just as the tragedy of Northern Ireland has centuries-old roots, so does the distinctly Irish outlook of the American Catholic Church and its thousands of parish communities.

Fundamental to the Irish Catholic experience is its sense of solidarity in the face of hostile forces. Sometimes those forces seemed intent on extermination, exemplified most vividly during the rampages of Oliver Cromwell in the seventeenth century, and other times they appeared more interested in winning over Catholics to the Protestant cause, an effort that led some well-intentioned humanitarians to offer soup to starving Catholics during the Famine if only they renounced their allegiance to the pope. In either case, the Church, though it had a claim on the devotion of 75 percent or more of Ireland's population, saw itself as eternally embattled.

And embattled it was in a land where a triumphant conqueror, in an age when Christian nations went to war over interpretations of the New Testament, ruled that Catholics were a political enemy and that Catholicism was a perversion of religion itself. Cromwell's bloody march through Ireland, intended to pacify the island's natives—nearly all of whom were Catholic—promised to dispatch Catholics "to hell or Connaught," the latter being the flinty western province where stones flourish and crops do not. A less violent, though perhaps more effective, solution to the Catholic problem that Ireland posed was a set of laws implemented in the late 1600s and early 1700s. Called the Penal Laws, the legislation essentially banned the practice of Catholicism in Ireland. Catholics could not acquire land—that all-important commodity—by either purchase, marriage, or inheritance. Catholics who already owned land were barred from passing a holding to a first son; the land instead was divided up among all sons, thus diluting the power that land held. (If a firstborn son suddenly discovered the joys of the Anglican faith, well, all was forgiven.) Catholic education was forbidden, and religious tests were applied to public offices so that no Catholic could serve. Catholics were barred from universities, juries, and the armed forces, and could neither vote nor teach school. The Irish language, associated with the native Catholics, was banned.

Having thus declared Catholics outcasts in their own land, the English Parliament made Catholic priests outlaws. They were ordered out of the country, and if they remained, they were subject to on-the-spot arrest, which could lead to either death or deportation. Nothing, of course, could have more forcefully welded together Irish identity and religion than the Penal Laws. The priests did not leave, and Catholics by and large remained true to their religion. Catholicism was driven underground, so that to attend a furtive mass was to defy an oppressor's laws, and to celebrate mass, as the priests did, was to put life and liberty at risk. Officially barred from schools, Catholics set up their own educational system that became known as "hedge schools," for they were conducted quite literally behind hedges. Not surprisingly, the priests who made their rounds through villages in defiance of the law, who suffered the same material deprivation as their flock, earned for themselves uncommon devotion and loyalty. The Catholic Church in Ireland was a people's church, a sharp contrast with the aristocratic Church of Italy and France, countries where the emotional and physical remoteness of priests and bishops inspired a tradition of anticlericalism.

The Penal Laws were on the books, though not rigidly enforced at all times, for 150 years. Their legacy of division between an Irish Protestant minority and an Irish Catholic majority was the foundation document of modern Ireland. The last of the punitive laws—the bar against Catholic admission to the English Parliament—fell only when Ireland's Catholics marched behind Daniel O'Connell, an apostle of nonviolent protest who marshaled masses of peasantry for the cause of what was called Catholic Emancipation. It was delivered, finally, in 1829. By the time of the Famine, Irish nationality and Catholic grievance were impossible to separate. It was a development that not all Irish nationalists welcomed; indeed, in 1848, a Protestant-led group known as Young Ireland made a token show of arms not in reaction to awful starvation, but as a gesture toward the ideal of a republic that was neither Catholic nor Protestant but simply Irish. To be Catholic was to be defiant, so it was that a Catholic priest, Father Tom Burke, would say: "Take an average Irishman. I don't care where you find him . . . you will find that the very first principle in his mind is, 'I am not an Englishman, because I am a Catholic.' Take an Irishman wherever he is found all over the earth, and any casual observer will at once come to the conclusion, 'Oh, he is an Irishman, he is a Catholic.' The two go together." And they would continue to go together in the New World. In 1960, when John Kennedy was running for president and reporters were dispatched to various Catholic strongholds to gather information about the parochial world of the parish, *Time* magazine noted that New York City's "Irish-Catholic population [is] 1,000,000 strong and pre-dominately Roman Catholic."

At least they allowed for the possibility that some Irish Catholics were Protestant.

✳

It soon became apparent that nothing about nineteenth-century America would change the Irish Catholic view of the outside world as a hostile, dangerous place to be kept at arm's length. If anything, America could be worse than Ireland, for here Catholics were a distinct minority in a nation that increasingly took the view that democracy and Protestantism were inseparable. Fears that Irish Catholics had simply traded locales in the move from Ireland to America seemed to be confirmed in the nativist riots of the Famine period and then, in a cruel reminder of history's ability to leap borders and oceans, in a bloody massacre that has gone down in history as the Orange Day riot.

In the Protestant-dominated areas of Ireland, most of them in what is now Northern Ireland, July 12 is the equivalent of Saint Patrick's Day, the Fourth of July, Memorial Day, and V-E Day rolled into one. On a battlefield near the River Boyne on July 12, 1690, the Protestant king William of Orange made Ireland safe for Protestantism by defeating the Catholic king James II. (James briefly was king of Britain, but his religion made him decidedly unwelcome, so he fled to Ireland in hopes of establishing a kingdom there.) The anniversary of the Battle of the Boyne was and is celebrated as a victory for liberty, Catholics being perceived as liberty's enemy. One of the ways liberty's victory is celebrated is by taunting the defeated Catholics with ditties concerning the personal habits of whatever pope is sitting on Saint Peter's throne. Generations of Irish Catholics have come to view the Orange Day proceedings as a display of prejudice and racial triumphalism.

Irish Catholics might have thought they had left behind this bit of historical baggage when they came to America, but, in a parable of history's portability, they discovered otherwise. Irish Protestants in New York marked July 12 with small commemorations, often under the banner of the anti-Catholic American Protestant Association. In 1870, however, Irish Protestants in New York were feeling overwhelmed by the presence of their Catholic kinsmen, and decided to march through the streets of New York near Central Park. The taunting of Irish Catholic laborers in the neighborhood, along with reports of Catholic churches under attack, led to a riot that left eight people dead.

New York's Irish Catholics, confident in their numbers and on the verge of achieving real polit-

Irish immigrant nuns went wherever the faithful needed them. Here, members of the Sisters of Mercy take a break on their journey west via covered wagon.

ical power in the city, vowed that the Orangemen would never again torment them, and as July 12, 1871, approached, the city decided to ban the march. Great howls of protest followed, with accusations made that City Hall was in the grasp of papists, so Governor Hoffman overrode the ban and allowed the march to proceed.

So it did, making its way down Manhattan's Eighth Avenue—home to many working-class Irish Catholics—under the careful eye of a militia called out for the occasion. As the march proceeded, Irish Catholics on the sidelines returned taunt for taunt. Stones began to descend on marcher and soldier alike. In such an overheated atmosphere, what came next seems inevitable: The soldiers opened fire on the Irish Catholic civilians, creating what the *New York Times* would describe as a "panorama of blood" and "a vista of gore." Sixty-two civilians were killed, twenty-eight of them Irish immigrants, and one hundred were wounded. A cartoon in *Harper's Weekly* after the massacre showed a stern-faced woman, representing Justice, grabbing the throat of an apelike Irishman armed with a knife and a shillelagh. The caption read: "Bravo! Bravo!"

It is hardly a wonder that priests encouraged their congregations to remain inside the parish's friendly confines.

✻

The very vastness of the American continent posed dangers for the defenders of the faith. Historian Thomas Beer noted that the Irish who forged inland from the port cities of the East Coast often were absorbed into the mainstream—as in Protestant—culture. "They melted easily into the westward movements . . . shedding their habits from prairie to prairie so that families named O'Donnell, Connor and Delehanty are now discovered drowsing in Protestant pews of Texas and Kansas," Beer wrote of the Irish in the American heartland.

The parish walls of urban America were designed to thwart this very danger. The parish, then, served not only to facilitate worship but also to preserve a tradition, culture, and value system seemingly at odds with mainstream American culture. Priests served as social arbiters; nuns would incul-

(continued on page 75)

JOHN T. RIDGE

IRISH SOCIETIES: TO BE UNITED AND KNOWN

Born in Brooklyn of Irish immigrant parents from County Galway and County Longford, John T. Ridge is the author of several books, including ERIN'S SONS IN AMERICA: THE ANCIENT ORDER OF HIBERNIANS.

Kate Murphy was just one of thousands of visitors to attend the 1897 Irish Fair at the Grand Central Palace in Manhattan. For several weeks people from all over the metropolitan region had come to see the handsome displays that the Irish societies had assembled in an attempt to present in capsule form something of Ireland's rich cultural heritage. One exhibit in particular, though, seemed to attract most of the attention. Irish soil, directly imported from the old country, had been laid out in sections, one for each of Ireland's thirty-two counties, to allow fairgoers to symbolically "set foot" in Ireland. In an age when relatively few Irish immigrants ever journeyed home again to see the old country, stepping on even a small piece of Ireland took on an almost mystical significance for many, particularly the elderly Irish immigrants who anxiously sought out the counties of their birth.

Eighty-year-old Kate Murphy, overcome by the emotion of the experience of stepping once again upon the ground of her native County Fermanagh, knelt down in prayer, oblivious to the crowds and the newspaper reporters around her. The flash of photographers' equipment surprised and startled this "simple-hearted creature" to such an extent that the light stunned her into awestruck silence as if it had been some sort of sign from heaven. Only reluctantly did she leave the exhibit, clinging all the time to the fence surrounding it, and looking back as if bidding a long farewell.

A lingering homesickness was something that many immigrants would carry with them all their lives, but it was rarely so publicly and poignantly expressed as in the case of Kate Murphy. The Irish societies exhibits at the Irish Fair were calculated to take a nostalgic look back at the Ireland the immigrants had left behind, and like their memories, it was a curious mixture of real and fanciful notions. But immigration in the nineteenth century was cruel in its finality, and faced with little chance of ever returning to Ireland, the Irish in America created the organizations that would try to create, in a small way, a surrogate Ireland in America.

*

Long before the American Revolution, Irish immigrants came together to form societies to allow a bit of the Old World to survive in the new. At first these groups were largely the domain of the prosperous middle and upper classes that emerged in coastal cities north and south, such as Boston, New York, Philadelphia, Charleston, and Savannah, but as the mid-nineteenth century approached, the fever for organizing spread to all classes, resulting in the formation of hundreds of local Irish societies in large cities and small towns across America.

While societies such as the Charitable Irish Society of Boston, independent societies called Friendly Sons of Saint Patrick in both Philadelphia and New York, and local Hibernian societies in Charleston and Savannah toasted Saint Patrick's Day with elaborate banquets in drawing-room fashion, most of the of Irish societies that emerged after the Great Hunger in the late 1840s and 1850s were composed of laborers and small tradesmen more interested in providing for their families in the event of sickness or death. A few of the local societies developed into national organizations that attempted to link together the far-flung elements of the Irish diaspora, but it was a slow process that took decades to develop.

Each branch of the larger Irish societies, such as the Ancient Order of Hibernians, the Father Matthew Total Abstinence and Benevolent Society, and the Saint Patrick's Mutual Alliance, functioned as a primitive insurance organization. The members pooled their limited resources together to allow benefits to be disbursed to members or their families in times of need. Typically one dollar a day for serious illness or between one hundred and one hundred fifty dollars to a widow in the case of death made things a bit easier for a member or his family to survive the calamities of nineteenth-century life. Public occasions such as the Saint Patrick's Day parades were used to hammer home the message of just how precarious life could be for the average immigrant.

The obligation to turn out on Saint Patrick's Day was often written into the requirements of membership, but it was not mere obligation alone that caused the Irish to demonstrate an almost fanatical desire to trudge along in the most horrendous storms and freezing temperatures. Just as the Irish societies used parades to preach that they could take care of their own, the long, orderly ranks of Irishmen marching in solemn attire and handsome regalia attempted to show their ofttimes critical non-Irish fellow citizens that the Irish could look every bit as prosperous as anyone else. The fact that so many of the early Saint Patrick's Day parades made a point of marching right by city hall for the official review by the mayor and the political leaders was no accident either. The thousands of disciplined paraders not only made for a pretty sight but strongly hinted at disciplined voters marching to the ballot box on election day as well.

*

The organization that grew to be the largest, the Ancient Order of Hibernians (AOH), traced its roots back to sixteenth-century Ireland and to the struggle between the English and the Irish for control of the country. The Hibernians served as a protective society for the Catholic Church and its clergy, and it was necessarily a secret society. The AOH came to America in 1836, and by the 1850s had spread across the country. It was organized in branches called divisions, and many of them quickly developed an identification with a particular neighborhood in the cities and frequently with a specific Catholic parish.

The Hibernians were not unknown in rural areas where the Irish were engaged in farming or in the West where the Irish were involved in ranching. Heading west from the East Coast one could even trace a pattern of branches from one mining area to another: from Pennsylvania to West Virginia to the upper peninsula of Michigan to Montana and to southwestern states such as Colorado, Utah, Nevada, and California. The Hibernian divisions formed a network that enabled the scattered communities of Irish to maintain their connection with others like themselves and to keep abreast of the social, cultural, and political developments affecting the Irish in Ireland and America.

*

The AOH was quick to involve itself in public issues that affected the Irish community, and it did not shy away from public wrangles with officialdom. Many of the local and independent Irish societies, however, avoided the

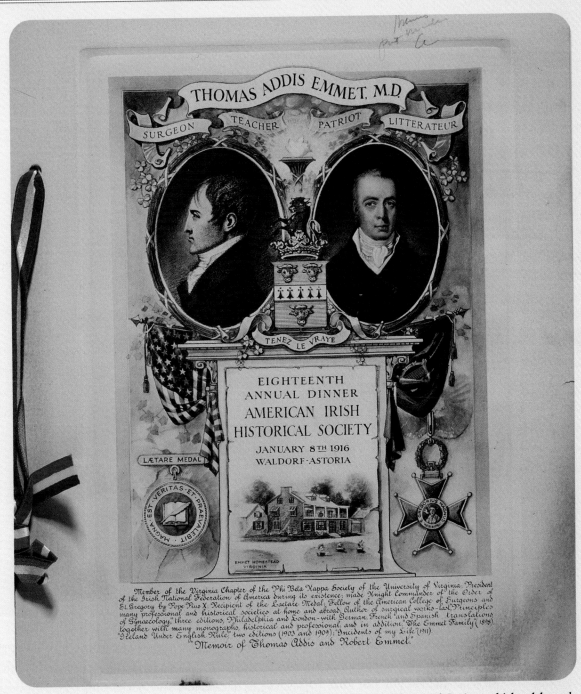

A program from the eighteenth annual dinner of the American Irish Historical Society, which celebrated its 100th anniversary in 1997. Groups like the Society have preserved Irish-American culture and tradition through the decades.

burned, he would see to it that New York's Catholics turned the city into a "second Moscow."

The reference was to the mobs in Russia who had burned Moscow rather than see it fall into Napoleon's hands, an image that was unsettling, to say the least. Dagger John's message was delivered, and heeded, at least to an extent. The Philadelphia rampage was not repeated in New York, but Harper's kindred spirits in the city's Know-Nothing movement did take to the streets. When they did, Hughes summoned the city's Catholics to protect their churches, and three thousand responded, many of them armed with shillelaghs. The clubs were not necessary, but Mayor Harper would never have cause to ask, as Stalin so contemptuously did of the pope, how many divisions John Hughes commanded. The answer presented itself outside Saint Patrick's Cathedral and other potentially besieged churches.

Hughes was imperious and authoritarian, a force for discipline in the chaotic quarter century (1836–64) during which he presided over New York's Catholics. His strong style of leadership and his aggressive advocacy on behalf of his faith, its beliefs, and its adherents set a tone for the Archdiocese of New York and, in fact, for a certain and persistent brand of leadership within the American Church. He has been described as a great Gaelic chieftain, transported through the mists from the time when Ireland's high kings walked the island's green fields. There was no question about the loyalty he could inspire and the empathy he could express, qualities that were tested in the anarchy and violence of the New York draft riots of July 1863, when predominantly Irish mobs rampaged through the city to protest the beginnings of conscription into the Union army. The riot, more like an uprising, went on for five days and killed at least 105 people, probably many more.

The city's elected officials and aristocracy turned to the only leader they thought capable of stopping the riots—Dagger John, the very man who had once threatened exactly the sort of violence that was tearing apart the city. Hughes was a grudging supporter of the draft, wary of the provision allowing the wealthy to purchase an exemption for three hundred dollars. The vast majority of Irish Catholics, of course, could hardly raise such a sum, and the blatant unfairness repelled his sense of social justice. It was, he said, nothing more than a provision to allow "the wealthy to become wealthier in their quiet homes." Nevertheless, he agreed to speak to his flock. He was in failing health, less than a year from death, but on July 17, 1863, he was the strongest man in the smoldering city of New York.

"They call you rioters, but I cannot see a riotous face among you," he told a crowd of three thousand Irish Catholic men gathered outside his residence not far from the worst of the looting and killings. "I thank God that I came to this country, where no oppression exists. If you are Irishmen—and your enemies say the rioters are Irishmen—I am also an Irishman, but not a rioter. If you are Catholics, as they have reported—then I am a Catholic, too . . . Every man has his troubles, but I think with the poet that it is better to bear our slight inconveniences than to rush to evils . . . When these so-called riots are over, and the blame is justly laid on Irish Catholics, I wish you to tell me in what country I could claim to be born . . . Ireland, that has been the mother of heroes and poets, but never the mother of cowards."

The riots came to an end after Federal troops were called in from Gettysburg. Even *Harper's*, a notoriously anti-Catholic periodical, took note of the archbishop's role in restoring the peace, and the "Roman Catholic priest-

Irish-Catholic immigrants found themselves a distinct minority in a country that was overwhelmingly Protestant. Fear and loathing of the newcomers burst into violence in Philadelphia in 1844. This daguerreotype shows the militia guarding a bank.

hood," whose efforts to end the riots "should teach us something more useful than a revival of Know-Nothing prejudices."

Hughes was not so conciliatory when dealing with his opponents. He set off an emotional political and cultural debate in New York when he attacked the city's public schools as a bastion of Protestantism—which they were—and demanded public funds for the establishment of a separate Catholic school system. In language that could easily be adapted to fit the arguments of the multiculturalists of the late twentieth century, Hughes charged that the school's curriculum recognized only Protestant cultural, Protestant history, and Protestant ideals, not to mention the King James version of the Bible—a Protestant, Reformation-inspired tract. Inside the classrooms, the history and culture of Irish Catholics received no mention; England was described as the Mother Country from whom all liberty and freedom flowed. A modern educator would describe the public school curricu-

lum of mid-nineteenth-century America as "irrelevant to the real-life experiences of minority students," the minority in this case being, of course, Irish Catholics.

Hughes lost the battle to win public money for Catholic schools, but he and his colleagues in other American cities were undeterred. Faced with what they regarded as anti-Catholic bias in public schools, Catholics built their own system, with their own scarce resources. The decision "meant a poor body of immigrants would have to make great sacrifices to build their own schools," noted author

Separate parish schools led to the building of Catholic universities and colleges. Among those built in the nineteenth century were Loyola of Chicago, Notre Dame, and Villanova.

Garry Wills. And sacrifice they did. Though not all parishes had schools, the Catholic education system became perhaps the most eloquent expression of Irish Catholic self-segregation. Well into the twentieth century, Cardinal William O'Connell of Boston asserted with the sort of self-assurance that Archbishop Hughes would recognize, that in the matter of Catholic schools, "there is . . . just one point of view, and that is, Catholic children should attend Catholic schools." Even into the 1960s, it was not unusual to hear Irish Catholic children refer to public schools as "Protestant schools."

Parish schools and Irish-American skepticism about mainstream American society led naturally to the establishment of Catholic universities and colleges, and many of the most famous Catholic centers of inquiry, research, and discovery owe their beginnings to attitudes that seem, at first glance,

the very opposite of a broad-minded pursuit of knowledge. Yet such institutions as Fordham University and Manhattan College in New York, Saint Joseph's College and Villanova University in Philadelphia, the College of the Holy Cross in Worcester, Loyola University in Chicago, Marquette University in Wisconsin, and Boston College all were founded during the great Irish immigration of the mid-nineteenth century, and all owed their beginnings to Irish-American church leaders who believed that, in fact, "Catholic children should attend Catholic schools." The Irish domination of Catholic education was advertised most famously when, in 1842, a French priest named Edward Sorin founded a small Catholic school in a village in Indiana called South Bend. Despite the priest's concern that Irish young men were "not obedient by nature," the University of Notre Dame quickly became a bastion of Irish Catholic culture and education in the American heartland. So dominant were the disobedient young men that when the time came to give the school's athletic teams a nickname, the choice was obvious: the Fighting Irish.

The schools and universities added bricks to the already thick parish walls and further cemented the Catholic notion of separatism. Not coincidentally, the education system provided a continuous stream of potential priests, nuns, and other religious, and decreased the chances that young men and

Conscription into the Union Army did not sit well with the Irish in New York City. What became known as the Draft Riots broke out in July 1863; more than a hundred people were killed. Bishop Hughes was widely claimed to have calmed the rioters, bringing the agitation to an end.

(continued on page 85)

MICHAEL P. QUINLIN

THE IRISH ACROSS AMERICA

Michael Quinlin is the author of GUIDE TO THE NEW ENGLAND IRISH. *He is a frequent contributor to the* IRISH ECHO. *He lives in Dorchester, Massachusetts.*

My hometown, Castle Shannon, in western Pennsylvania, was an early outpost of the "Irish Nation in America," a phrase coined in 1892 by journalist John Deignan to describe hundreds of places named Eire, Dublin, Belfast, Tyrone, and Cork sprouting up across the American landscape. Irish settlers looking for adventure and prosperity were harking back to the towns they loved so well, even as they were creating new ones. "The presence of the Irish," Deignan said, "is felt in the nomenclature of cities and towns."

Where is the Irish Nation in America today? Certainly in Boston, New York, Chicago, and San Francisco, where waves of new Irish pilgrims have been settling for generations. But it is also embedded in America's heartland, where the Irish have nestled in more intimate and less strident surroundings, cultivating their heritage amid the mainstream of American life. In a string of well-worn routes crisscrossing the continent, trailblazed by earlier travelers, the Irish have established conduits for music, dance, sports, education, and self-identity. In these nooks and crannies throughout the country there lies an authentic, unbroken cultural tradition that has helped to shape the Irish-American persona.

✻

Savannah, Georgia, dates its Irish tradition back to 1733, when the British first colonized the area. Early settlers included wealthy Irish Protestants who were awarded land in the New World by the Crown, followed by poor Irish Catholics who helped build the railroad lines in the 1830s. Thousands more settled there after fleeing the Famine of the 1840s, especially from Mayo, Cork, and Kerry. Others came from County Wexford, which had a direct shipping line to Savannah.

Jimmy Ray, head of the city's parade committee, says Savannah has been celebrating Saint Patrick's Day continuously since 1824, with a few exceptions. "We didn't have the parade for a few years, like during the Civil War, and one year when Saint Patrick's Day landed on Easter Week, but we always observed the holy day," he says.

His Irish great-grandparents, Mathias H. Ray and Mary Elizabeth Mahany, came to Savannah in the 1850s, when 70 percent of immigration to the city was Irish, and they settled there. A century and a half later, Irish-American clans such as the Rays maintain their sense of Irishness, not just from family tradition, but from the Irish Sisters of Mercy and Irish priests who have had a constant presence there. "We were taught Irish history by the nuns," Ray says proudly.

That awareness extends to descendants of Protestant Irish, who also participate in the parade activities, and to local Scottish Americans, who consider Saint Patrick's Day part of their Celtic tradition, too. It extends to Savannah's sizable Jewish and Greek communities, who don green and partake in the annual parade, which is the second largest in America next to New York City's. Floyd Adams, the African-American mayor, is seen at every Irish event, wearing his green topcoat.

Examples abound of such coexistence. New Orleans, whose Irish Channel section dates back to the 1840s, was the largest port of destination after New York for the Irish during most of the nineteenth century, and also sported large German, French, and black communities. Peter Hand, a local Hibernian and police lieutenant, describes New Orleans as "a big gumbo," referring to the fish stew that blends various spices, sauces, and ingredients to form a distinctly local dish. "The Irish just added a little more seasoning."

Even so, the Irish sustained an identity often based on more exact criteria than just one's Irishness. Since the eighteenth century, Irish immigrants have been quick to start associations and societies to ease their loneliness. Every one of Ireland's thirty-two counties has a club somewhere in America. County Mayo has a huge following in Cleveland, while Tyrone rules in Philadelphia, and Galway claims Portland, Maine. Dubliners and Kerrymen, of course, are everywhere.

But immigrants create new affiliations, too. When Peter Shovlin of Donegal and his wife, Sheila, immigrated to Pittsburgh in 1957, there was sparse Irish activity, other than the Saint Patrick's Day Parade and an Irish picnic each summer. The Shovlins and some friends "saw a need for something, and said let's do it." They established the Irish Cultural Center of Pittsburgh in 1966 as a meeting place for Irish immigrants and their families.

The center provided social and economic networks for new immigrants and promoted Irish culture. Seven of the Shovlin children delved heavily into Irish dancing, competing around the region—in Youngstown, Dayton, Buffalo, and Syracuse—against Irish clubs in those cities. Their father traveled with them, playing fiddle for the competitions.

Shovlin and friends also began building currachs, small boats made of either canvas or wood that have been used along the west coast of Ireland for centuries.

"I used to row at home a lot," says Shovlin, a master carpenter by trade, "and there were a lot of Galway men in Pittsburgh who had lived on the [Aran] islands and had rowed everywhere, to school, to church, to the store. So we built some currach boats, from scratch, trial and error, and began racing on the Allegheny River." They joined the Irish Currach Association, which took them to Annapolis, Boston, New

Keeping the tradition alive, young step-dancers at the St. Patrick's Day celebration in Savannah, Georgia, perform steps their great-grandparents would recognize.

York, and Philadelphia to pit their carpentry and rowing skills against other Irish teams.

There is also the Irish festival circuit, a marketplace where authentic and facsimile Irish culture converge. This movable feast of great and awful music, beer tents, and tea-and-scone huts, featuring vendors hawking books, coats of arms, T-shirts, and imported crystal, is where the struggle for the Irish-American imagination is played out. Having spent a few years on this circuit, I still recall how people arrived from miles around, gleefully anticipating some shared cultural celebration. Open-air tents and stages plopped in mountain pastures or on remote college

campuses give the feeling of an American county fair or a tailgate party at a football game. Onstage the precise little feet of boys and girls dressed in heavy woolen suits earnestly keep beat to some mysterious cultural rite they will one day insist their children learn. In a grove of trees around a picnic bench musicians gather together in casual repose to play tunes that roll into the cool night air as bystanders chatter amid the smoke, drink, and laughter.

These festivals wind their way through Wolf Trap, Scranton, Glastonbury, Newport, and to bigger venues in Milwaukee, Philadelphia, and Brooklyn. Invariably they land in the Catskill Mountains in Greene County, New York, where the Irish busloads from Boston and the Bronx have been summer vacationing for decades.

Some cultural endeavors fade from popularity, only to return decades later. A century ago, W. B. Yeats and Douglas Hyde spawned a Celtic revival out of Dublin that salvaged the ancient culture of Ireland from near extinction. In America, Philo-Celtic societies "devoted to the language, literature, history, music, sports and pastimes of the Gael" flourished for a decade before waning to the dictates of time.

Today there is a renewed Irish-language movement across America. Irish immersion weekends offering intensive language classes take place in Ohio, Texas, New York, and Wisconsin. At the annual Gaeltacht Gathering on Cape Cod, dozens of Irish Americans such as Richard O'Eigeartaigh convene for a weekend of Gaelic conversation, songs, mass, and instruction: The goal is to speak Irish as much as possible.

Bill Mahon of Paterson, New Jersey, was a forerunner of this trend. He learned to speak Irish from instructional tapes in the early 1970s as a high school student, then went on to get his Ph.D. in Celtic languages from Harvard. "Learning Irish is a way of expressing a commitment to preserve small things of value," he notes. Mahon is part of an academic movement that has done much to enrich the study of Irish culture in the United States. The American Conference of Irish Studies, founded in 1962, boasts more than sixteen hundred members, including Irish professors from colleges in every state in the union, and has succeeded in keeping Irish studies a legitimate academic field of inquiry.

Pioneers of this educational front were Eoin and Jeannette McKiernan of Saint Paul, founders of the Irish American Cultural Institute in 1964. Now based in New Jersey, IACI regularly sends troupes of Irish poets, storytellers, politicians, genealogists, and professors into the heartland. In places such as Charlotte, Cincinnati, Dayton, Detroit, Grand Rapids, St. Louis, and Tulsa, these bards encounter a well-educated group of Irish Americans pursuing their heritage on an intellectual plane.

"When my father first started the Institute, there were charges of elitism early on. Being of Irish descent was not a source of pride in those days," says daughter Eithne McKiernan. "Eoin's goal was to change that."

✼

While many Irish Americans, like the Shovlins and McKiernans, are nurtured in an environment where Irish culture is actively pursued, others discover their heritage quite unexpectedly. Dr. Larry McCullough retrieved his Irish cultural identity as a third-generation Irish American after it had been put aside by his ancestors, "who felt compelled to dispel their heritage" in order to succeed economically in America.

"My family had become completely Americanized and assimilated, and I was looking for something more specific," McCullough recalls. "When I discovered Irish music, I said, 'This is mine, I belong here.'"

The Indianapolis native traded in his saxophone for the tin whistle as a teenager, and went on to win an All-Ireland championship on the whistle, a rare feat for an American. He later became an ethnomusicologist, writing his dissertation on Irish music in Chicago. His book, *The Complete Irish Tinwhistle Tutor*, still sells well after two decades, and he has recorded four solo albums that fuse Irish music with jazz, rock, Cajun, and salsa. After musical stints in Pittsburgh, Austin, and upstate New York, McCullough returned to Indianapolis, where he is writing plays but still teaching tin whistle to local children. "I've considered myself a cultural conduit for the last two decades," he says proudly.

✼

The Irish Nation in America, once defined by Irish place-names, is more accurately a vast network of cultural conduits linked not only by events and traditions but by the steadfast devotion of individuals who simply are the culture.

Which brings me to a final word about Castle Shannon, and its three phases of Irish immigration. It was founded on the outskirts of Pittsburgh in 1784 by David Strawbridge, an Irish Methodist who stopped short of the larger frontier beckoning westward. It remained a sleepy farm land until the 1890s, when industrial barons discovered coal in the ground. Then it became an overnight mining town with shanty villages of Irish, Polish, and German immigrants, optimistic souls who left their homelands to dig black gold but ended up with black lung.

But then no Irish settled there for decades, until Mary Campbell, my mother, emigrated in 1950 from the green hills of Armagh in Northern Ireland to join her Irish-American husband. And though she may have been the last Irish native to settle into this town once brimming with Irish ways, in some sense she restored its Irishness. Through her manner and her stories, she fashioned for her family, neighbors, and friends an Irish world of music, history, and customs. The value she placed on her heritage was made more poignant by her separation from it, and that poignancy is what gives Irishness such special meaning for so many Americans. ❖

women would marry outside the faith. It was a parochial world, sometimes maddeningly so, but for the immigrants and their families, it was a reassurance, a touchstone, and a symbol of a shared culture and value system.

*

If a screenwriter or novelist were to revisit Chicago's fictional Saint Patrick's or O'Malley's Saint Dominic's, he or she would discover that the Irish were gone, but that their institutions remain. The pastor might have a name such as O'Malley, for the Irish priest has hardly disappeared, but it very easily could be López or Martini. And surely the urban parish of the twenty-first century will be Irish only in its history and its institutional memory.

Still, there are pockets where Dagger John Hughes would feel right at home, assuming he listened only to familiar accents and paid little heed to changed views of verbal decorum. Parishes from Woodside, Queens, to South Boston to Chicago and San Francisco saw an influx of new Irish immigrants in the 1980s, when the Irish economy collapsed. The new immigrants were young and, even in this day of mass culture, often confused and uncertain in their new home. The parish was among the first to reach out with help, through such organizations as New York's Emerald Isle Immigration Center in Queens and similar organizations in other historically Irish cities.

The names of old urban parishes inspire great nostalgia among the Irish who grew to adulthood in midcentury America, a golden age for the country and for the Irish themselves as they continued a journey toward acceptance that began at the barricades of Saint Patrick's Cathedral and ended, so it seemed, with the election of John F. Kennedy in 1960. But the decline of the old Irish urban parish has not meant an end to the link between the Irish Catholics of America and their Church. In fact, there is ample evidence that the baby-boomer Irish and their successors have retained their faith and traditions even in their leafy postwar communities. Research by the Reverend Andrew Greeley showed that the Irish remain more devout and more attached to the parish than other

(continued on page 89)

WHEN NEW YORK WAS IRISH

I'll sing you a song of days long ago
When people from Galway and County Mayo
And all over Ireland came over to stay
And take up a new life in Americay

Chorus:
They were ever so happy, they were ever so sad
To grow old in a new world through good times and bad
All the parties and weddings, the ceilis and wakes
When New York was Irish, full of joys and heartbreaks

We worked on the subways, we ran the saloons
We built all the bridges, we played all the tunes
We put out the fires and controlled City Hall
We started with nothing and wound up with it all.

[Chorus]
They were ever so happy . . .

You could travel from Kingsbridge to Queens or mid-town
From Highbridge to Bay Ridge, from uptown to down
From the East Side to the seaside's sweet summer scenes—
We made New York City our island of dreams

[Chorus]
They were ever so happy . . .

I look at the photos, now brittle with time
Of the people I cherished when the city was mine
O how I loved all those radiant smiles
How I long for the days when we danced in the aisles

[Chorus]
They were ever so happy . . .

—TERENCE WINCH

JAMES CARROLL

"WHAT PARISH?" : AN EXPERIENCE OF CHURCH

Carroll is the author, most recently, of AN AMERICAN REQUIEM: GOD, MY FATHER AND THE WAR THAT CAME BETWEEN US, *which won the National Book Award for Nonfiction in 1996.*

What parish? With that question we were always asked to identify our home neighborhoods of Chicago, Boston, Pittsburgh, New York, or a dozen other cities. Saint Gabe's, we'd say, referring to the parish near the Chicago stockyards. Or Gate of Heaven, on the highest hill of South Boston. Or Good Shepherd, on the Inwood tip of Manhattan. Wherever the Irish settled in America, we identified ourselves, even to outsiders, by the parish in which we lived. Beginning years ago, when the post-Famine immigrants found themselves in a less-than-hospitable America, the parish was the safe harbor, usually an urban enclave in which auld sod customs, manners, mores, and beliefs were valued even while being derided by the larger society outside the parish.

We Irish had our parish schools, parish bazaars, parish picnics, and the Holy Name societies and sodalities that served as parish clubs. We had our priests, often Irish-born themselves, who, chain smoking and hard drinking, nevertheless gave us images of intellect, erudition, holiness, and affability. We had our nuns, who taught us penmanship and who embodied the virtue of freely chosen selflessness. And above all, we had Our Lord and His Mother, figures simultaneously of transcendence and intimacy. The parish church dependably located us in space, not only in a country we were otherwise unsure of, but in the cosmos itself. On our knees before the tabernacle or the bank of blue votive lights at Mary's feet, we knew exactly where we were and where we belonged. At the grand moments of deep significance—birth, death, illness, marriage, passage into adulthood, as well as at the more mundane yet pointed moments of failure and success—the parish, through its elegantly simple sacraments, assured us that we were not alone. The taste of an unleavened wafer; the sound of a warbling soloist; the aromas of candle wax, stale incense, and altar wine; the male odor of a priest's cassock; the scent of soap on Sister; the feel of a tattered bingo card—it all meant home to us. Indeed, the word "parish" itself comes from Greek roots meaning "near the house."

But in addition to space, the parish also located us in time, providing a felt sense of history that extended back beyond the rough arrival on these shores, beyond the dread colonial past, beyond the unmentioned horror of the English-sponsored Hunger, beyond the still painful breach of the Reformation to the glories of true Catholic triumphs—the Gothic cathedral, the five proofs of God's existence—that seemed our own. The parish helped us touch a time when God walked among us not just as a man but as a Catholic. We could taste the very beginning, when Adam and Eve lived in what we always thought of as the first draft of Ireland. And, conversely, the parish pointed us to trustworthy futures when we would once more be with lost loved ones; when the truth of our position would be proved; when, by the grace of God, "beatitude" would be ours. Hell was lurking in that future, too, as ferocious parish missionaries reminded us once a year, but, despite temptations of the flesh, we did not believe it was really for us. The future was the absolute in which we put our faith because we had the promise of it in our parish. Thus, we could be scorned or ignored by people outside the boundaries of this precious turf, but we felt immune to their condescension and could even regard it as their veiled envy.

When, in the postwar economic boom, the children and grandchildren of the immigrants left the cities for suburbs, even while leaving the closed Irish Catholic subculture for a full participation in the American consensus, we still planted ourselves in parishes, now centered on bright modern churches in former pastures. Their cheerful names—"Our Lady of Good Hope" instead of "Sorrows"; "Queen of Angels" instead of "Martyrs"—reflected the Irish version of midcentury American optimism, a sure signal that our exile was at an end. The Irish had arrived, not just in the New World, but in its universities, boardrooms, executive suites, and country clubs, and its Oval Office. We may have kept our names on the parish register—defying patterns of other groups, Irish Americans remain overwhelmingly religious—but we stopped identifying ourselves with the name of our church. Despite continued high levels of attendance at mass, for example, the parish is no longer the central institution of Irish-American life. It is a source for the Eucharist, and perhaps for religious education of the young, but not much else. Ironically, that is a precise measure of the once all-encompassing immigrant parish's success, for no institution was more important in sustaining the energy and confidence first of insecure newcomers, then of their ambitious progeny. The parish itself, more than any other factor, enabled the Irish in America to leave the parish behind.

✳

And only now do we begin to see the thing clearly. In addition to being a wonderfully consoling and nurturing institution, wasn't the parish also in some way inhibiting? Once, we proudly identified ourselves as, in that odd phrase, "products of parochial schools," but then we began to hear the pejorative note in the word "parochial." "Merely local," the *Oxford American Dictionary* says, "showing interest in a limited area only." And, yes, we realized, that was true. We Irish had made a kind of bastion of the parish at times of real threat. After all, we first began to arrive in this country knowing that the British had just caused the starvation deaths of millions of us; Know-Nothing Americans had lumped us in with the despised Negroes and Jews. The Irish-American parish was born in an era when we had as much to fear as they. In our case, the era passed quickly, but did our fear of those who were not local? And how, exactly, did our suspicion extend to include those selfsame Negroes and Jews?

There are two problems with orienting one's entire life "near the house." The first is that the world is so much larger and more varied than we ever imagined. Think what we were missing! In the parish they told us, "There is no salvation outside the Church." But then we learned that there is no salvation *inside* any rigidly self-referential institution, precisely because salvation is itself the opposite of such narrowness. Indeed, American Catholics, by embracing the values of democracy and pluralism, defied the values of the hierarchical and exclusivist parish, even while finding a way to be loyal to it. American Catholicism was a key influence in the democratizing reforms of the Second Vatican Council, which began weaning the Church away from the garrison values to which the "merely local" parish gave such efficient expression. The opening of the Church to the broader world—implied by a shift in the council's rhetoric from "the Church and the World" to "the Church *in* the world"—has changed forever the meaning of the parish. No longer a place to retreat to, it becomes a place from which to go. Why? Because God is available not only in the sanctuary but everywhere. This theologically enlivening idea restates the basic human principle that the particular opens up into the universal—or it shrivels and dies.

And among human beings, the form that death takes is hatred, which brings us to the second problem. There is a tragedy built into any life lived exclusively "near the house." In America, it has been a Catholic tragedy, never more so than when those outside the parish have been regarded as enemies even when they weren't. The habit of seeing the "other" as a threat has been a hard one for Irish Americans to break. Whether rooted in the deep past of Old World wounds or not, leering Irish suspicion of those who are not local has periodically been dramatic, from Coughlinite anti-Semitism in the 1930s, to McCarthyite red-baiting in the 1950s. In the 1970s, Irish Catholics were among the most vociferous resisters of racial integration when the Civil Rights movement made its way north, and in the 1990s it seems less than pure coincidence that the most strident voice of anti-immigrant isolationism has been a proudly parochial Irish Catholic by the name of Patrick Buchanan.

✻

Some say the old-fashioned Irish Catholic parish is dying because of the shortage of priests to administer it, and indeed whereas most parishes were once staffed by a pastor and numerous curates, now a parish is lucky to have a pastor to itself. But isn't it possible that the cause and effect here are reversed? Isn't it possible that young Irish Catholics and other young Catholics decline to become priests because their faith invites a broader taste of life—if not necessarily cosmopolitan, not parochial? Once such figures of inspiration, manliness, and integrity, priests, by clinging fearfully to an outmoded exclusivity, are becoming increasingly anachronous. Catholics, the Irish included, have increasingly left behind the structure of a parish centered on male, celibate clergy devoted to a last-ditch defense of a patriarchy the parish has so long epitomized. These same people may still faithfully attend mass to taste the goodness of the Lord, but they will no longer confine themselves "near the house," nor will they define their Church as a parochial institution that claims to have a lock on the truth, much less on God. ❖

Carney Hospital has been an institution in Boston since the nineteenth century, a manifestation of Irish-Catholic determination to care for their own. Like many such institutions, it now tends to the needs of Catholics and non-Catholics alike.

Catholic ethnic groups. In his book *Irish Americans: The Rise to Money and Power,* Father Greeley notes that even in the face of material success and a more secular world, "Irish Catholics are more certain than other Americans that life is not chance, that there is purpose in human existence, that love is at the heart of the universe, and that prayers are heard."

No doubt the day is coming when a non-Irish cardinal will succeed to the see of Saint Patrick in New York, America's wealthiest and most powerful archdiocese. Perhaps that prelate will be of Latino background, which would seem only fitting in a city in which Latinos have replaced the Irish as a dominant and growing Catholic ethnic group. The Irish already have surrendered so much in the cities they used to run that a change in Saint Patrick's Cathedral seems not only inevitable but appropriate.

That day will be a milestone in the American Church's history. When it comes, it will be the occasion for Irish sentiment and nostalgia, qualities rarely in short supply. To the extent, though, that the Catholic Church remains a vital advocate for immigrants and a voice for social justice and a force for inner-city education, it retains an Irish accent.

The walls are gone. The Irish have fled into suburbs and intermarried. The parish has changed, utterly. Yet it is impossible to imagine the Church and the parish without the Irish. Within the parish walls, they built a piece of America that continues to serve those who have come later.

PETE HAMILL

THE INTERRUPTED NARRATIVE

Pete Hamill is the author, most recently, of the novel SNOW IN AUGUST, *and is editor of the* DAILY NEWS *in New York.*

They came across oceans, leaving everything behind: relatives, friends, landscape. Departure, for those voyagers, was often painful. In Ireland, too many families gathered in the ritual of the American Wake, saying farewells that were often as final as death. They danced, drank, embraced one another, said good-byes, wept. And then it was the cold morning and they were going down streets or lanes that would bring them to the sea. In the songs, there was a final glimpse of Ireland. The coasts of Donegal. The abrupt shores of Dingle. And then the cold heartsick Atlantic journey, chilly with doubt and separation, warmed only by the promise of what lay ahead. At last, they arrived in the new places, to have their documents examined and their bodies inspected for disease, and they stepped ashore. Everything had been left behind, except memory.

For the Irish immigrants, as it was for all others who came to America, memory was at once a curse and a goad. Many things had driven these men and women from the lands where they were born: hunger, bigotry, tyranny. Often, when faced with the disappointments of America, its harshness or indifference, they drew on such memories to remember why they had come. As bad as it might be in some tough slum, life was usually better than it had been in the places they left behind. My own parents were from Belfast. My father arrived in 1923, convinced that the old dream of a united Ireland had died with Michael Collins at Beal na mBlath, County Cork. "He was the only man in Ireland," he once said, "with the guts to bring an army north and make the British keep their word." This was, of course, unprovable, but in my father's view of the old country, myth and history had a way of entwining themselves.

My mother arrived in 1929, on the very day that the stock market crashed. Her fare had been paid by a rich family, and for a few years she worked for them as a maid and nanny. She did not do this job in a victimized state of mind; as a Catholic from Belfast, she was delighted to have any work at all. Her memory of the bigotry that had driven so many of her neighbors to despair was at the root of her American optimism. She believed that work was central to an honorable, decent life, and she would keep working for almost all of her life, as a department store clerk, a nurse's aide in a hospital, a cashier in a movie house, a clerk in an insurance company. In her late sixties, when everyone she knew had retired, she went back to work at Off Track Betting. For her, there was no such thing as a "meaningless" job; work was the meaning. Somehow, without government help, she and my father also managed to raise seven children.

In many ways, theirs was not an unusual story; in the long history of the Irish in America, it has been duplicated many times. The details are always different. But there were always certain constants. Work was one of them. So was a kind of invincible optimism. After all, this was the United States of America, a country that believed in the limitless future. Never look back, said Satchel Paige. Someone might be gainin' on you.

And yet . . .

And yet the past was not entirely dead. For millions of Irish immigrants, including my parents, the old country remained vividly alive. It was often sentimentalized, time and distance blurring the hard edges of the abandoned reality. Since most had gone away when young, the emotions were also tangled with a nostalgia for youth. These feelings were often expressed most poignantly in songs, from the music and lyrics of Percy French to the manufactured nostalgias of Tin Pan Alley. There was a huge market for these songs, and many of them drove deep into the immigrant experience. It didn't matter that a certain amount of cynicism led to their existence; the emotions they expressed, or unleashed, were genuine. When my father stood up at a family party, or at the bar of a saloon, to sing about the sun going down on Galway Bay, or the glories of the green glens of Antrim, he was evoking both a lost land and an altered youth.

In a way, those songs served another purpose. They stated clearly that those Irish men and women who had become Americans still lived with their Irishness. Ireland had been left behind, but it still lived in their memories, their accents, their dreams. They could pledge allegiance to the flag of the United States of America. But in the mysterious places of the heart, that allegiance was never total. This was almost never a question of divided loyalties; the Irish fought in American wars; they gladly called themselves Americans. But it was not easy to erase memory.

Almost universally, Irish immigrants of my parents' generation found themselves mysteriously separated from their American children. Fathers and sons, mothers and daughters lived together in the same apartments.

They went to the same churches. They heard the same radio programs. They knew the same people. But their stories were crucially different. Most of those stories were, in fact, told by the children. That is, by the Americans. For reasons that are not clear to me (although education is surely a major reason), there isn't much of an Irish-American literature told by the immigrants themselves. Some of this might transcend the Irish experience; stories of fathers and sons are almost always narrated by the sons. But many Irish-American writers (myself included) have found themselves trying to remember for two separate generations, our own and that of our parents. One is a form of personal history; the other is an act of the imagination. We can relate what we remember of our own lives; we can only imagine the lives our parents had led before we came to know them.

In the end, one large truth separates us. Our parents, the immigrants, were the products of an interrupted narrative. My parents could trace their families' presence in Ireland back through the generations into the mists of time. They had lived in one place, or one region, all their lives. They knew people down the street who had suffered for their religion. They knew rebels and cowards and informers. They knew old men and women who spoke Irish in the mountains. They carried with them the surviving fragments of the older religions, worshipping through superstitions the pagan gods who lived in the Irish narrative before Christianity swept the island. The chapters of the Irish narrative were told around hearth fires. They were passed from one generation to another, traveling across stone-cursed fields to the hard streets of Irish cities. Sometimes, that narrative took the form of song, other times of poetry. Sometimes it was continued in a tin box full of yellowing documents. Almost always, it ended with the great interruption of emigration.

The story of the American children was a much different narrative. We took America for granted. It was our country, a right of birth. In many of us, the sense of discovering America each day was permanent. We had been granted a kind of invincible optimism, believing that we could do anything in this marvelous place if only we worked for it. It didn't matter that some of us failed, or were embarrassed later by our idealism. What did matter is that we believed it. We were the beginning of a process, not its end. The future was ours. Or so we thought at ten or fifteen or thirty. It never occurred to us that we might have to move to another country to eat. Or to vote. Or to make something real of our American dreams.

That was at the heart of the differences. My parents' myths were not my myths. My father remembered music hall songs and clandestine meetings of Sinn Fein. He remembered playing soccer on the fields of Belfast.

My mother remembered British army patrols and their boots crunching the streets of the Short Strand. They lived with those myths. Years later, in her seventies, my mother was mugged by two "brave" hoodlums and was thrown into shock. She kept speaking about a Sergeant Butler, and none of us who gathered beside her bed could recognize his name. The next day, having come out of shock, she told us. Sergeant Butler was the leader of the British patrol in her neighborhood in Belfast.

I had other memories and different myths. My mythic figures were named Batman or Captain Marvel, Roy Rogers or Jackie Robinson. I heard the Irish songs on Saturday nights or Sunday afternoons, and was infused with their sense of longing and melancholy. But if the sun was shining, I wanted to hurry to the street to play stickball. If the sun was gone, I wanted to travel through abandoned subway tunnels with Billy Batson to meet the wizard named Shazam. I was from Brooklyn, not Belfast. In my imagination I roamed through Ebbets Field or Monument Valley. I went with Bomba the Jungle Boy to the Giant Cataract. I went down the Mississippi with Huck and Jim. I was mercifully free of the grieving drizzle of Northern Ireland.

And yet, as I grew older, as I listened to Hank Williams and Charlie Parker and the blues, as I became more deeply American, I began to think more about that interrupted narrative. When I was twenty-one, I went off to Mexico for a year on the GI Bill, to study painting. For the first time, I went through the experience of being a stranger in a strange land. I loved Mexico and Mexicans, but I knew I could never be a Mexican. Their myths were not my myths. A strange thing happened: In Mexico, I often found myself thinking about my mother and father in Ireland and New York. When I came home, I often questioned them, trying to pry from them the life they had lived before they had come to America. Later, I traveled to Ireland, lived there for long periods, trying to piece together the frayed ends of the narrative.

Of course, I failed. There were too many blank places in the story, too many names that meant nothing to me, too many people who had died. I could never hope to grasp the dailiness of my parents' lives in the city they'd left behind because Belfast itself had changed. They left before the development of two technologies that changed the world: television and the transatlantic passenger jet. Television opened the world to the young people of modern Belfast. Catholics saw Martin Luther King marching at Selma and felt a sense of connection. The airplane ended the America Wake, because the journey was no longer so final; the Irish young could now go off for a year or two and fly home for Christmas. The old parochialism was waning. The myths were quickly shifting. Irish kids knew Batman. They played rock and roll. They too dreamed of the canyons and mesas of the American West. In some irreversible ways, the distance between the Irish and the Irish Americans had been diminished.

That does not mean that the distance had been permanently bridged. The young Irish now growing up in Belfast and Derry, Dublin or Cork might be more connected to Irish Americans through the grinding force of popular culture. But for the moment, their narrative remains uninterrupted. They can trace their families through the tombstones in local cemeteries and can continue to hear the tales of the Irish past. They might wander the world. They might choose for a while to become some newer version of the wild geese. But they will not go off in the same permanent way. The jet plane is waiting. The *Irish Times* is on the Internet. Some new narrative is almost certainly being imagined. I just hope I live long enough to read it. ❖

CHAPTER 3

THE
PRECINCT

WORKING FROM
THE INSIDE

MORE THAN any other institution, the precinct—the smallest unit of local political organization and influence, be it a voting district, a municipal ward, a party clubhouse, a firehouse, or even a saloon—provided the economic stability and the power that enabled Irish Americans to progress into the middle class and beyond. For Irish Catholic America in particular, the precinct was the political equivalent, and sometime partner, of the parish. Political and parochial influence built churches and orphanages and schools; it built politicians and, ultimately, it built what came to be known as "machines."

Tammany Hall in New York City, which began innocently enough in the late eighteenth century as an institution to help the poor and was named after Delaware Indian chief Tamawend, fell under the sway of the Irish and became a political force—a machine—in the early nineteenth century. In many respects, Tammany was the embodiment of the grassroots urban political organizations that sprang up in other American cities where the Irish congregated: the Pendergast organization in Kansas City, the Hague machine in Jersey City, the latter-day Daley machine in Chicago. To define Tammany, or to define a machine, one has to contend with mercurial structures enveloped in shadows. The very informality of many of these often unofficial political organizations combined with often brazen politicking, arm-twisting, and civic activities makes definition elusive. Consequently, the so-called Irish-American political machines mean different things to different people. To some, they

John F. Kennedy's election to the presidency in 1960 was a transcendent culmination of Irish-American politicking that began in the local wards and ended on Pennsylvania Avenue.

Tammany Hall, on 17th Street in New York City, may look like just another nineteenth century building front; in fact it has come to symbolize the very idea of an urban political machine. Within its walls the Irish in New York succeeded in organizing their political interests into power and influence.

were a legitimate means to political ends; to others, they represent all that is corrupt in politics. In truth, they were both.

Some aspects of these machines, however, are incontrovertible. Any organization deserving of the moniker "machine" operated at a grassroots urban level on behalf (usually) of the Democratic Party. Often, an elected official (such as Jersey City mayor Frank Hague) would be at the helm; in other cases, Tammany Hall, for example, the "chieftain" would be unelected, but not without political influence. The organization would fan out into the neighborhoods, especially in poor areas, and assign a person as the local "ward heeler" to serve as the eyes and ears on the street. He might be on the city payroll, he might be unpaid, he might be a saloonkeeper, but whatever his status, he was plugged into the community. Residents in need of a job, an interview, a vendor's license, some official paperwork, or perhaps the ministrations of a doctor they could not afford would appeal to the ward heeler, who would appeal to the leaders of the political club, who would employ their influence with the powers that be to see what could be done. What everyone expected in return was the vote of the beneficiary and those he could influence in coming elections. That was the quid pro quo that fueled the early Irish-American political machines. And a ward heeler was judged by how many votes he could deliver on election day.

Poor immigrants understandably were attracted to a political presence that promised the delivery of services. And the Irish were particularly drawn to this method of organizing, with the result

that the political machine is considered an Irish gift to American politics.

That is not to say that these networks were purely public-spirited; plenty of shady deals were going on, ranging from the "honest graft" that Tammany leader George Washington Plunkitt spoke of (a kind of insider trading) to kickback schemes from the various vice peddlers who were willing to pay money to enjoy the protection from prosecution that a good political machine could offer (the Albany novels of William Kennedy give ample evidence of the darker side of a machine).

At their best, though, these organizations, functioning from the bottom up, effectively gave voice at city hall to the humblest members of the local neighborhoods and precincts. In the nineteenth century, Tammany in particular brought people into the political process who had never felt part of it or were newly arrived to America. The machine was not about elites and their concerns; it was not about maintaining the order that reigned before new immigrants began to change the complexion of the poorest precincts of the city. In fact at Tammany Hall the leaders were constantly bumping heads with the elites, fighting and cajoling to extract from government the favors it felt its constituents deserved, and ultimately fighting to get its own into city government. And in 1828, Andrew Jackson brought this kind of grassroots precinct populism, this irreverent feistiness, to the presidency. Jackson, the son of Protestant Irish immigrants, was an antiestablishment candidate who commanded the loyalty of the disenfranchised by dint of an active antielitism. Jacksonian Democracy, as his style of politics came to be known, dispensed favors to supporters, a tactic that brought the bottom-up ethic into federal politics. His administration came to be identified with the spoils system, and his very election was in part made possible by the churning engine of Tammany, the

Davey Crockett, of Irish Protestant stock, was poor, humble, and bright. From Obion County in Western Tennessee near Reelfoot Lake he traveled far, all the way into America's very image of the frontiersman; but along the way he served as a distinguished United States senator and was a valued confidant of his fellow Irishman, Andrew Jackson.

nineteenth century's ultimate machine. And there is no story of the rise to the American presidency that can outdo Jackson's in moving from the bottom up.

✻

Andrew Jackson was only thirteen years old when a squad of British soldiers took him prisoner in South Carolina during the Revolution and ordered him to shine the commanding officer's boots. The boy would have none of it. "I am a prisoner of war, and claim to be treated as such," he is reported to have said with stubborn defiance—not to mention a precocious eloquence. The officer drew his sword and took aim at the boy's head. The boy ducked and threw up his left arm, but the weapon found its mark. The sword slashed both arm and head, opening wounds that would leave lasting scars. This son of Irish immigrants would carry a reminder of a British soldier's cruelty to his grave.

As president, Jackson would be hailed as a man of the people who had challenged and defeated starchy old elites. He would shock the nation's ruling classes by appointing trusted cronies, people much like himself, to offices that had been regarded as the personal property of the American aristocracy from Virginia and Massachusetts. He asserted that nobody was *entitled* to public office, convinced as he was that republican government was best served when jobholders frequently were changed. He sought the abolition of the electoral college and advocated for the direct election of U.S. senators (a democratic reform that was still more than seventy years away), the election of all judges, and a one-term limit for presidents. The people, not the politicians, were the sovereigns of a repub-

Andrew Jackson was the first Irish-American to serve in the White House. He shook up the ruling elites with his populist politics and his habit of sharing the spoils with those of like mind.

lican democracy, Jackson said. Such attitudes in the early nineteenth century were radical and not a little frightening. One society matron expressed the thoughts of America's established order: "Why, if Andrew Jackson can be president, anybody can!" Her tone suggested that she approved of neither Jackson nor the very idea that anybody could become president.

The familiar narrative of Irish-American political history often excludes Andrew Jackson and yet is filled with men very much like him. While Jackson remains outside the Irish political pantheon, there was in his life a positively Irish quality of tragedy and triumph. His parents left the town of Castlereagh on the east coast of Ireland in 1765, settling in the Carolinas because so many other Irish immigrants, Protestant like the Jacksons, lived there. Jackson never laid eyes on his father, who died after two years of backbreaking effort, trying literally to carve out a new life for his immigrant family. As a final indignity, his body fell from a wagon bound for the local cemetery. Nobody noticed until the procession arrived at the grave, and members of the funeral party were dispatched to find and retrieve it. Several days later, and two days before Saint Patrick's Day, the widowed Elizabeth Jackson gave birth to her third and last child. He was named Andrew in honor of the father he would never know.

Young Andrew's life was as difficult as that of any of the Irish Catholic politicians who would later write such moving rags-to-power, if not riches, stories. His oldest brother died while serving with the American army during the Revolution. He and his remaining brother, Robert, were taken prisoner during bitter fighting near their home—leading to the confrontation that ended with sword-

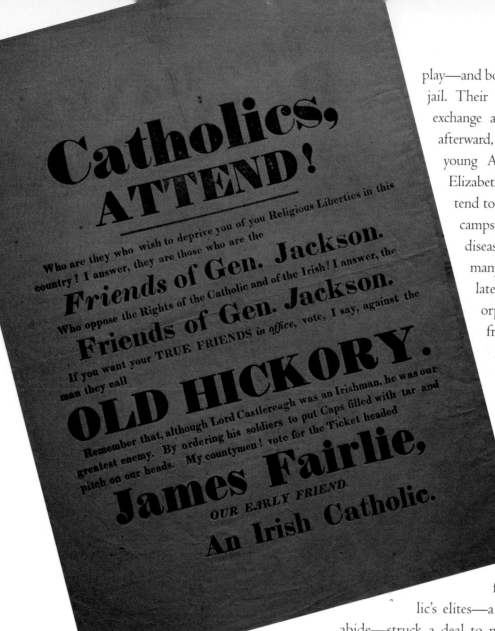

Catholics, ATTEND!

Who are they who wish to deprive you of you Religious Liberties in this country! I answer, they are those who are the

Friends of Gen. Jackson.

Who oppose the Rights of the Catholic and of the Irish? I answer, the

Friends of Gen. Jackson.

If you want your TRUE FRIENDS in office, vote. I say, against the man they call

OLD HICKORY.

Remember that, although Lord Castlereagh was an Irishman, he was our greatest enemy. By ordering his soldiers to put Caps filled with tar and pitch on our heads. My countymen! vote for the Ticket headed

James Fairlie,

OUR EARLY FRIEND.

An Irish Catholic.

play—and both became ill with smallpox while in jail. Their mother helped arrange for their exchange and return, but Robert died soon afterward, and only Elizabeth's nursing kept young Andrew alive. Some months later, Elizabeth Jackson traveled to Charleston to tend to other American prisoners in British camps; she developed cholera, the same disease that killed Patrick Kennedy and so many Irish immigrants a half century later. She died, leaving Andrew an orphan at fifteen in the backwoods of frontier America.

Jackson's path to political power began its ascent following his triumph over the British at the conclusion of the War of 1812, but he met resistance nearly every step of the way. Part of the Irish political legacy is to take particular pride in winning despite the odds, despite the barriers. Andrew Jackson had the presidency stolen from him in 1824 when the republic's elites—a phrase no Irish republican would abide—struck a deal to make John Quincy Adams, son of starchy John Adams, president. Talk about an aristocracy looking after its own! Andrew Jackson had won the election handily in the popular vote, with 152,900 votes to Adams's 114,020, but when the electoral college met, the fix was in. The son of Irish immigrants went down to defeat in a backroom deal that would go down in American history as the "corrupt bargain."

Jackson's opponents feared his supposed lack of polish and education, his temper, and his combativeness. They feared his supporters, whom they regarded as uncouth and unwashed. Perhaps they were. But the uneducated (and undoubtedly corrupt) Tammany chieftain Richard Croker answered similar criticisms of his own supporters in a fashion Jackson surely would have appreciated: "If we go down into the gutter, it is because there are men in the gutter, and you have got to go where they are if you are to do anything with them," Croker said. Tammany and Jackson got their way in 1828, but everything that was said about Jackson might have been said, and indeed was said, of the Irish politicians who would come later.

(continued on page 105)

ROBERT SHRUM

THE GREENING OF THE PRESIDENCY

Robert Shrum is a Democratic strategist and longtime political consultant based in Washington, D.C. He was raised by a mother, he says, who convinced him that he was actually all Irish.

James Farley, pictured here at the 1932 Democratic convention, helped build an organization that propelled Franklin Roosevelt to the presidency.

The Scotch Irish got to the presidency early on—and from Andrew Jackson, have stayed there off and on ever since. But it was different with the Irish Irish, the Irish Catholics, in part because they came later to America and even more because of their religion.

In 1927, just a year before New York governor Al Smith became the first Irish Catholic nominee for president, even the progressive *New Republic* could write: "The Catholic Church will remain an alien guest in the American body politic as long as it tries to form the minds of American Catholics by educational methods different from those which are used to form the minds of other Americans." Smith was denied the 1924 presidential nomination by Democrats who openly defended the Ku Klux Klan. When he was finally nominated in 1928, on his third try, Smith had to run not only into the gale force of the last economic grasp of the roaring twenties but against a religious and cultural bigotry that cost this cigar-smoking, brown-derbied, quintessential urban Catholic a host of normally reliable Democratic states. And the prejudice didn't come just from the fringes. The legendary newspaper editor William Allen White denounced Smith as a danger to "the whole Puritan civilization, which has built a sturdy, orderly nation."

In 1932, Democratic leaders had concluded that Smith could never win, even in the depths of the depression, because he was urban and Catholic, and too many voters would prefer poverty to the pope. But almost unnoticed, Smith's 1928 loss had altered the landscape of presidential politics and laid the groundwork for forty years of Democratic ascendancy. Roosevelt's victory in 1932 was built upon the decisive shift of urban voters to the Democratic line that Smith's candidacy had inspired.

But first, FDR, once Smith's protégé, had to beat him for the nomination. He did it with the decisive help of two Irishmen.

The first was James A. Farley, a tall, balding political organizer who maintained a massive political correspondence handwritten in green ink. Virtually every delegate to the convention saw one or more of these Irish-green letters. Farley systematically organized for years before in anticipation of the 1932 Democratic Convention in Chicago. He had Roosevelt officially declare his candidacy at what was then an early and unprecedented date—five months before Chicago.

The Roosevelt forces entered the convention hall with a clear majority, but for generations, the Democratic Party had required a two-thirds vote for nomination. A dominant Roosevelt would order that changed in 1936, but for now, he kept falling short of the two-thirds on ballot after ballot. This is where another Irishman came in. Joseph P. Kennedy had broken with the Massachusetts Irish establishment to back Roosevelt over Smith. He didn't really care— his path had been finance, not politics—and he'd known Roosevelt since the then assistant secretary of the navy had enlisted Kennedy in World War I to whip one of the nation's leading shipyards into fighting trim. Kennedy now went to his fellow mogul, the newspaper publisher William Randolph Hearst, to broker a deal. If Roosevelt didn't make it, he suggested, the compromise nominee could be utility executive Newton Baker, Woodrow Wilson's secretary of war, an internationalist despised by the isolationist Hearst. At least Roosevelt wouldn't try to take the United States into the League of Nations. A deal was struck: Texas would throw its votes to Roosevelt, and in return, the vice presidency would go to Hearst's friend, John Nance Garner, a Texan who was Speaker of the House. (Garner, who would later bitterly regret the deal, left us with just one famous line: "The vice-presidency isn't worth a pitcher of warm piss.")

*

Roosevelt's administration was an almost Irish presidency. He chose an Irish attorney general, Senator Thomas Walsh of Montana, an aging populist workhorse who died before taking office while honeymooning with his young wife. Thomas Corcoran—"Tommy the Cork"—became speechwriter, spinmeister, and strategist, and his influence would continue into Lyndon Johnson's presidency. Joseph Kennedy became chairman of the Maritime Commission and the first chairman of the Securities and Exchange Commission, where he cleaned up Wall Street; he himself had made millions there and knew every trick of the financial trade. He finally became ambassador to Britain, a post he coveted both for its immense prestige at the time and for the discomfort the appointment gave to the WASP establishment at home as well as the anti-Irish power elite in London. Frank Murphy became attorney general and a Supreme Court justice. James A. Farley was in the cabinet as postmaster general and in politics as chairman of the Democratic National Committee—and there was no Common Cause to object. FDR built close ties to the Irish-dominated labor movement and urban machines while he denounced the old anti-Irish, anti-Catholic nativism as unpatriotic, addressing a shocked convocation of the Daughters of the American Revolution as "fellow immigrants."

In temperament, wit, sympathy, and policy, and most conspicuously by offering appointments, apparent respect, and a share of power, Roosevelt struck a deep chord with Irish voters. But the 1940 campaign brought dissonance. First, Farley himself challenged Roosevelt's reach for an unprecedented—and today unconstitutional—

Will it be peace or war: Two quintessential Irish-American pols, Ned Kelly and James Farley, huddle over an uneaten meal.

third term. Roosevelt spoke by radio to the convention, disclaiming any interest in the presidency; he was, in effect, inviting the delegates to draft him. As they sat there stunned and silent, the third-term strategy was consummated by Chicago's Irish mayor Ed Kelly, who had wired the sound system to a bullhorn in the sewers underneath the convention hall. The "voice from the sewer" suddenly blared out: "We want Roosevelt." The Irish urban machine delivered again. The delegates took up the cry, as they were supposed to, and Farley—as well as Garner, who also challenged the president—lost decisively.

✻

One young Massachusetts delegate who refused at the end of the roll call to change his vote and make the nomination unanimous signaled Roosevelt's underlying problem with the Irish. Joseph P. Kennedy Jr., very much his father's son, reflected the ambassador's disillusion with Roosevelt's increasingly interventionist policy in World War II. Britain, Ambassador Kennedy said, was "finished." And Irish Americans in general didn't see much reason to rescue the British. But in the fight to hold the Irish vote, Roosevelt still commanded most of the Irish political elite: almost all elected officials; New York leader Ed Flynn, a Farley protégé who took Farley's place; and Robert Hannegan, who in turn would become chairman of the Democratic National Committee. Ambassador Kennedy, who would be unceremoniously dismissed after the election, was pressured to give a last-minute national radio address endorsing Roosevelt. The president himself, facing defections on the war issue from Germans in the Midwest and the Irish everywhere, traveled to Boston only days after the first draft numbers had been drawn from a fish bowl and days before the election to deliver one of his most famous and disingenuous lines: "I have said this before, but I shall say it again, and again, and again. Your boys are not going to be sent into any foreign wars." But before, he had always added "except in case of attack." Now, worried about a closing margin and the ethnic vote, he had gone to the heart of Irish America to promise that Americans would not be fighting and dying for Britain.

It was enough, although the Irish and Catholic vote for Roosevelt and consequently his overall majorities declined sharply in both 1940 and 1944. The fervor was gone. But Roosevelt's presidency had marked the turning point. The Irish were in the White House, in the corridors of power, at the levers of the Democratic Party's machine. It was the Irish chieftains who insisted on Harry Truman for vice president in 1944 and who drafted Adlai Stevenson in 1952. Many of them were, ironically, the principal doubters about John Kennedy in 1960; they were old enough to remember Al Smith. Better they be close to the throne than risk losing it by attempting to seat one of their own on it. Kennedy, however, had taken his case to the people in the primaries— and, far more important for the chieftains, built a clear popular strength among their people, a sense of both preference and pride that could be politically perilous to resist. Mayor Daley didn't decide until convention week, but then he took almost all the Illinois delegates away from Stevenson and delivered them to Kennedy.

Pennsylvania's governor David Lawrence capitulated when the Kennedy forces were about to organize his delegation out from under him. Quite simply, they wanted one of their own. Other Catholics, ethnic groups, and Jews—the core of the northern Democratic Party—saw Kennedy as the standard-bearer of their claims to equal status. The southerners and Stevenson diehards like Eleanor Roosevelt, who was bitterly suspicious of Joe Kennedy's son, were simply swamped on the first ballot.

*

John F. Kennedy's election completed the long march of the Irish to the center of the Oval Office. They were no longer sitting outside as petitioners; they were no longer just T. S. Eliot's "attendant lords," with power as derivative as Farley's. An Irishman was president; his staff was nicknamed the Irish mafia. He might be a product of private and not parochial schools, of Harvard and not Holy Cross; he might be urbane and not urban; but he was fiercely, proudly Irish, combining the pols' sense of power with the Irish love of language, turning political prose into poetry. When he traced the immigrants' trail back across the Atlantic and went to Ireland as president, it was one of the island's most stirring moments in a thousand years. The wakes of the nineteenth century, still remembered, had been redeemed. And when he was killed after a thousand days in office, the event had a very Irish sense of fatalism and tragedy.

No matter how many other presidents of Irish descent there may be, the Kennedy presidency was a unique Irish passage, the end of second-class citizenship in America for the Irish and for Catholics in general. Kennedy's lilt and language also reshaped the way we see the nation's highest office. Perhaps it's no accident that our two best presidential communicators since then—Ronald Reagan and Bill Clinton—have been Irish; their families may have long since lost the religion, but their way with words, their wit and fluency, have been Irish to the core.

With both Reagan and Clinton, we've also seen an American activism on Northern Ireland never present in the White House before. Reagan, reluctant to offend his friend Margaret Thatcher, nonetheless tried to nudge the process along on the basis of discussions with Irish-American leaders in Congress, including House Speaker Tip O'Neill, Senator Daniel Patrick Moynihan, and Senator Ted Kennedy. The Irishness often proved stronger than ideological differences: Reagan and O'Neill would share a nip after a long day of partisan combat and the president happily traveled to Kennedy's home to give one of his most eloquent speeches at a fundraiser for the John F. Kennedy Library. And with Clinton, the nudge on Northern Ireland has become an overt push, over British objections, and the fevered remonstrances of his own Anglophilic State Department; Clinton's popularity in Ireland is higher than it ever has been in the United States.

*

Not long ago, Congressman Joe Kennedy, one of a new generation of Irish politicians, one or more of whom could end up in the Oval Office, was in Northern Ireland when a British soldier walked up to him and snarled: "Why don't you go back to your own country?" Kennedy shot back: "And why don't you go back to yours?" But no American president of Irish descent will ever be a foreigner in Ireland. The Irish had no colonies—except Boston, New York, Philadelphia, Chicago, and countless other American places, and then, after a long time, the White House. The United States is the largest Irish nation in the world—and for any American president who symbolizes that, the Irish will always say: "Céad Mille Fáilte"—a hundred thousand welcomes. Or how about "Hail to the [Irish] chief"? ❖

"What's the use of being Irish if you don't know the world is going to break your heart?" Daniel Patrick Moynihan once asked, after the death of JFK, expecting no reply.

If such knowledge defines Irishness, then who could deny Andrew Jackson his Irish roots, for the world had broken his heart several times over during the course of his eventful life. The man who practiced his own style of precinct politics, who brought his friends into government and defiantly gave the boot to entrenched elites, all in the face of defeat and tragedy, easily could be regarded as the founder of the Irish-American political tradition. During Jackson's last year in the White House, a traveler en route to Washington, D.C., on the National Road (the superhighway of its day) was surprised to find the president's coach parked outside a roadside tavern in Maryland. The traveler, his curiosity piqued, paused in his journey, wandered into the place, and found the seventh president alone at a table, puffing on a pipe. While others merely watched in awe, an Irish immigrant, dressed in laborer's clothes, approached the president, asked his age (sixty-nine at the time), and noted that Jackson had been criticized for excessive pride. "It is like a great many other things folks say of me," the president replied. "There is no truth in it." And the two men, president and immigrant laborer, continued their discussions, apparently long after the witness left. A Jackson biographer said of the incident, and of the new world of Jacksonian Democracy: "There could be no doubt that, in some remarkable and marvelous way, the average American, the 'common man,' had been admitted into the mainstream of the nation's political life."

The admission came less than a decade before the Irish fled a land where the political mainstream remained safely guarded, where politics consigned the "common man," not to mention the "common" women and their "common" children, to the mercies of the marketplace. The coming of the Famine Irish only accentuated the need for a dialogue that could be carried on in the gutter, in the streets, and in whatever precincts the poor might gather.

If the Irish rushed into American politics with unseemly speed, it had everything to do with numbers, and the numbers increasingly favored the Irish—by 1870, New York was home to two hundred thousand people of Irish birth, more than any other city in the world, including Dublin, and the Irish were assuming dominant roles in Chicago, Boston (where the Irish population of thirty-five thousand Irish in 1850 increased by 200 percent by 1855), and elsewhere. And unlike Ireland, where a privileged minority was permanently installed in office, America and its democratic institutions could not ignore the preponderance of Irish in its biggest cities, nor, for that matter, would the Irish consent to being ignored.

When George Washington Plunkitt, the son of immigrants who grew up in a New York shanty town, became a leading figure of Tammany Hall in the late nineteenth century, he summed up his view of politics and government in a single phrase that has survived the ages: "I seen my opportunities, and I took 'em." The same could be said for the Irish as a whole after the Famine, although the opportunities Jacksonian Democracy presented the average Irish voter and the opportunities pre-

From GRAMMUDDER
for Ann McCardy Murphy

*1943. You hummed
"Over There" absently,
but another war*

*throbbed in memory.
You poured Irish tea
into white enamel cups*

*steaming pale rinds
of smoke into casks
of afternoon silence.*

*I ate scones and heard
pipers, Robert Emmett's last
speech on the dock.*

*Fenians, republicans
lined up, your brother
Jack beaten with a horse*

*crop, bleeding in his own
velvet fields, the brocade
lands of Mullingar.*

*Your stories held onto
that world, useless
as the blind collie*

*sleeping at your feet.
You gave us stories
like hidden tongues*

*that might speak later on,
might wake a partisan heart.
I have always remained Irish,*

*missing something
I cannot name.
It has given me an edge.*

—RENNY GOLDEN

sented to Plunkitt were of a decidedly different sort. Plunkitt became a millionaire by privately speculating on what he knew from his political connections; the Irish as a group saw their opportunities, too, and took 'em, and rode them to the heights of urban power.

*

While the Irish came to America with few material possessions and even fewer marketable skills, they were supplied with qualities that were a perfect match for the new era of populist democracy in America. They were a gregarious, sociable people—with the conspicuous exception of several Tammany leaders, who craved the anonymity of the back room and whose work habits were as sober and joyless as any banker's. When the businesslike Charles Francis Murphy was at the helm of Tammany Hall, he was spotted close-mouthed as "The Star-Spangled Banner" was being played. An aide explained that the boss simply didn't want to commit himself in public.

Of course, running an operation such as the urban political machine no doubt required all of the colorless sobriety associated with the leadership of a corporation. But the mass of foot soldiers, and possible recruits, were under no such pressing constraints, and they quickly established ready-made bases of operations in their parishes and their saloons. To say as much is to walk on the edge of ethnic stereotype, but history speaks for itself. In her study of the Chicago Irish community, historian Eileen M. McMahon noted the key role of the close-knit parish that served as a staging ground for local politicians. One parish's boundaries corresponded, perhaps coincidentally, with an Irish-dominated election ward or election district. Another parish served as a community powerbroker for the Back of the Yards neighborhood, while the Irish parishes of Chicago's Bridgeport section were home to numerous politicians, the most notable being Richard Daley, who lived in Bridgeport until the day he died.

The saloon culture, meanwhile, may have been the bane of temperance lecturers such as Father Theobald Matthew, an Irish priest who toured America in the early

1850s to preach about the evils of demon whiskey, but as a vehicle for political organizing, it was as custom-made as the parish.

The neighborhood saloon acted, as the village pub did in Ireland, not simply as a place to drink but as a community social center or ad hoc precinct headquarters, providing a ready-made constituency for the bold face-to-face politics of the times. Commonly referred to as "grog shops" or, in a bit of the Irish language transported to America, shebeens, they were where Irish workers gathered after a long day of labor. New York had more than two thousand of them by 1840, nearly all concentrated in what is now downtown Manhattan. Boston's blue bloods were horrified, as no fewer than twelve hundred saloons opened for business by the time the Famine immigration eased. Their number continued to grow as the Irish poured into the city. In the 1870s, Patrick Kennedy, namesake of the Patrick Kennedy who left County Wexford during the Famine only to find an early grave in cholera-infested East Boston, decided to try his hand at business by opening his own saloon. Whether he realized it or not, it was the beginning of his political career.

Bartenders were respected members of the parish, yet another example of Irish indifference to the social pecking order of Protestant America. (When Patrick Kennedy's son Joseph was turned down for membership in an old-money country club in Brookline, Massachusetts, he spoke not only for himself but for a defiantly Irish-American point of view: "Those narrow-minded bigoted sons of bitches barred me because I was an Irish Catholic and the son of a barkeep.")

Tammany and similar machines in other cities had no intention of being so selective, which is good enough reason why the machine prevailed over aristocracy and many a reform movement. The machines were quick to incorporate barkeeps like Patrick Kennedy and saloon owners like the future Tammany chief Charles Murphy into local leadership positions, and were more than happy to support the grandson of a barkeep when he ran for president in 1960.

Colorful though it sounds, the saloon culture clearly had terrible drawbacks, and for every deal cut over friendly glasses in the name of the masses, there were dozens of lives wasted and families ruined within the walls of this particular outpost. Another, less savory side to the saloon's role in neighborhood politics was its ties to the violent gangland culture that was developing in urban Irish America. Just as the saloon served as a recruiting hall for Tammany, so it became a gathering place for gangs with such names as the Dead Rabbits, the Bowery Boys, and the Plug Uglies. And in this era of the common man, the gangs, too, found themselves enmeshed in urban America's chaotic democracy, often being called upon to flex their muscles on behalf of their political benefactors. In some Irish neighborhoods, far from those of the ruling elites, the saloon was where the underworld met democracy's underlings, forging a relationship that had its roots in the age of Jackson and has since served as the starting point for many a motion picture.

John Morrissey, a native of Tipperary, was a one-man symbol for the way in which the Irish used the available social structure to at first shock and then replace the old-stock ruling elites. As a young man in the Hudson River city of Troy, New York, he was a barroom brawler whose fists were fast enough to earn him fame as a heavyweight champion. From the saloon and the ring, Morrissey grabbed the next available rung and parlayed his fame as a fighter to win election as a congressman from New York, and from that position he became an owner of racehorses and a gambling salon in Saratoga. His

In the early years of the twentieth century, Irish Americans ruled urban America from east to west. Above, Thomas J. Pendergast (left) and his nephew James M. Pendergast ruled Kansas City. Frank Hague (left, inset) of Jersey City proclaimed "I am the law," and served as both mayor and head of the local machine. (oppsite) Al Smith and Charles F. Murphy combined to implement a social safety net in New York.

background, with its aroma of sweat, liquor, and cigar smoke, confirmed every aristocrat's image of the emerging Irish-American pol. But he was wildly popular, ever more so when it became known that he had been turned away from Troy's city hall by a newly installed mayor who insisted that visitors first present their cards. Morrissey had no card, but he showed up at city hall next time in formal dress, feigning an interest in speaking French, since, he pointed out, that was now the style at city hall.

Such styles, however, were about to go out of fashion. Mass, popular democracy, exemplified at its best and at its worst by a machine that depended on a grass-roots knowledge of the people it served, had little use for politicians who considered themselves above the struggle for power that was taking place every day, in every ward and precinct.

*

The litany of powerful Irish-American political figures, some elected, some not, reads like a guidebook to a vanished America: the Pendergasts of Kansas City, Daniel O'Connell of Albany, Frank Hague of Jersey City, Richard Daley of Chicago, "Blind Boss" Chris Buckley of San Francisco, and the likes of Honest John Kelly, Richard Croker, and Charles Francis Murphy of Tammany in New York. These figures functioned very much as "bosses," and the organizations over which they presided, whether a mayoral administration or a Democratic club, steered the cities of which they were a part. Although their names were seldom affixed to pieces of legislation or great public works projects, their services, no doubt, were remembered by generations of poor immigrants, Irish and otherwise. The turkeys at Christmas, the coal on a bitter winter's night, the job that forestalled eviction, the word to a judge or cop that prevented calamity—such was the work of these influential machine politicians.

On occasion, such work inspired the ambitious and the gifted to greater heights. Alfred E. Smith came out of Tammany Hall, became governor of New York, and introduced sweeping social legislation. Harry Truman was an out-of-work haberdasher when he became a cog in the Pendergast machine, and while he was as un-Irish as could be imagined, he understood the machine's principle of loyalty. The Pendergast family was in disrepute when Truman became vice president, but when Thomas Pendergast died, Truman went to the funeral despite the outcries of reformers.

Ironically enough, the politician who came to symbolize a distinctly Irish style was not a machine politician but a loner who prospered on his own. Boston's James Michael Curley, his father from famished County Galway, spoke to the Boston Irish sense of having to fight for every scrap of power, a defensiveness New Yorkers never quite adopted thanks to Tammany's welcome. "The Massachusetts of the Puritans is as dead as Caesar, but there is no reason to mourn the fact," Curley said in a typical thumb-in-the-eye blast at his commonwealth's aristocrats. "It took the Irish to make Massachusetts a fit place to live in."

Curley expanded workers' compensation, cut the work week at state institutions from sixty hours to forty-eight, advocated a progressive state income tax, and pushed through a bill ensuring that workers on state construction projects were paid a living wage. Curley's two-year stint as a depression-era governor of Massachusetts was credited with passing more social legislation than administrations that served a decade. During his long, and interrupted, tenure as Boston's mayor (the interruptions were caused by defeat and term limits, but not at all by his short spell in prison—he governed from his cell), he built housing, hospitals, schools, and recreational facilities in the city's poor neighborhoods, and he wore his working-class roots on his sleeve. His mother had been a scrubwoman, toiling on her knees to support the family after her husband died. When he discovered a woman scrubbing city hall's floors, he told her to get off her knees, and the next day he ordered long-handled mops.

With chips on their shoulders the size of Gibraltar, these Irish-American political leaders, these men who trafficked in influence and votes, reconfigured American politics during the time the nation itself was being transformed into a melting pot. In a nation whose cities were becoming home to poor, confused newcomers, these urban, neighborhood-based political networks offered a service, and whether it was tainted with the expectation of quid pro quo mattered little to a bewildered immigrant. Armed with a sense of grievance and an appreciation for the rough-and-tumble of mass democracy, they re-created the machine as a parish, a separate entity that followed the form and substance of government but remained distinct and apart.

*

When Al Smith ran for president, he was succeeded by Franklin Roosevelt as governor of New York. Smith lost, but in 1932, it was Roosevelt's time, and he benefited mightily from many of the coalitions Smith had forged in his unsuccessful run. Here they are in 1931, in Hampton Bays, Long Island, sharing some political talk sotto voce.

Unlike the parish, the precinct is not a place associated in the public mind with the search for social justice. The typical ward heeler and boss had more pragmatic business to attend to, whether it was arranging favors for friends or cutting deals for themselves. And yet, just as Irish Catholic clergymen, representatives of an institution regarded in the nineteenth century as utterly un-American, raised their voices on behalf of democracy and republican virtues, the communal and democratic values of the precinct eventually were enshrined in social legislation that marked the end of nineteenth-century laissez-faire capitalism in America.

For the average Irish machine politician, there was no fouler word in the English language than "reform." Reformers represented the interests of those who had been beaten at the ballot box and who now sought to reestablish their control under the cover of objective disinterest and detached nonpartisanship. Reformers were the antithesis of the machine, which prized loyalty above all else. When the notably taciturn Charles Francis Murphy chose to speak of the virtues of George Washington Plunkitt, he started with the highest compliment he could think of: "Senator Plunkitt is a straight organization man." In other words, he was a man you could count on.

Reformers were no such creature. Plunkitt called them "morning glories" because they "looked lovely in the mornin' and withered up in a short time, while the regular machines went on flourishin' forever, like fine old oaks."

Yet it was in the golden age of Irish control of urban politics that the rugged individualism and regulation-free economy of nineteenth-century Yankee America fell to the swift sword of twentieth-century social reform. Of course, some reforms were put in place over the machine's objections, and some, like women's suffrage and the direct election of U.S. senators, were enacted because of pressure from progressives and reformers who wanted nothing to do with Irish machine politics.

It was Tammany, with its ear always close to the ground, that first heard the pleas for economic reform and social justice, though it took a near disaster before it paid attention. In 1886, Tammany found itself fending off a remarkable challenge from the economic reformer Henry George, who ran for mayor on a third-party ticket, the Workingman's Party. George already had endeared himself to the Irish in America by going to Ireland, preaching against landlordism, and getting himself arrested in the process. His crusade against the Gilded Age moneyed interests in New York and his advocacy of a single tax on property persuaded thousands of working-class Irish to abandon Tammany and its recent alliance with conservative business interests.

The pro-George rebellion found its most eloquent champion in the voice of Father Edward McGlynn, a priest from a working-class parish who knew firsthand the poverty and misery of New York's Irish neighborhoods. McGlynn's role in the George campaign and the larger crusade for social equity won him the admiration of many Irish Catholics and a reprimand from New York's archbishop Michael Corrigan, who eventually suspended the priest.

George finished an uncomfortably close second to Abram Hewitt, a millionaire reformer who would go on to complain about the rates of Irish incarceration and would refuse to take part in Saint Patrick's Day festivities. He was pushed aside after a single two-year term. But the size of George's support, and the eagerness with which the Irish flocked to him, were a shock to Tammany's system. Irish discontent, the machine learned, could no longer be assuaged by cheap identity politics. And the organization's perceptive eyes and ears picked up something else, something new: Jewish voters, mostly from Russia, were moving into the Lower East Side. They supported George, too, and would bear watching.

In 1886, Al Smith was eleven years old and was growing up fast on the sidewalks of the Lower East Side, on its way to becoming the most crowded corner on earth. Smith lived in a tenement under the Brooklyn Bridge, a vantage point that allowed his Irish-American mother to witness the bridge's cost in human lives. Dozens of workers died during the decade it took to build the bridge, and many of those workers left behind large families. There was a safety net for neither worker nor family. Both were left, as Charles Trevelyan might have said, to the forces of nature and the marketplace.

Young Al Smith got his start in politics through the good graces of Tammany Hall, which found a low-level job in the court system for him until he won promotion to the state assembly in 1903. What Murphy said of Plunkitt could have been said of Smith and his Tammany colleague, Robert F. Wagner Sr.—both were straight organization men. And both would go on to become two of the century's greatest social reformers. The two young politicians were united by the common experience of investigating workplace conditions throughout New York after a fire at the Triangle Shirtwaist Factory in Manhattan killed 145 young women seamstresses. Smith, Wagner, and Frances Perkins, who became Franklin Roosevelt's secretary of labor, issued a landmark report that marked the beginning of a government-led assault on the abuses and privileges of private capital.

Smith, the very picture of the Irish urban politico, turned state government into a laboratory of social reform. This creature of Tammany introduced what would become the model for Franklin Roosevelt's New Deal. Under Smith, New York began clearing slums and making workplaces safer.

(continued on page 119)

T. J. ENGLISH

THE ORIGINAL IRISH GANGSTERS

T. J. English was born in Tacoma, Washington, the son of a steelworker and a social worker for Catholic Charities. One of ten children, he traces his family roots to Counties Tipperary and Kerry. He is the author of THE WESTIES.

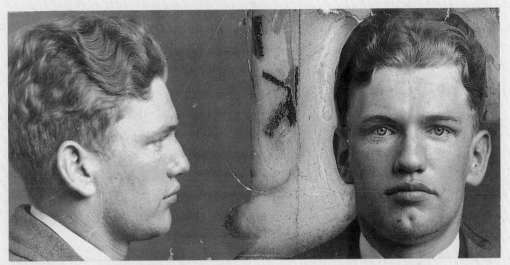

Vincent "Mad Dog" Coll got his nickname the old-fashioned way: He acted like one.

I guess we thought we had to be crazier than everybody else because we were the Irish guys."
   The speaker was Francis "Mickey" Featherstone, hit man extraordinaire for the Westies, the notorious Hell's Kitchen Irish mob in New York City. Featherstone was speaking during an interview I conducted with him while researching a book on the rise and fall of the gang. In the course of our interviews, Mickey often reminded me that he had been involved in more than a dozen murders as a member of the Hell's Kitchen mob. He was found not guilty of one murder by reason of insanity. Eventually, in a convoluted sequence of events, he turned against his criminal cohorts in early 1988, spilling his guts on the stand and revealing, for the first time, the full scope of the gang's terrifying twenty-year reign.

   With their ghoulish penchant for making their murder victims' bodies "do the Houdini" (i.e., disappear), the Westies may have been the most violent Irish-American criminal group ever. But they were not an anomaly.

Owney Madden, seen here (left) with a detective in 1934, worked with gangsters of all creeds and ethnicities, which made him a popular fellow.

Deanie O'Banion didn't get along with Al Capone, a development that could have only one ending. Here it is in 1924.

In many ways, their savagery had an evolutionary logic. From the beginning the saga of the Irish gangster has contained examples of mad behavior, a tendency toward impulsive, counterproductive mayhem that runs like a corrosive wire through the megawatt theatrics of America's brutal gangland history. It is a story that many of today's Irish Americans would like to believe never existed.

Like nearly all criminal groups organized along ethnic lines, the earliest Irish gangs were by-products of the immigrant experience. Around the turn of the century, in teeming urban slums in Boston, Chicago, Philadelphia, New York, and elsewhere, becoming a gangster was a semilegitimate form of employment. It was not uncommon for hungry, recently arrived Irish immigrants to hire themselves out as political "leg breakers" in an attempt to curry favor with the local establishment.

In Saint Louis, a feared early mob was Egan's Rats. Founded around 1900 by one Jellyroll Egan, the Rats practiced the fine art of political persuasion, stuffing ballot boxes and staging violent raids against political organizations on behalf of the local Democratic Party machine. In Chicago there was Ragen's Colts, the largest ethnic gang in the city. Described as racists, jingoists, political sluggers, rumrunners, and murderers, in 1908 they even adopted a motto, "Hit me and you hit two thousand," which was probably only a slight exaggeration. In New York City, a gang known as the Gophers met in tenement basements hatching robbery schemes and staging gang wars—mostly internecine battles that amazed and appalled the more genteel Dutch and German settlers of the era.

None of these turn-of-the-century gangs engaged in what would later be commonly referred to as organized crime; they were basically glorified street gangs. At the time, there were none of the lucrative rackets that would flourish later in the twenties with passage of the Volstead Act.

Among other things, Prohibition ushered in the era of the urban gangster as celebrity, with visionary mobsters such as Lucky Luciano, Al Capone, and others becoming famous through colorful, larger-than-life profiles on the radio and in the newspapers. In most cities, Irish gangsters remained a factor, but only in relation to highly organized, rapidly expanding bootlegging syndicates controlled in most cases by Sicilian immigrants, Jews, and Italian Americans.

Perhaps the most successful Irish-American criminal organization of the era existed on Chicago's North Side and was led by Charles Dion "Deanie" O'Banion. O'Banion was Al Capone's toughest competitor in the latter's struggle for power in Chicago, the gangster capital of the world. Even after he was assassinated in 1924 in a Capone–Johnny Torrio coup, O'Banion's ghost continued to haunt Capone.

As a youngster growing up on the city's North Side, O'Banion lived a double life as an acolyte and choirboy at Holy Name Cathedral and as a street punk in a tenement district known as Little Hell. Thanks to his training in the church choir, Deanie became a singing waiter in tough dives on Clark and Erie. After hours, O'Banion labored as a street mugger, robber, bootlegger, and political fixer. He did numerous stints in prison, and by the time he had established himself as the leader of the North Side gang, local police designated him "Chicago's archcriminal," claiming he was a suspect in at least twenty-five murders.

Deanie had a kind of perverse charisma. He was known for his elaborate practical jokes, which he liked to play on fellow gang members. Behind the cheery facade was a steely, stubborn businessman with a fierce loyalty to his North Side neighborhood.

O'Banion's approach to Prohibition, even before it went into effect, was to stockpile supplies by hijacking booze from legitimate sources. This eventually brought him into direct conflict with the Torrio-Capone mob. His unwillingness to play along with the syndicate sealed his fate.

After a series of outrageous tit-for-tat gangland murders that galvanized the city throughout the early 1920s, the inevitable finally came to pass. On the evening of November 9, 1924, O'Banion was in his florist shop on North State Street, directly opposite the church where he had once been a choirboy. The shop was partly a dodge to provide him with a legitimate front, but O'Banion also derived a perverse pleasure from selling his flowers for the city's many gangland funerals. It was there, surrounded by tulips and roses, that he was gunned down at close range by hit men imported from New York.

The murder of Deanie O'Banion did not solve Al Capone's Irish problem. One of O'Banion's favored henchmen was another North Side Irish American, George "Bugs" Moran. Although he had gained his nickname from his sometimes bizarre and flaky behavior, Bugs was known, especially to Capone, as a serious and efficient killer.

Moran always considered Capone a lowly human, referring to him as "The Beast" or "The Behemoth." Like his mentor O'Banion, Bugs was a regular churchgoer who refused to let whorehouses operate on the North Side. Capone kept trying to set up shops, sending offers to split the profits evenly with the Irishman. Irate, Bugs reportedly once thundered, "We don't peddle flesh. We think anyone who does is lower than a rat's ass. Can't Capone get that through his thick skull?"

When historians talk of Chicago's infamous gangland wars, they are referring to Moran's reckless all-out assault against Torrio and Capone. After the murder of O'Banion, Moran could never trust the Italians. He tried to kill Torrio himself. He led a machine-gun motorcade that sprayed Capone's Hawthorne Inn in Cicero with more than one thousand slugs.

The war came to an end, of course, with the most famous mob hit in history, the Saint Valentine's Day Massacre. On the morning of February 14, 1929, Capone hit men murdered seven of Moran's people. Bugs, the intended target, was supposed to have been there that day, but he overslept. Effectively defanged by Capone, Moran died of cancer thirty years later in Leavenworth prison, an impoverished, forgotten figure from Chi-town's infamous gangland era.

*

In New York City, the nation's other gangland capital, the war between the Italians and the Irish was waged in a slightly different manner. The most prominent Irish-American mobsters of the era, divided on the question of whether or not they should cooperate with the Italian syndicates, turned their violence inward—a tendency that characterized New York's Irish gangsters right up until the demise of the Westies.

Manhattan's most successful Irish mobster during the Prohibition era was none other than Owney "the Killer" Madden. Born in Liverpool of Irish parentage, Madden made it through his turbulent youth (five arrests for murder by the time he was twenty-three) as a ruling member of the Gophers. Eventually, he controlled the entire West Side of Manhattan, including Hell's Kitchen, probably the most boisterous Prohibition-era district in the United States.

Unlike an earlier generation of Gophers, who were mostly back-alley toughs who preferred to stay that way, Madden aspired to the highest levels of New York society. His nights were usually spent making the rounds at local speakeasies and clubs, where he was known as the Duke of the West Side. An average evening might be spent at his own Winona Club or at one of the swankier West Side dance halls like the Eldorado or the Hotsy Totsy Club, owned by Jack "Legs" Diamond, another prominent Irish-American gangster.

The secret of Madden's success was his willingness to cooperate with the Italian-Jewish consortium that made New York's underworld a relatively smooth-running operation. For an Irish gangster, Madden's willingness to play along with the big boys was unusual. Far more typical was the reaction of Vincent "Mad Dog" Coll.

Born in County Kildare, Coll was brought to New York at an early age and raised by his sister in a cold-water flat on Eleventh Avenue. After years of bouncing from one Catholic reform school to another, he went to work for the notorious Dutch Schultz before he was even old enough to shave.

For a time, Coll distinguished himself as a gleeful hit man for Schultz, who controlled the rackets in Harlem and parts of New Jersey. With his thick mane of red hair and toothy grin, Coll seemed to enjoy his work, though he exhibited a pronounced disregard for authority, be it Schultz's or anyone else's. Before long, Vincent sought to establish himself as a freelance operator.

Over a series of bloody months in late 1931, Coll proceeded to make himself a major annoyance to Schultz, Owney Madden, and the rest of the New York syndicate. He kidnapped Madden's closest associate and held him for ransom. He hijacked Schultz's beer trucks, trashed his speakeasies, and moved in on the Harlem rackets. In broad daylight, he tried to gun down a Schultz protégé in a drive-by shooting, missing and killing an innocent five-year-old boy and injuring four other children.

The botched hit turned the entire underworld against Coll. Newspaper headlines the next day christened him "the Baby Killer." Both Madden and Schultz put out a twenty-five-thousand-dollar contract on the infamous Mad Dog who was giving the underworld a bad name.

Finally, on the night of February 23, 1932, Coll's reign of terror came to an end. At a drugstore on West

"Mad Dog" Coll met his end in this phone booth in a drugstore on 23rd Street in New York City. Dr. Leo Latz, seen here, was having ice cream at the time when Coll was sprayed with bullets. Keeping Coll on the line until the killers did their deed was the reliable Owney Madden.

Twenty-third Street and Eighth Avenue, he was in a phone booth carrying on a protracted conversation. Four gunmen entered the store with Thompson submachine guns and riddled the phone booth with a cacophonous fusillade, leaving Coll for dead.

It was Owney Madden on the phone with Coll at the time, holding him on the line until the hit men arrived. Madden's willingness to set up and eliminate his fellow Irishman endeared him to the Italians. With Prohibition coming to a close, Lucky Luciano was in the process of forming an organized crime "commission." In a radical departure from the closed-door policy of earlier generations of "mafiosi," it was Luciano's intention to allow other ethnic mobsters to take part in a nationwide ruling body. Madden was included as a personal friend of Luciano's and as a representative of New York's Irish mob. These were nice guys. ❖

Fantasy and reality: Spencer Tracy played the role of feisty Frank Skeffington in the movie version of Edwin O'Connor's novel *The Last Hurrah*. The Skeffington character bore a close resemblance to a certain Boston mayor named James Michael Curley, shown at right paying due homage to Franklin Roosevelt.

He fought for child labor restrictions even as some of New York's most prominent Catholic clergy argued that such legislation trampled on the rights of private property owners. He reached out well beyond the precinct and parish, giving high-profile appointments to two Jews, Robert Moses and an anti-Tammany suffragette, Belle Moskowitz, who became one of Governor Smith's principal aides. But suggestions that somehow Smith outgrew Tammany—after all, no creature of Tammany could be so progressive—betray the prejudices of the machine's tormentors. For Tammany chieftain Charles Francis Murphy remained one of Smith's closest advisors and was a full partner in the creation of Smith's far-reaching social reforms.

Such was the legacy Smith would pass on to his successor, Franklin Roosevelt, in 1928, when he left Albany to embark on his historic, but bitterly disappointing, presidential campaign. America was not yet prepared for a Catholic president.

✥

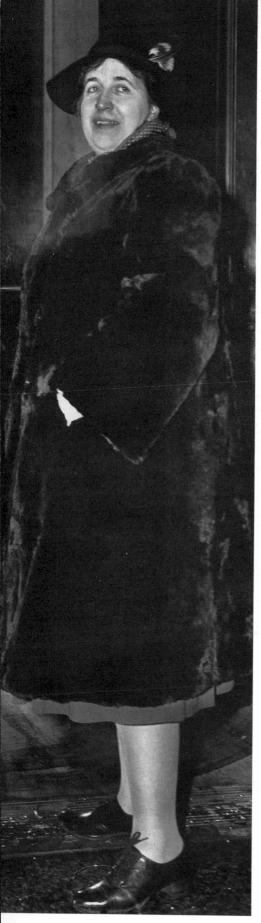

Irish-American women not only were the backbone of immigrant families, they were activists and, at times, radicals. Elizabeth Gurley Flynn (left) was the head of the American Communist Party at a time when John F. Kennedy was engaged in his "twilight struggle" against communism. Margaret Higgins Sanger (left of center, above), born to lapsed Catholic parents from Ireland, was a pioneer in the birth-control movement.

Mary Harris (Mother) Jones was a militant union organizer. She led a thousand marchers through the snows of Colorado to demand the withdrawal of troops from a strike-torn mining area.

THOUSANDS ARE SAILING

The island is silent now, but the ghosts still haunt the waves
And the torch lights up a famished man who fortune could not save
Did you work upon the railroad? Did you rid the streets of crime?
Were your dollars from the White House? Were they from the five and dime?

Did the old songs taunt or cheer you? And did they still make you cry?
Did you count the months and years? Or did your teardrops quickly dry?
Ah, no says he, 'twas not to be. On a coffin ship I came here
And I never even got so far that they could change my name

Thousands are sailing across the Western ocean
To a land of opportunity that some of them will never see
Fortune prevailing across the Western ocean
Their bellies full, their spirits free
They'll break the chains of poverty. And they'll dance to the music.

—PHIL CHEVRON
recorded by The Pogues

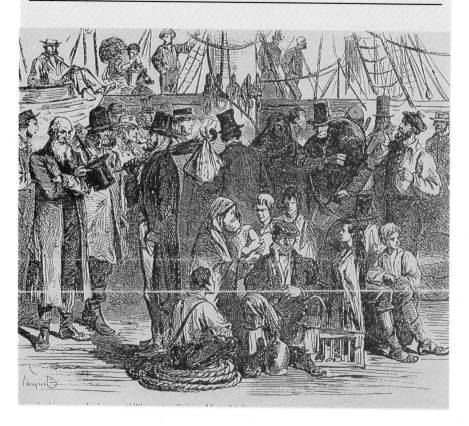

In supporting the vast social reforms of the 1920s and 1930s, the old Irish urban network essentially handed over its power to the local government agencies, authorities, departments, and other entities that assumed control of the social welfare state. The neighborhood ward heelers were replaced by legions of bureaucrats chosen not for their political connections but for their administrative qualifications (or so it was believed, anyway).

It was, ironically enough, the Irish who provided a fair amount of the brainpower and horsepower required to implement the New Deal and thus doom the old machine. Smith, of course, had established the model, and such Irish-American politicians as Thomas Corcoran of Rhode Island and Ed Flynn of the Bronx helped implement it. In fact, it was during the New Deal that Irish Catholics began showing up in places—like the cabinet—where they had not often been before. James Farley of New York was FDR's postmaster general, and Thomas Walsh, a senator from Montana and a vigorous supporter of Irish freedom in the 1920s, was nominated to be Roosevelt's first attorney general.

The New Deal itself did not destroy all vestiges of the old ways, but clearly the times were changing. *The Last Hurrah*, Edwin O'Connor's classic fictional study of Irish-American politics and culture, was published in 1956, a time when any clear-eyed observer could see that Tammany's long show was drawing to a close, and with it a complex and often misunderstood chapter in American political history.

Early in the twentieth century, Irish-American political power still had a long

(continued on page 127)

DENNIS DUGGAN

AT THE CENTER IS McMANUS: A DEMOCRATIC CLUBHOUSE

Dennis Duggan is a columnist for NEWSDAY *and has covered politics in New York City for thirty years.*

The Tammany tiger has been an endangered political species for decades, but you wouldn't know it from the bustling crowd inside the McManus Midtown Democratic Association Club on West Forty-fourth Street in Hell's Kitchen on a recent visit.

In one corner of the clubhouse, an affable Bronx cop named Manny Torres, who grew up in Hell's Kitchen, is fingerprinting mostly Spanish-speaking immigrants on a portable fingerprint machine. In another, Democratic district leader and current mantle wearer of the politically famed McManus family is James R. McManus, talking politics with wheelchair-bound Hunter College professor Phyllis Rubenfeld. "I heard about this club through friends," she says. " 'Tis marvelous. These people actually listen to you. I want to help them on disability issues."

In a room at the rear, several eager recent immigrants, speaking mostly Spanish, are listening to an immigration expert calm their fears about losing benefits and telling them how to go about getting their citizenship papers. At the door, a clubhouse regular passes out new membership forms along with a calendar from the McManus and Ahern funeral home on West Forty-third Street. The funeral home is owned by the McManus family, and legend would have it that voters who have passed into eternity still manage to pull the lever from there.

McManus himself is the last of the working Irish "bosses," and he fumes over the fact that the political clubs have lost the clout they once held. He blames this on the so-called mornin' glory reformers that George Washington Plunkitt lambasted in one of the great books on American politics, *Plunkitt of Tammany Hall.*

That book was written around the turn of the century, when the McManus family entered city politics. One of them got more votes for district leader than Plunkitt, and Plunkitt moaned, "Caesar had his Brutus . . . I've got The McManus."

The current McManus is a sixty-three-year-old Irish American who has been steeped in the tea of the city's politics. Senator Daniel Patrick Moynihan affectionately refers to this family political dynasty as the "McMani."

There isn't much James McManus doesn't know about the city and especially about Hell's Kitchen. He may be an artifact, a leftover from the era of daylong picnics, of torchlight marches through the city's streets, and of hands-on control of the election machinery, but McManus can still do favors for people, can still call in chits, and can still do "contracts" with politicians who need his help.

McManus knows the political sun has all but set on the old-time clubs. Politicians now look to the pollsters and consultants who spend huge sums of money on television commercials to try to get their clients elected. The community boards were another nail in the coffins of the clubs. They have taken on many of the duties the clubs once performed.

"You don't need foot soldiers like you once did," says George Arzt, a political consultant. "Today, it's all television."

Still, McManus says his club has twelve hundred dues-paying members paying twenty-five dollars a year, and he is able to stage fund-raisers to defray club expenses, including the monthly rent for the clubhouse. About half the club members today are Hispanics; the rest are what's left of the old Irish crowd and a smattering of immigrants from China and Spain as well as some recent Irish immigrants. Surveying the crowd, McManus vows that "our day will come again because the people who run things now are greedy and they will someday go too far."

*

The McManus clubhouse is open to one and all Mondays and Thursdays from 6 to 10 P.M. It gives off the flavor of the *Cheers* bar but without the booze. People from the neighborhood stream into the place seeking this favor or that favor from McManus—an apartment in a public housing project, a job, a loan. The phones ring with calls from political bosses and the walls are festooned with posters, proclamations, invitations to a White House inaugural for William Jefferson Clinton, old photos, and most important of all, maps of the West Side election, assembly, and city council districts.

There is a feeling of bonhomie and well-being here, of people looking for help and people trying to offer it. The clubhouse features a giant American flag and a real voting machine on which first-timers are taught to vote. For McManus, there is nothing as precious as the right to vote. His club is on a block filled with nightclubs, including the new Birdland, and is across the street from a saloon with a political name—the Bull Moose Saloon.

Other clubs in the city may be moribund or draw sparse crowds to their events, but the McManus club seems like an oasis in a city that to many seems impersonal. Here, newcomers sit on folding chairs in the center of the room and chat with the old-timers. No one is left unattended.

And at the center of things is McManus, who Manhattan Borough President Ruth Messinger hailed in a 1993 proclamation as still "the man to see" in Hell's Kitchen.

It is a typical evening. Officer Torres is present. Ask why he is here, and he speaks of his long-term friendship with McManus. "I grew up in this neighborhood," says Torres, forty-one, who now lives in the Bronx. This night he is fingerprinting people to comply with immigration requirements. "Usually, this is done in police precincts," he says, "but many of these people are intimidated by the precinct houses and many of them can't speak English. It's easier for them here."

Torres says he learned about politics from McManus. "Jimmy taught me all I know. I ran petitions for him, and worked doing odd jobs in the clubhouse. Jimmy is a prince of this city. He is also godfather to my twin girls."

There are Sri Lankan cab drivers and newly arrived Ecuadorans here this night seeking help in getting an apartment or with filing their taxes. Some want to find employment, and all keep an eye on McManus, who works the room, talking, laughing, telling stories, and giving advice.

There are always the regulars who have made the McManus clubhouse their second home. One is Lenny Kane, a neighborhood resident and club gofer for McManus who tells me his big job is getting petitions signed.

The clubhouse lives: James McManus, center, with two fledgling politicians, Lenny Kane (left) and Carlos Manzano. The McManus Club serves new generations of immigrants, whose problems are similar to those of the Old Irish.

"I grew up here on the same block as Jimmy," says Kane, who wears a button that reads "Friends don't let friends vote Republican." He adds, "This is my second home." Kane, who walks with a limp he got as the result of a bar fight years ago, has a title: Chairman of Petitions. In a day when the pollsters and television commercials have all but driven the clubhouses out of business, you still need strong legs to carry petitions up and down the stairs inside elevator-challenged tenements.

"People ask me what do we do," says McManus, wearing his trademark suspenders, a white shirt and a tie, and a neatly pressed suit, "and I tell them that this club is like a law firm that does pro bono work for the poor and the disenfranchised." McManus makes it clear in conversations at his club and at Gallagher's, a nearby steak house he frequents, that politics was taken away from the clubs by reformers because "no one wants the people to have a say in things that affect them."

It was his great-uncle, Thomas J. McManus—known as "The McManus"—a New York State assembly-man and then state senator, who in 1905 was elected district leader. He is the "Brutus" Plunkitt was talking about. In 1926 he was succeeded by another great-uncle, Charles A. McManus, a vice president of the city council. Family members ruled the club until 1941, when Eugene McManus, Jim's father, became district leader.

McManus says that when his father died in 1963, he acted quickly to replace him as club president, relying on his father's sage deathbed advice to "move quickly after I'm gone because they'll be planning your demise at my wake." And so he did, stopping in to get the votes of several Manhattan Democratic county leaders on the way back from seeing his father's body into the grave.

McManus has a knack for telling stories that almost always picture him on the right side of justice. He rails at the antilabor legislation passed, he says, by both Democrats and Republicans in the past thirty years. "Now people have to work two jobs to survive," he says. "Whatever happened to the forty-hour week?"

He is a "street-pickled New Yorker," he says, sounding like one of those kids from the Jimmy Cagney movie *Angels with Dirty Faces*. His talk is almost always about politics. There isn't much he doesn't know about who got elected and how. He is still the "go-to man," and his members regard him with a mixture of awe and respect.

McManus's all-time political hero is Harry S. Truman. Pointedly, he refers to the fact that Truman came out of the Boss Pendergast political machine. "We worked hard for his election," he recalls of the Truman-Dewey cliff-hanger in 1948. "There were a lot of McManuses working for him and that's why he got elected."

Over lunch at Gallagher's, where a huge picture of an old McManus picnic at a grove on Long Island hangs over the restaurant's meat case, McManus introduces Carlos Manzano, a Colombian and young Democratic state committeeman who is now president of the McManus club.

"Carlos runs the club," he says. "I just sit around looking pretty." Manzano is thirty years old and has been president of the club for three years. He says that one day he walked in off the street and asked McManus to "teach me about politics." He says the McManus clubhouse has survived "because when people come in off the street, Jimmy doesn't see different ethnics, he sees people who are in need of help and who can also help us." McManus complains that voters aren't as interested in voting as they once were. "It's down to twenty-five percent of the registered voters," he says, "and that's because there are no street campaigns. The politicians today are in Washington or in Albany. You hardly ever see them. Now it's all television sound bites. When is the last time you heard a discussion of the great issues?"

He concedes that corruption flourished in some of the clubhouses, but he insists that "the savings and loan scandals make those people look like pikers. The rascals are still here, only they work for the white-shoe law firms and the banks. The bottom line," he says, " is that these people don't want the little people to have any power. But I have great faith in human greed. These rascals don't know when to stop."

McManus has no regrets about a life spent in politics. He once worked in the production control side of the composing room of the *New York Times*, but when the time came to take up his father's political mantle, he didn't falter.

"My dad never pushed me into politics," he says, "and it has been a good life for me. I am able to do things for people who can't help themselves. I am a good politician because I am just an average guy. I know how people feel and what they need. I know how to deal with the bureaucrats, too. The bureaucracy is like the army. You should always get to know the corporals, not the generals, because the generals are too busy trying to look and sound like generals to listen to anyone." ❖

way to go. Irish America's conflicting emotions about its role in American society—the palpable hunger for acceptance matched by an aggressive defiance of entrenched elites—finally were resolved on January 20, 1961.

On that cold day in Washington, D.C., John F. Kennedy completed the journey begun when Patrick Kennedy left his home in County Wexford in 1849. His brief administration was the undeniable height of Irish Catholic political power, and in a more diverse America, it is possible that no single group ever again will amass the power that Irish America wielded during those Camelot days. As Daniel Patrick Moynihan and others have noted, the president, the majority leader of the U.S. Senate (Mike Mansfield), the Speaker of the House of Representatives (John McCormack), the chairman of the Democratic National Committee (John M. Bailey), and the president of the AFL-CIO (George Meany) all were Irish Catholic.

It is said that a generation of Americans changed on the day that Kennedy took the oath of office. To be sure, the Irish did. The struggle for acceptance was over. The ultimate barrier had been broken. Irish Americans would run for president afterward; in fact, the horrible, tragic campaign of 1968 was a contest between two Irishmen, Robert F. Kennedy and Eugene McCarthy, until bullets rang out in a hotel kitchen in Los Angeles.

✻

In late October 1966, Senator Robert Kennedy, grandson of Patrick the barkeep, was touring California to perk up the flagging reelection campaign of incumbent governor Edmund (Pat) Brown, the descendant of Irish immigrants who was desperately fighting off a challenger with a decidedly different view of the way the world worked. His name was Ronald Reagan, great-grandson of Michael Reagan of County Tipperary. Kennedy's cross-country journey inspired rumors, which he denied, that he planned to run for president in 1972.

While Kennedy campaigned for Brown and against Reagan, an Irish immigrant priest in Santa Monica named Brendan Nagle attracted headlines when he and a colleague announced the formation of a union for Roman Catholic clergy. Father Nagle already had drawn upon him the wrath of the Irish-American cardinal and archbishop of Los Angeles, James McIntyre, for preaching in support of the Civil Rights movement.

In New York that fall, the Democratic nominee for governor, Frank O'Connor, accidentally crossed paths with a bitter rival who answered to the name of Franklin D. Roosevelt Jr., the nominee of the Liberal Party who seemed destined to split the Democratic vote and hand Republican governor Nelson Rockefeller an easy reelection. In a hallway at Columbia University's journalism school, O'Connor accused Roosevelt of trying to destroy the Democratic Party. Roosevelt replied that he was merely trying to save it from "bosses." Roosevelt made no mention of the "bosses" who were frequent visitors to his father's White House, particularly Ed Flynn of the Bronx, the man who had persuaded Franklin Roosevelt Sr. that he ought to put Harry Truman on the ticket in 1944.

The preelection excitement was hardly restricted to politics that autumn. Macy's department store on Manhattan's Herald Square was displaying in its showpiece window the crown worn by Pope Paul VI during his coronation in 1963. Less than a century after Catholics were regarded as grave

When Robert Kennedy campaigned with Hubert Humphrey in 1964, there were signs of change in Irish-American political loyalties. Note the posters for Republican candidate Barry Goldwater.

threats to the republic, Macy's placed a full-page advertisement in the *New York Times* to celebrate the presence of a papal crown in its windows, representing, the ad said, "the concern of the Pope for the hungry, the sick, the hopeless millions who still exist in our own affluence."

Something, it seemed, was about to change. The 1960s migration from city to suburb marked the beginning of a new chapter in the Irish-American narrative even as the power and influence of Irish America seemed at its height. Old neighborhoods were giving way to suburban backyards, priests were marching for civil rights, and the few remaining political bosses were on the run. The defensiveness that so marked Irish-American politics had become an embarrassing relic of another age. The pope's crown, after all, was on display at Macy's, and two Irish Americans were running for governor in, of all places, California, where the yearlong sun melded old ethnic groups together to produce westerners. Irish Catholic America, which had produced one president and seemed likely to produce another in the near future, seemed very much a part of mainstream America.

Although no Irish Catholic has headed a major party ticket sine John Kennedy, his accomplishment changed the national political landscape. A barrier had been broken, so much so that the Irishness of Ronald Reagan was considered part of his charisma. (True, he was Protestant, but he clearly was a Gael through and through.) Since Kennedy's death, three Catholics have run (unsuccessfully) for vice president—Edmund Muskie, Sargent Shriver and Geraldine Ferraro. The Irish showed the way for other ethnic groups, and eventually, in city after city, they passed the torch of leadership to others. There was a time when politics was all the Irish had. And clearly that time has passed.

THOMAS MALLON

POLITICAL MIGRATIONS: A FAMILY STORY

Thomas Mallon is the author, most recently, of the novel DEWEY DEFEATS TRUMAN.

Two days after the attempted assassination of Ronald Reagan, a *New York Times* editorial discerned a "paradigm for the emergence of the Irish in America" in the names of the four men shot outside the Washington Hilton: "McCarthy and Delahanty are in police work. Reagan and Brady are in politics. All four, then, have their feet set on the two ladders that traditionally led the descendants of Irish immigrants out of poverty." This warmhearted squib, slugged "Sons of Ireland," seemed unaware of the longer editorial right above it, a serious meditation on presidential incapacity that ended with praise for George Washington

University Hospital's dean for clinical affairs, "the remarkably fluent Dr. Dennis O'Leary," whose "candor, knowledge and charm" had helped to calm the country.

Dr. O'Leary could himself have fit easily into the second editorial, given that his trinity of qualities have rarely gone unnoticed in the emergence of Irish Americans. In fact, it was the last of these three, practiced that day by Reagan himself, that did more than anything to reassure citizens of the president's likely survival. "Please tell me you're all Republicans," he said to his surgeons as they prepared to administer anesthesia.

He had achieved his political faith by conversion, and by 1981, most of his ethnic tribe could have answered him in the affirmative. They were Republicans now, by registration or voting habit, even if millions of them had reached their middle-class perches with a series of Democratic assists: the ward-heeler's wad, the GI Bill, the sort of student loans that had helped some of the president's surgeons to acquire their skills. After "rum, Romanism, and rebellion"—and then Roosevelt—they had traveled the same route through and out of the New Deal that Reagan had taken, and by 1981 they were delighted to have him at the head of their parade.

My father, Arthur Mallon, had died a year before—in fact, just a week before Reagan won the New Hampshire primary and set in motion the victory that capped his own fifty-year political odyssey. He had been born in Hell's Kitchen in 1913, grandson of an Eleventh Avenue saloonkeeper, son of a process server who later became a doorman at the Hotel Roosevelt. His mother was Irish-born, but only because her father, already in New York, had taken his wife back to Ireland to have the baby on his native soil. (Or so family legend had it—a legend that didn't interest my grandmother at all: She always let the census taker believe she'd come into the world stateside.)

To my father's generation of New York Irish, prosperity came not with a bold American move west but a series of small, counterintuitive steps east, the first of them made by the Mallons in 1924, when they bought a house in Woodside, Queens, on Forty-first Drive. (Fifty years later, one magazine would select the street as the one best typifying the world of Archie Bunker.) The family's new comfort, shared by thousands like them who commuted back to the city by the still-new subway line, might have ended when Mr. Mallon (as my grandmother usually referred to him) died suddenly in 1928. But my father, not yet fifteen, joined his older brothers in the workforce, as a publisher's office boy and eventually as a traveling salesman, where he was lucky enough to remain through most of the depression. Even so, he watched some of his closest friends having to idle out the thirties playing stickball, and he himself did a short stint in the Civilian Conservation Corps.

The day he went off to the army and World War II (the only time he could remember being kissed by my powerfully reserved grandmother), he was a convinced New Dealer, and he remained one in the years just after the war, when he took his Italian-American bride one county farther east, into Nassau, and began raising his family. On our block in Stewart Manor, bursting with McLindens and Clares and Nolans, most of the families we knew had taken the same small steps we had. Sunday afternoons everyone would backtrack toward grandparents still in Brooklyn or Queens, but come Monday our fathers would walk under the green sycamore trees in their new white collars to the Long Island Rail Road, a conveyance respectably above the now murderous subway, heading off to their jobs in the city. At home we children mastered the simple suburban pleasures around our sixty-by-one-hundred-foot tracts. I played in Little League with Richie Walker, a descendant of New York's gentleman mayor.

With all this new prosperity came a predictable sort of political self-protection. My father voted for his last Democratic presidential candidate in 1952, and even then he was hardly mad for Adlai. In 1960 he passed

The picture of suburban stability: a boy, his dad, a lawnmower. Young Tom Mallon, age eight, and his father, Arthur, in Stewart Manor, Long Island.

up, without regret, the chance to vote for the first Irish Catholic president. It was Robert Frost who advised JFK to be "more Irish than Harvard," but to some in his ethnic group it was too late for the candidate to do that. Jack Kennedy, the epitome of keep-your-distance Brahminism, was no Al Smith. Not only had he gone to Harvard, his father had gone to Harvard! For millions of middle-class men like Arthur Mallon, paying the mortgage on their new green mansions, Richard Nixon was an easier figure with whom to identify and sympathize. Back in Woodside, my uncle Tom—another sort of Irish paradigm, who never married and lived on, decade after decade, with his widowed mother—remained a Democrat for a couple of elections longer than my father, but he crossed over to vote against Kennedy in 1960 precisely because JFK was a Catholic. My uncle and grandmother nursed one of those obscure, persistent quarrels with the Church, whose exact nature my father would learn only in 1974, when his mother died at ninety-seven. At the funeral, my uncle Tom told him that Mr. Mallon had been already married and divorced when he married their mother—a set of circumstances for which the Church had never ceased to make Loretta McNaughton Mallon, along with the eldest son who knew the story, feel small. Thus did Richard Nixon, a half century after this defining moment of family history, become, to my uncle, the anticlerical candidate.

It was during Kennedy's brief administration that my father's conservatism took on its fervency. "Less profile, more courage" was a favorite refrain, and Barry Goldwater, that Jewish Episcopalian, his fondest presidential hope. He attended, I remember, at least one organizational meeting of the new New York State Conservative Party, whose founders included Kieran O'Doherty and Daniel Mahoney (later appointed to the federal bench by Reagan). The party's first gubernatorial nominee, who it was hoped would siphon votes from the liberal Nelson Rockefeller, was a businessman named David Jaquith, and I can still hear my mother, emerging from the voting booth in 1962, sweetly telling my father that she had voted for Mr. Javits—the Republicans' sound-alike senatorial incumbent, even more liberal than Rockefeller—just as she thought he'd asked her to. The Conservatives never succeeded in getting rid of either Senator Javits or Governor Rockefeller, though by 1970 they would elect James Buckley, elder brother of William F., to a single term in the U.S. Senate.

But that came later. The '64 election produced some schizophrenic ticket-splitting in Stewart Manor. Goldwater polled over 60 percent against LBJ, but a fair number of those Goldwater voters also pulled the lever for Bobby Kennedy, who unseated the Republican senator Kenneth Keating. This burst of tribal grief by Irish Manorites for JFK, murdered less than a year before, did not carry away my father, who was as much of a Bobby-hater as his otherwise mild personality would permit. He told me that he had given him a thumbs-down when his '64 campaign car passed beneath his Fifth Avenue office window, and four years later, the morning after the shooting in Los Angeles, I said a silent prayer as my father, on his way out the door to the train, stopped in front of the television, which was updating the news from LA. I knew that if he said the wrong thing, a part of me would never forgive him, and I can still recall my relief when he just shook his head in evident sorrow. The following Sunday, however, when the priests at Saint Anne's chose "The Battle Hymn of the Republic" for the recessional, he objected.

My father did not like any kind of political lecture from the pulpit, but the days when Cardinal Francis Spellman, "Vicar of the Armed Forces," had flown around in military transport were preferable to a new era of pacifist priests whose liturgical "handshake of peace" seemed as subversive as it was smarmy. The Irish now seemed as AWOL from the Church as from the Democratic Party. My parents had been married by Father Murphy, and I had taken Communion from Father O'Donnell, but by the early 1970s the priest giving the anti-war homily was often enough a visitor from India or the Far East.

It was Nixon, not Eisenhower or Ronald Reagan, who really made Republicans out of the postwar Irish, and Vietnam was the kiln in which their new loyalties were hardened. At the moment they and Nixon himself at last seemed to have it made, the air was split with cries of revolution. No wonder those well-paid New York construction workers, many of them Irish, lost their tempers in the spring of 1970 and famously assaulted some students demonstrating down near Wall Street. The prosperous, status-quo "hard hats" became a new political metonymy, and their white-collar kin in the suburbs, beneath a new veneer of sophistication, quietly applauded their fisticuffs, even while hoping their own sons—the first in the family to go to college, however ungratefully—didn't catch any of the blows.

In those days of near insurrection, Arthur Mallon's admiration for Franklin Roosevelt only deepened. When we talked politics, as we often did, he spoke seriously of how Roosevelt, in the 1930s, had saved the country from a revolution. Now that we seemed faced with the possibility of another, my father turned Roosevelt, by dint of his reforms, into a conservative, someone who had modified the social order in order to save it. My father was the first person I ever heard articulate this view, though it would later become a commonplace among Reaganites and Newt dealers.

My father died in the middle of reading Theodore White's *In Search of History*. Seventeen years later I still have his bookmark where he left it. By the end of his days he liked to call himself a "Jeffersonian Democrat," a strange-seeming label for a suburb dweller out of Hell's Kitchen, but one he had a better understanding of than most people who went years further in school than he did. The term had applications to his truest hero, Goldwater, and were he still here, I imagine that my father, even while saving most of his breath for attacks on Bill Clinton, would be curling his lip in libertarian disdain toward the more zealous religious rightists: He had, after all, believed that the priests of Saint Anne's had no more business telling their congregation to write its legislators in oppostion to abortion than they did in opposition to Vietnam.

In the years he has missed, my mother has migrated across one more county line: into Suffolk, at the eastern end of Long Island, where family-size suburban houses have been exchanged for small retirement condos. My sister became the first member of our family to return to Ireland since my grandmother left it in 1876. She married an Irishman named Oliver Harney and lived for two years in Ballinasloe, in County Galway. At their wedding, a month before his death, my father pointed to them on the dance floor and whispered to me, "A hundred and forty years, and back to square one."

I moved back, for many years, to Manhattan, at first to a walk-up apartment on Archbishop Fulton J. Sheen Place (East Forty-third Street), and then to a better spot near the United Nations. (You don't want to know what my father thought of the later Eleanor.) Most recently, and inevitably, I've gone to the Connecticut suburbs, where I, too, vote Republican. But all the way along I've carried with me a black scrapbook of news clippings, its pages rippled with paste, which my father, still a teenager, kept during the first hundred days of the New Deal. The "rendezvous with destiny" that he and Ronald Reagan and millions of other American Irish showed up for was not the political one envisioned by FDR when he used that phrase in accepting his first nomination. Still, history may judge their inconsistencies as more apparent than real. When the long view takes over, their resolute anti-Communism—maintained through the Democrats' long McGovernite lapse from it—will likely be viewed as noble, and by tempering the excesses of the welfare state, that genial Irishman Ronald Reagan may someday be recognized as its improbable savior, another counterrevolutionary and, for all we yet know, FDR's truest heir. ❖

CHAPTER 4

THE

WORK

WHERE

THE IRISH

DID APPLY

WORK WAS, and remains, a central theme in the story of American immigration. It has been true as long as the Irish (not to mention every other immigrant group) have been coming to America. Ironically enough, while they endured the great hardships of a transatlantic voyage and tore themselves from all that they knew and cherished just for the chance to work, their colonial masters at home regarded them as lazy and feckless by nature, without the requisite qualities of ambition and diligence to succeed in a world that rewarded effort.

In a measure of just how much the Irish wanted the chance to work and the opportunity to succeed, some of the first immigrants landed in the New World prepared to sacrifice even their freedom in exchange for the assurance of a job. In 1678 ships landed off the coast of Virginia and the Carolinas to drop off Irish indentured servants who were willing to sell their liberty to their employers, at least for a fixed number of years, in exchange for a chance to work. Afterward, servants received either some land or some money to help them begin an independent life.

Indentured servitude, a common method for seventeenth-century Irish to get to America, was a cruel bargain beyond the obvious. In Virginia, the colonial governor said that as many as 80 percent of indentured servants in the late 1600s died soon after landing in the colonies. Letters survive that attest to savage whippings, backbreaking toil, and poor food doled out to the unfortunate indentured.

A worker espies a photographer at 125th and Lenox Avenue in New York City in 1904 during cut-and-cover construction of the first IRT subway line. The Irish not only ran America's cities, they helped build them too.

Scorned as lazy and feckless by Victorian Britain, the Irish came to America and immediately went to work. At left, an Irish domestic tends to kitchen duty, proudly wearing a shamrock. Contracting offered Irish entrepreneurs a chance to own their own businesses (bottom left). Canal work (opposite, top) was dangerous and exhausting, but the Irish flocked to it. Irish women, meanwhile, dominated domestic service, and gave birth to a stereotype. The employer of the women pictured opposite (bottom) called each one of the women by the same name: Bridget.

WM. J. DELANEY
BUILDING
CONTRACTOR
LAWRENCE MASS.

mercial center of the American republic, a title it continues to hold even in the dawn of the information superhighway.

Clinton himself wore his Irish roots proudly and very likely would have abhorred the conscious distinction a later generation of Irish Protestants sought to make by calling themselves Scotch Irish. His canal project not only found employment for thousands of fellow Irish Americans but suggested a pattern that later Irish politicians, and later Irish immigrants, would embrace. Public works projects, separate from the private economy although not immune to the boom-and-bust cycle, became another important source of work for Irish America. Not as stable as the civil service and often just as dangerous as pounding a beat or putting out fires, public works projects from the Erie Canal to the New Deal's Works Progress Administration provided blue-collar Irish America with opportunities that were denied them not only in Ireland but in America's hostile cathedrals of commerce. DeWitt Clinton and his successors, as well as the Irish immigrants who eagerly grabbed shovels and picks, no doubt would be curious to know that in late-twentieth-century America, the notion of public works projects, and public employment in general, is regarded with distaste, an anachronism, even as commentators lament the disappearance of work from urban America and the seemingly insoluble problems of the urban underclass.

The first of the pre-Famine immigrants understood immediately what Clinton and America itself were offering. Despite the awful conditions, they flocked to the most difficult, worst-paid jobs they could find, simply because it was work and it was better than anything they had in Ireland.

While the canal workers and other laborers might welcome their new employ, they could also die long before they sprouted their first gray hair. Men died of accidents and, inevitably, of disease, often cholera. A ballad about Irish canal workers laboring in the bayou near New Orleans took grim note of the toll that cholera took:

Ten thousand Micks, they swung their picks,
To dig the New Canal
But the choleray was stronger 'n they,
An' twice it killed them all.

But by the time the Erie Canal was finished in 1826, more than five thousand Irish laborers armed with shovels were digging the nation's first transportation network, a tradition that would take the Irish laborer from the flatlands of central New York to the swamps outside New Orleans to the railroad towns of the West to the subway tunnels underneath Boston and New York.

The Irish laborer went from building canals to building railroads without a respite, and found conditions no better and often worse, since railroad work involved large-scale use of explosives, as America defied nature in its attempt to link east to west. With reason, it was said that an Irishman lay buried underneath every railroad tie, and an Irish newspaper in Boston, the *Pilot*, warned immigrants against canal and railroad work, saying it was the ruin "of thousands of our poor people." Irish workers struck the Erie Railroad in 1853 in an effort to win a daily wage of $1.25 and a ten-hour

(continued on page 146)

MAUREEN MURPHY

BRIDIE, WE HARDLY KNEW YE: THE IRISH DOMESTICS

Maureen Murphy, a professor at Hofstra University, is at work on a biography of Asenath Nicholson.

An Irish servant in a Chicago household, circa 1888.

Kate Liam put down her two buckets of water, leaned back against the stone wall, and looked out across Galway Bay to the Clare hills. "So you're going to Dublin, *a stór.*"

"I am, Kate. Have you ever been to Dublin?"

"*Arrah*, I've never been that far, but I've been to America."

For Kate, as well as for the nearly seven hundred thousand Irishwomen who immigrated to America between 1885 and 1920, America was indeed closer than cities like Cork or Dublin. The Aran poet Máirtín O'Direáin, born in 1910, recalled that in his boyhood there wasn't a mother who hadn't spent time in America and that places like Boston, Dorchester, and Woburn were more familiar to him than even Galway. What accounted for this phenomenon of young Irishwomen going to America? The pattern of young Irishwomen outnumbering Irishmen as emigrants in the quarter century between 1884 and 1910 was an exception to male-dominated western European emigration that resulted in family re-formation in America. Irish parents stayed on the land and Irish daughters and sons emigrated, alone or with siblings. These siblings could no longer expect to inherit family land. After the Famine, the inheritance pattern changed from one that divided land among sons to one that privileged a single inheriting son and set aside a dowry for one daughter who was married in an arranged match. For nondowered daughters who did not want to stay on as unpaid workers in the households of their fathers or brothers, there was the Church or there was emigration. In many ways leaving home was the most attractive alternative for these "surplus" daughters.

*

Personal histories and immigration records indicate that those coming to America often shepherded younger siblings, cousins, and neighbors later on, which gave courage to girls who yearned to try their luck in cities such as New York, Boston, Philadelphia, Chicago, or San Francisco. Letters home, cash remittances, prepaid tickets, and parcels reinforced the image of America as the place of opportunity. Nora Curtin's sister sent clothes. She said, "I was dressed to kill in Tralee and thought the United States would be great if there were clothes like that." She emigrated in 1927.

Photographs were especially enticing. Annie O'Donnell, who left Spiddal in 1898 and worked as a children's nurse for the W. L. Mellon family in Pittsburgh, sent back a studio portrait of herself beautifully dressed with a glamorous hat and posed against a lush floral photographer's backdrop. It must have been a sensation back home in villages where girls dressed in traditional petticoats and shawls and went barefoot. (Mrs. Mellon gave Annie a camera in 1902, and she became an enthusiastic photographer. A family story describes Annie asking old Andrew Mellon when he visited the household whether she should invest some of her savings in Kodak. "Keep your money, Annie," he cautioned. "It is only a toy.")

For all the attractions of America and for the support of family and friends to ease the journey and the settling in, emigration took courage, independence, and spunk. Many girls traveled as part of a group: siblings, cousins, neighbors, and friends forming a cohort of young people from a village or townland. And the numbers are wrenching. In a single month, April 1898, Cunard and White Star liners calling at Queenstown (Cobh) carried 342 young women from small towns in east Mayo to New York. Passenger records indicate that the emigrating girls described themselves as servants and that they joined family members or friends employed in households or they went to homes of family or friends and looked for employment.

Irish girls arrived in America knowing that there was a demand for domestic servants. The *Longford Independent* for August 17, 1912, carried the story of the servant problem in New York promising that girls could expect to earn five pounds a month (about twenty dollars) for general housekeeping and ten pounds a month for cooking. The article further encouraged emigration, saying that the scarcity of servants made it necessary for employers to tolerate shortcomings. Mona Hearn's study of domestic service in Ireland surveys the "help wanted" advertisements in the *Freeman's Journal* between 1910 and 1920; they offered wages of between nine and twenty pounds *a year* for ordinary servants and thirty to forty pounds per year for a cook.

While most Irish girls went to some sort of sponsor, there were some who arrived without family or friends or who had no job prospects. Of the 307,823 Irish females between the ages of fourteen and forty-four who arrived in New York between 1883 and 1908, some 100,000 were assisted in some way by the Mission of Our Lady of the Rosary for the Protection of Irish Immigrant Girls. They found positions in households for 12,000 domestic servants. Some Irish girls went through the labor exchange at Castle Garden or used employment agencies such as the New York Labor Exchange located at 10 Washington Street, which issued a receipt to Mr. T. F. Green on November 28, 1891, for two-dollar fee for hiring Annie O'Brien at the rate of eight dollars per month. Annie O'Brien paid the agency one dollar from her first month's wages. Others placed "work wanted" ads like the ones that appeared in the *New York Herald Tribune* on September 24, 1908:

> IRISH GIRL, 18, lately landed, as chambermaid or waitress in private family, no cards. Malone, 70 Bedford St.

> YOUNG IRISH GIRL as chambermaid or chambermaid and waitress in small private family, wages $18-20. Andrews, 250 E. 50th.

> A YOUNG GIRL, lately landed, in small apartment, willing to learn. Smith, 1077 First Ave. corner of 59th.

Finding employment could be complicated by anti-Irish or anti-Catholic prejudice. The idea that Catholic domestics had been dispatched to spy for the pope had been promulgated in tracts such as *The Female Jesuit* or *The Spy in the Family*. Signs reading NO IRISH NEED APPLY or ONLY PROTESTANTS NEED APPLY reflected the suspicion that Irish girls would report family behavior to their priests or that they would secretly baptize the children of the household. Oral tradition collected from former Irish servant girls suggests that such fears were not unfounded. When the mistress of the house died in childbirth, Nora and Josie Enright rushed the infant off to church to be baptized; other devout servant girls concerned about the souls of their charges report baptizing unbaptized children also.

Despite prejudice, Irish girls found a ready market for their services. According to the immigration historian Oscar Handlin, it was the Irish girls' reputation for loyalty and cheerfulness and their willingness to work for low wages that made them welcome in Boston households. Handlin estimated that there were more than two thousand Irish domestic servants in Boston by the 1850s.

The girls who went to households where they were the only help were expected to be maids of all work. Bridget Curran, who came to America in 1911, worked from six in the morning till midnight cleaning, doing the laundry, stoking the furnace, and shoveling snow on winter mornings. She drew the line at walking her employers' three dachshunds. "I wouldn't have people laughing at me dragging them up the street."

While Irish girls did not want people laughing at them, they could laugh at themselves. Householders may have called their servant girls "simple," but it was more innocence abroad than ignorance. Former servant girls recalled trying to boil melons and dealing with other unfamiliar fruits and vegetables. One woman recalled spending a Saturday making little woolen coats after her employer asked her to prepare potatoes baked in their jackets for a dinner party.

*

Irish girls who found work in the smaller households were often treated as members of the family, albeit as children. They report they had a ten o'clock curfew or had to present their young men to their employers. Some of these girls married from their places of employment as if they were daughters of the house. The girls who went into service in big houses often found the work was easier: Their time off was respected, there was the excitement of entertaining high society, and there was company and fun "below the stairs." In 1927, Nora Curtin joined her sister Hannah who was second cook for the Blairs in Peapack, New Jersey. Nora started in the kitchen and worked her way up from chambermaid to laundry maid to head laundress in the household. "It was a terrific job. The machines did all the work and I was off from Friday night until Sunday night."

She later worked as third chambermaid for the Vanderbilts, "a gorgeous job." Nora and the other girls watched from the balcony as the Vanderbilts and their guests danced below in the ballroom and, then, with the cook's permission, entertained their own friends in the kitchen. Nora only saw Mrs. Vanderbilt coming and going; the senior staff, mainly English, supervised the young maids. In other large households, the mistress of the house often did not bother to learn the names of the Irish girls, adopting instead the generic name of Maggie or Bridget for any female Irish servant. Servant girls, like most domestic servants of any age, were addressed by their first names.

*

Religion was often a test of independence for Irish servant girls. Women who worked as servants report that time off for mass, for some, was only reluctantly given or given at great hardship to the girls. Even Annie O'Donnell, who always praised the Mellons for their kindness and consideration, wrote in 1901 that she hoped she would be let off to go to mass on Christmas morning, but it was not certain.

A frequently told story describes leaving a job rather than missing mass, a departure depicted by an image, perhaps apocryphal, of the servant girl whipping off her apron, throwing it on the kitchen floor, and walking out. A servant girl in Mary Anne Sadlier's novel *The Blakes and the Flanagans* finishes an argument with her employer who had told her it would be no harm to miss early mass, saying:

> It would be that much harm, that I wouldn't do it for all you're mistress of—No Ma'am! I know I'm foolish an' light enough in some things, and I'm a poor, ignorant girl in the bargain, but I wouldn't miss mass, ma'am, not for all the money in New York.

Catholicism was not only a measure of the Irish servant girl's autonomy, it was also the one significant aspect of home that traveled with the girls when they emigrated. Mass and devotions were also the social center of many lives, for the church was a place for meeting and for courting in the Irish countryside. Parish women's organizations often were scheduled for the servant girls' night off. Irish girls were legendary for their generosity to the Church, which was second only to their generosity to their families in Ireland. New York tradition credits Irish maids with building Saint Patrick's Cathedral and the Dominican Church of Saint Catherine of Siena, and they were the major support of the Mission of Our Lady of the Rosary for the Protection of Irish Immigrant Girls.

Irish servant girls also contributed to church-building funds at home. When Saint Éanna's Church in Spiddal, County Galway, was being built in 1903 at the cost of some three thousand pounds, the parish priest collected one thousand dollars from America. Annie O'Donnell sent forty-five dollars from Pittsburgh, a sum that included her contribution as well as money she collected from the Mellon staff.

Most women gave up full-time domestic service when they married; however, some women who were widowed or abandoned or who were responsible for their families because their husbands were ill or incapacitated went back into service. John F. Kennedy's great-grandmother went to work when her husband died of cholera, James Michael Curley's mother became a charwoman after Curley's father's death, and Eugene O'Neill's paternal grandmother returned to domestic service when she was abandoned. Sometimes such women left their own children with family members while they worked in service. Perhaps the most famous example of this is Catherine Coll, who placed her son with a Limerick neighbor in New York until she sent him back to Ireland with her brother to be raised by her family in Bruree, County Limerick. The boy was Eamon De Valera, who would go on to become prime minister and president of Ireland.

*

Women who had worked as domestic servants brought the taste and style they learned in the households to their own families. They knew how to dress; they knew fine linen and the lines of good furniture; they could set a beautiful table. Having arrived in America with a good basic education and a courtesy natural to people in the Irish countryside, they realized that education, a good appearance, and social graces would carry their children a long way.

The servant girls had ambitions for their children, and the children of turn-of-the-century Irish immigrants moved into professions and into leadership positions in business and politics in a single generation. Educated themselves, they supported parish schools and sent their daughters as well as their sons to the Catholic secondary schools. Servant girls' daughters became the schoolteachers of Boston, Chicago, and New York. Realizing their Irish mothers' dreams for vocations among their children, these daughters entered religious life in record numbers and consolidated the Irish dominance of the Catholic Church in America through the twentieth century.

The servant-girl immigrants of the turn of the century were uniquely women of their time. As they looked back to the nineteenth century and forward to the twentieth, they also looked Janus-like back to Ireland and forward to America. They honored their obligations to their families at home; they gave their own children the education that provided opportunities to move into the American middle class. They followed the struggle for Irish independence and were active in Irish-American organizations that supported Irish causes. They created Irish America. Their world spanned their past and their present, Ireland and America, and they created images to define that world. Mary O'Keeffe spoke for many Irish servant girls when she said, "Not a day goes by that I don't look at the moon and say it's the same in Ireland." They were Irish, but they lived in America. ❖

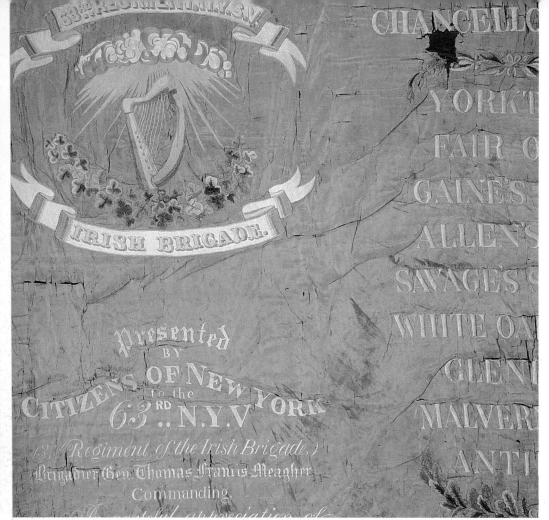

The flag of the Irish Brigade's 63rd New York Regiment, an outfit known for its bravery on the Union's behalf during the Civil War.

born Niall O'Dowd, publisher of *Irish America* magazine and the *Irish Voice* newspaper, helped forge an alliance of Irish-American politicians and business leaders behind an effort to bring Sinn Fein's Gerry Adams, regarded as the political voice of the Irish Republican Army, into a fledgling peace process. The effort led to a cease-fire in Northern Ireland, but it was short-lived. It was restored in July 1997. Without O'Dowd's version of a New Departure, Adams would have remained a pariah, and Northern Ireland's troubles would have remained out of the world's spotlight.

Between the unions and the Land League, the mass of Irish workers found an expression of their discontent and their determination to change the status quo in Ireland as well as America. The *Irish World*'s Patrick Ford preached that there was no difference between the poorly paid coal miner in Pennsylvania and the impoverished tenant farmer in County Mayo. The cause of their suffering, Ford said, was oppression and exploitation. It was a message the Irish in America were ready to hear.

By the 1880s, however, some Irish already were in position to grab the next rung. Many of the skilled workers who helped build the Brooklyn Bridge were Irish, and the beginnings of an Irish middle class were appearing in the ethnic cities of the Northeast. The Irish were beginning to show up among the ranks of carpenters, machinists, masons, and other skilled, blue-collar professions. Not coincidentally, the Irish began to make their way out of the canal ditches and railroad beds just as a great mass of new immigrants from southern and eastern Europe was beginning to transform the old neighborhood—and compete for low-skilled jobs.

The Irish found themselves on both sides of America's great dispute; in the South, there are monuments to the efforts of the Irish on the Confederate side.

In the closing decades of the nineteenth century, popular Irish-American literature was filled with stories about economic success, either its actual achievement or its possibilities. Before long, there were lace curtains on some windows.

*

But the Irish did not work only for themselves. They worked and fought for their country, too, however new it was to them. Beginning with the Famine wave of Catholic immigrants, the Irish were confronted with accusations that their fidelity to the pope took precedence over their devotion to the nation and its constitution. "The Constitution is a Protestant Constitution," declared a clergyman named Harvey Springer in 1960. In fact, despite the sacrifices of generations of Irish Americans on the nation's battlefields, it was the hoary old charge of divided loyalty that John Kennedy confronted during his presidential campaign when he addressed Protestant ministers in Houston. It was Harry Truman, though, who got to the heart of the matter. Nobody, he said, had asked Joseph Kennedy Jr.'s religion when he signed up for duty in World War II. The remark spoke to the sacrifice of generations of Irish-American Catholics. The elder Kennedy brother, of course, had been killed over the English Channel while serving in the army air forces.

Beginning with the Irish who filled the ranks of George Washington's band of rebels, the armed services have provided not so much a chance to work but an opportunity for the Irish to prove themselves to a skeptical nation. They seized the chance with notable and often poignant enthusiasm during the Civil War, when 144,000 Irish immigrants joined the Union army, many of them fighting under the banners of the Irish Brigade. One of those who answered the call was an Irishwoman from Michigan named Bridget Divers, who served as a nurse in her husband's regiment and had several horses shot out from under her as she tended to her battlefield duties.

When the war broke out, a Famine immigrant named Michael Corcoran was given command of an Irish-Catholic unit known as the 69th New York Regiment, soon to gain fame as the Fighting 69th. In 1860, Corcoran had gained an equal measure of fame and notoriety when he refused to allow the 69th to march in a parade honoring Britain's Prince of Wales (the future King Edward VI) while he was visiting New York. He was court-martialed and relieved of his command, but his offenses suddenly were forgiven once cannons opened fire on Fort Sumter.

River, Massachusetts, Irish men and women tended the machines that would propel America toward industrial supremacy by century's end. In port cities from Newport to New Orleans, from Savannah to San Francisco, Irish longshoremen loaded and off-loaded the nation's imports and exports, while Irish teamsters and transport workers moved people and goods to their appointed destinations.

One crucial area of occupational growth was in the public sector. The Irish took advantage of their family and ethnic networks, familiarity with English, universal white male suffrage, and the sweeping expansion of cities and municipal governments to achieve political empowerment. They soon translated that into economic opportunity. In a word, while no more than a few dozen Irishmen held elective office at any given moment in an American city, thousands, even tens of thousands of Irish men and women derived direct economic benefit, principally in the form of jobs. As early as 1855, one-fourth of New York City's police force was Irish-born. By the 1880s, American cities had ever growing payrolls of inspectors, clerks, experts, teachers, and secretaries. Even allowing for the possibility of a modest amount of "honest graft," few of these jobs offered much money. They did, however, provide something that appealed to countless Irish workers seeking to avoid the harsh and quixotic realities of the industrial economy: security.

An equally important economic benefit of political power were the tens of thousands of construction jobs generated by the rapid growth of American cities. One of the principal forms of Irish entrepreneurship was contracting, owing to the large numbers of Irish in the building trades and the fact that it required only small amounts of capital. With Irish friends and family in office, Irish contractors received the lion's share of municipal contracts for laying out streets, building mass transit systems, erecting public buildings, and constructing sewer, water, and gas lines. Irish politicians rewarded Irish contractors, who in turn employed thousands of Irish workers of every rank and skill.

Patrick Murphy, an Irish immigrant, captured this spirit in a letter to his family in 1885:

> New York is a grand handsome city. But you would hardly know you had left Ireland, there are so many Irish people here. Some of them are become rich. Some of them are big men in government. For most of us it is hard work, but there is plenty of it and the pay is all right. They are always building things here. Tom worked on the great bridge they made over the river to Brooklyn a year or two ago. Now he has got me a job working with him on the new streets they are making in this city. There is always something going on if a man wants work.

Indeed there was. The bridge he wrote of was the Brooklyn Bridge, an epic fourteen-year project presided over by Irish-born contractor William Kingsley and built with the labor of both skilled Irish workers (bricklayers, masons, and carpenters) and unskilled laborers. Of the latter, dozens died in the excavation of the foundation under the East River while earning 12.5 cents per hour. Such an example reminds us that while Irish contractors provided many Irish workers with jobs, they also were not above exploiting them.

In exchange for lucrative city contracts, contractors gave lavishly to politicians and the organizations that placed them in office. Undoubtedly the finest symbol of this system is the mansion of Boston mayor James Michael Curley, built for him gratis by the city's contractors, replete with shamrock cutouts in the window shutters.

*

The Knights of Labor made a special effort to organize women in the work force. Here, women delegates (including one new mother) gather for the union's convention in 1886.

As Irish workers spread throughout the workforce, they quickly assumed an important role in organized labor. Historian Carl Wittke noted that "the same qualities that made the Irish successful organizers and leaders in politics and the Church, helped them to become successful labor leaders." Among those qualities was the ability to speak English and strong traditions of ethnic solidarity and neighborhood cohesion.

The prime example of this was the Knights of Labor, the foremost labor organization in the nineteenth century. Key to its rise to prominence in the 1880s was Terence Powderly, son of Irish immigrants and a mechanic, who became the Knights leader, or Grand Master Workman, in 1879. Under his stewardship, the Knights were transformed from an obscure, secret labor society of Philadelphia tailors in 1869 to the first national industrial union with more than seven hundred thousand members at its peak in 1886. Powderly's decision to lift the Order's vow of secrecy in 1881 and a subsequent victory by Knights railroad workers against industrial giant Jay Gould were instrumental in enlisting more members. So, too, was the organization's willingness to welcome unskilled women and black workers (anathema to skilled trade organizations) and its ideology of mutuality: "An injury to one is an injury to all" was its motto.

Irish workers by the hundreds of thousands joined the Knights for these reasons and one more: the close association between the Irish struggle for independence and the workingmen's struggle for justice in the 1880s. A substantial number of Irish labor activists were also members of the Land League, the nationalist movement led by Charles Stewart Parnell that promised both independence for Ireland and land reform to relieve its oppressed farmers. Powderly himself was an active Land Leaguer and a leader in Clan na Gael, a secret militant nationalist organization. Another prominent labor leader who drew inspiration from the struggle for Irish independence was P. J. McGuire. Born of Irish parents in New York City, McGuire rose to become the secretary of the International Brotherhood of Carpenters and Joiners and later a cofounder of the American Federation of Labor with Sam Gompers, as well as an ardent Land Leaguer. The leading Irish-American newspaper in the late nineteenth century was Patrick Ford's *Irish World*, which devoted so much attention to labor issues that he changed the name in 1878 to *Irish World and Industrial Liberator*. For these and countless Irish workers and labor leaders, the connection between Irish nationalism and the American labor movement was clear. "The struggle in Ireland," declared Ford, "is radically and essentially the same as the struggle in America." P. J. McGuire concurred, "It is no longer an Irish question. . . We [Americans] have known of people driven from their homes at the point of a bayonet. The railroad companies have repeatedly turned out workmen from their homes." In their minds, American robber barons were cut from the same cloth as British landlords.

One powerful vestige of this Irish-labor connection remains a key element of American protest strategy today: the boycott. Begun as a practice of social ostracization of oppressive landlords by Irish tenant farmers, it was transformed by Irish workers in industrial America into a potent form of economic shunning. Another vestige is Labor Day, the first celebration of which took place in 1882 in New York City at the suggestion of P. J. McGuire. At the head of the parade making its way up Broadway was William McCabe of the International Typographers Union. On the reviewing stand in Union Square were Terence Powderly and Patrick Ford.

*

America entered the twentieth century with its industrial power ranked first in the world and its unions ever more firmly in the control of Irish leaders. By 1910 nearly half the 110 member unions of the AFL were led by Irish-born or Irish-American men. Overwhelmingly they represented a constituency that was non-Irish, reflecting both Irish upward mobility and vast immigration from eastern and southern Europe. Though buffeted by war, depression, and antiunion policies of employers, union membership rose from nearly 1 million in 1900 to more than 5 million in 1920. Irish union leaders were known for their oratory, organizing skills, and tough negotiating tactics, but also for pursuing the moderate ideological course laid down by AFL founder Sam Gompers. Known as "pure and simple" unionism, it shunned radicalism and stressed high wages, shorter hours, and job security. Such a policy often ran afoul of the interests and outlook of more radical Jewish, Italian, and Slavic workers.

And yet, some of the most outspoken radicals of the day were Irish. Elizabeth Gurley Flynn, born in the Bronx to immigrant parents, joined the Industrial Workers of the World (IWW) in 1905 and rallied workers in the massive strikes in Lawrence, Massachusetts, and Paterson and Passaic, New Jersey. Two of her compatriots in New York were the exiled Irish socialists James Connolly and James Larkin. Another of her contemporaries was Kate Richards O'Hare, known as the "First Lady" of American socialism. Mary Harris "Mother" Jones was one of the most revered orators and organizers in the nation's coal mining districts. In 1903 she led a dramatic march of stunted and injured children from the Pennsylvania coalfields to the New York home of President Theodore Roosevelt. Also active in organizing Jewish and Italian garment workers was Leonora O'Reilly. William Z. Foster, a former IWW leader and Communist, led a successful drive to organize the Chicago meatpackers in 1918. Later that year, he and John Fitzpatrick organized thousands of steelworkers, few of whom were Irish, who in late 1919 would engage in the largest industrial strike to that time.

The Catholic Church remained staunchly antiradical and antisocialist, but the rights of Catholic workers

George Meany presided over the AFL-CIO in the years just before America's labor movement began losing members and political clout.

to organize into unions was firmly established. So, too, was the right of priests to speak more freely on social and labor issues. Father John A. Ryan emerged as a leading spokesman for economic justice with the publication in 1906 of *A Living Wage*. In this and subsequent works he summoned the authority of Pope Leo XIII's *Rerum Novarum* and other teachings to call for Social Security, a living minimum wage, public housing, and a more equitable tax system. In 1911 he authored Minnesota's minimum wage bill, which became law in 1913.

American labor and its Irish aspect entered a new phase with the stock market crash of 1929. Many of the gains of the last two decades, both material and institutional, were swept aside by the economic earthquake known as the Great Depression. With massive job losses, noted Pulp and Paper Workers Union president John Burke, "The only thing the unions can do during these times is hang on and . . . try to save our organization."

But the crisis of the depression turned out to be a moment of opportunity for American labor. In Washington D.C., New York senator Robert Wagner successfully pushed for landmark labor legislation granting workers the right to organize, elect their representatives, and strike, boycott, and picket, as well as prohibiting unfair practices by employers, such as blacklisting. This led to a flurry of labor union activity and the reemergence of the industrial union movement that had died with the Knights of Labor in the 1880s. The Congress of Industrial Organizations (CIO) committed itself to unionizing mass-production workers in key industries such as automobile, appliance, and rubber manufacturing. When it broke from the AFL in 1936, it was led by Irish Americans John Brophy as Director and James B. Carey as secretary-treasurer. One of the CIO's vice presidents was Mike Quill, a radical Irish immigrant and former IRA member who founded the heavily Irish Transport Workers Union in 1934.

✵

The combination of federal protections for organized labor in the 1930s and the economic boom brought on by World War II produced a period of unprecedented worker prosperity and union growth. The massive strikes in 1946 were as much a sign of worker discontent as they were of strong worker organization. Irish leadership in organized labor remained strong and highly visible. Maurice J. Tobin, son of an Irish carpenter in Boston, embodied this prominence when he was selected by President Truman to serve as secretary of labor.

The forties, however, witnessed the onset of the cold war and a fear of Communism that culminated in the improbable rise to national prominence of an obscure first-term Irish-American senator from Wisconsin named Joseph McCarthy. While McCarthy's targets were primarily officials in government and Hollywood, organized labor felt the sting of the Red Scare, too. Many Irish-American union leaders, either out of personal anti-Communism or public pressure, purged radicals from their ranks and supported similar purges of radical unions from the AFL and CIO. Mike Quill, for example, who had allied himself with the Communists in the CIO, shocked the organization in 1948 when he adopted an outspoken anti-Communist position. For this Quill and others earned praise from the Catholic Church and the American middle class, but also the derision of many more radical union leaders.

While some Irish-American labor leaders became negatively associated with union conservatism, others came to symbolize growing union corruption. In 1953 the AFL suspended the International Longshoremen's Association, headed by Joseph P. Ryan, for its corruption and links to organized crime. Tony Boyle, who succeeded John Lewis as president of the United Mine Workers, was also accused of corrupt activities.

These questions aside, American labor was in its heyday in the 1950s. Wages were high, strikes were rare, and union membership reached its historic highpoint with 39 percent of the American workforce enrolled. The AFL and CIO reconciled their differences and joined forces once again.

And yet the harmony, strength, and Irish leadership of American labor would quickly begin to erode. In the coming decades union membership declined steadily, especially among groups like the Irish, who occupied many of the traditional trades most affected by American deindustrialization. By 1990, about 12 percent of the American workforce was in a union. Moreover, the one area of the economy where union organization was growing—public sector jobs such as teaching—was no longer the province of the Irish.

More telling than the fate of organized labor was the new status of Irish America. Irish Americans, by the 1970s and 1980s, were far removed from the world of their parents and even further removed from their grandparents. On the whole, they were more suburban, better educated, more cosmopolitan, more wealthy, and, dare it be said, more Republican. Whether there are more Irish-American heads of *Fortune* 500 companies than major unions is anybody's guess.

This is not to say that organized labor, Irish-American or otherwise, is destined for oblivion. In the early 1990s Ron Carey was elected president of the Teamsters Union on a pledge to root out corruption and restore its dwindling ranks. John Sweeney, a building services veteran from the Bronx, bested Tom Donahue, another Irish American, for the top spot at the AFL, which in 1996 posted its first gain in membership in decades.

Yet even if the Irish were to disappear completely from the American labor movement (an unlikely possibility), their contributions to America as workers will endure. ❖

Irish America no longer dominates the labor movement, but when John Sweeney was elected president of the AFL-CIO in 1995, unions began to show signs of resurgence.

Dunne and Jimmy Cannon (the celebrated sportswriter of midcentury America) of yester-year, to celebrate their heritage and define them-selves as part of a tradition that has deep and proud roots in the history of American argu-ment. The Irish have been shouting at each other, and at America, in newsprint since the first Irish-American newspaper, the *Shamrock*, began publishing in New York in 1810.

The *Shamrock* set a tone that many other Irish newspapers would follow, from the *Chicago Citizen* to the *Boston Pilot* to the *Irish Press* of Philadelphia. It was militant on the subject of Irish freedom and saw as part of its mission the creation in America of a voice for the cause of Ireland's liberty. As if anticipating the issues that would haunt Irish America until well into the twentieth century, the newspaper's publish-ers adopted the harp of Ireland and the eagle of America as its signature symbols, and the paper's editors advised readers to become enthusiastic American citizens.

Irish-American journalism, like the rest of the ethnic press, fostered a sense of the familiar for immigrants who found themselves in new and decidedly strange surroundings. The *Boston Pilot*, under the guidance of the remarkable John Boyle O'Reilly, best exemplified this mission of socialization. Boyle O'Reilly himself was a sin-gular example of Irish-American achievement and acceptance at a time when his adopted hometown of Boston was rife with conflict between old-line Yankee Boston and the Irish who were reshaping the city in their own image.

O'Reilly started with the *Pilot* as a writer and eventually became its editor, and soon became a staunch American even as he argued on behalf of Irish independence and the rights of Irish immigrants. He saw no conflict between his embrace of America and his support for Ireland.

'TO MRS. MOORE AT INISHANNON'

No. 1, Fifth Avenue, New York City, Sept. 14th, 1895
—and Mother, dear, I'm glad to be alive
after a whole week on the crowded Oceanic—
tho' I got here all right without being sick.
We boarded in the rain, St. Colman's spire
shrinking ashore, a few lamps glimm'ring there
('Will the last to leave please put out the lights?'),
and slept behind the engines for six nights.
A big gull sat at the masthead all the way
from Roche's Point to Montock, till one day
it stagger'd up and vanish'd with the breeze
in the mass'd rigging by the Hudson quays . . .
Downtown, dear God, is like a glimpse of Hell
in a 'hot wave': drunken men, the roaring 'El,'
the noise and squalor indescribable.
(Manners are rough and speech indelicate;
more teeming shore / or ashore than you cd. shake a stick at.)
However, the Kellys' guest-house; church and tram;
now, thanks to Mrs. O'Brien, here I am
at last, install'd amid the kitchenware
in a fine house a short step from Washington Square.
Protestants, mind you, and a bit serious
much like the Bandon sort, not fun like us,
the older children too big for their britches
tho' Sam, the 4-yr.-old, has me in stitches:
in any case, the whole country's under age.
I get each Sunday off and use the privilege
to explore Broadway, the new Brooklyn Bridge
or the Statue of Liberty, copper torch on top
which, wd. you believe it, actually lights up,
and look at the Jersey shore-line, blue and gold:
it's all fire and sunlight here in the New World.
Eagles and bugles! Curious their simple faith
that stars and stripes are all of life and death—
as if Earth's centre lay in Central Park
when we both know it runs thro Co. Cork.
Sometimes at night, in my imagination,
I hear you calling me across the ocean;
but the money's good, tho' I've had to buy new clothes
for the equatorial climate. I enclose
ten dollars, more to come (here, for God's sake,
they fling the stuff around like snuff at a wake).
'Bye now; and Mother, dear, you may be sure
I remain
yr. loving daughter,
—Bridget Moore

—DEREK MAHON

LIST OF FUGITIVE MOLLIE MAGUIRES,
1879.

WILLIAM LOVE.—Murderer of Thos. Gwyther, at Girardville, Pa., August 14th, 1875. Is a miner and boatman: 26 years old; 5 ft. 9 in. high; medium build; weighs about 150 lbs.; light complexion; grey eyes; yellow hair; light mustache; has a scar from burn on left side of neck under chin, and coal marks on hands; thin and sharp features; generally dresses well. Lived at Girardville, Schuylkill Co., Pa.

THOMAS HURLEY.—Murderer of Gomer Jamas, August 14th, 1875. Is a miner: 25 years old; 5 ft. 8 in. high; well built; weighs about 160 lbs.; sandy complexion and hair; small piercing eyes; smooth face; sharp features; large hands and feet; wears black hat and dark clothes; lived at Shenandoah, Schuylkill Co., Pa.

MICHAEL DOYLE.—Murderer of Thomas Sanger and Wm. Uren, September 1st, 1875. Is a miner: 25 years old; 5 ft. 5 in. high; medium built; dark complexion; black hair and eyes; full round face and head; smooth face and boyish looking generally; wears a cap. Lived at Shenandoah.

JAMES, ALIAS FRIDAY O'DONNELL.—Murderer of Sanger and Uren, is 26 years old; 5 ft. 10¼ in. high; slim built; fair complexion; smooth face; dark eyes; brown hair; generally wears a cap; dresses well; is a miner and lived at Wiggan's Patch, Pa.

JAMES McALLISTER.—Murderer of Sanger and Uren, is 27 years old; 5 ft. 8 in. high; stout built; florid complexion; full broad face, somewhat freckled; light hair and moustache; wears a cap and dark clothes, lived at Wiggan's Patch, Pa.

JOHN, ALIAS HUMPTY FLYNN.—Murderer of Thomas Devine, October 11th, 1875, and Geo. K. Smith, at Audenreid, November 5th, 1863. Is 53 years old; 5 ft. 7 or 8 in high; heavy built; sandy hair and complexion; smooth face; large nose; round shouldered and almost humpbacked. Is a miner and lived at New Philadelphia, Schuylkill Co., Pa.

JERRY KANE.—Charged with conspiracy to murder. Is 38 years old; 5 ft. 7 in. high; dark complexion; short brown hair; sharp features; sunken eyes; roman nose; coal marks on face and hands; wears black slouch hat; has coarse gruff voice. Is a miner and lived at Mount Laffee, Pa.

FRANK KEENAN.—Charged with conspiracy to murder. Is 31 years old; 5 ft. 7 in. high; dark complexion; black hair, inclined to curl and parted in the middle; sharp features; slender but compactly built; wears a cap and dark clothes. Is a miner and lived at Forrestville, Pa.

WILLIAM GAVIN.—Charged with conspiracy to murder. Is 42 year old; 5 ft. 8 in. high; sandy hair and complexion; stout built; red chin whiskers; face badly pock-marked; has but one eye; large nose; formerly lived at Big Mine Run, Pa. Is a miner. Wears a cap and dark clothes.

JOHN REAGAN.—Murderer of Patrick Burns at Tuscarora, April 15th, 1870. About 5 ft. 10 or 11 in. high; 40 years old; small goatee; stoop shouldered; dark hair, cut short; coal marks on hands and face; has a swinging walk; wears shirt collar open at the neck.

THOMAS O'NEILL.—Murderer of Patrick Burns, at Tuscarora, April 15th, 1870. About 5 ft. 9 in. high; 35 years old; light hair; very florid complexion; red moustache and think red goatee; stoop shouldered; walks with a kind of a jerk; think has some shot marks on back of neck and wounded in right thigh.

PATRICK B. GALLAGHER, ALIAS PUG NOSE PAT.—Murderer of George K. Smith, at Audenreid, November 5th, 1863. About 5 ft. 8 in. high; medium built; dark complexion and hair; latter inclined to curl; turned up nose; thick lips; wears a frown on his countenance; large coal cut across the temple; from 32 to 35 years old; has been shot in the thigh.

Information may be sent to me at either of the above offices.

ALLAN PINKERTON.

The Molly Maguires of Pennsylvania got their name from a secret society active in Ireland just before the Famine. According to one popular story, Molly Maguire was an old woman threatened with eviction from her cottage. In Pennsylvania, a powerful trade union movement, the Workingmen's Benevolent Association (WBA), became the largest union in the nation. In a series of strikes in the late 1860s and early 1870s, the union won important victories, not least of which was recognition by the employers and the linking of wages to the price of coal. But in the 1870s it met its nemesis in the person of Franklin B. Gowen.

President of the Philadelphia & Reading Railroad Company, Gowen was determined to destroy all obstacles in his way, including small-scale entrepreneurs, trade unionists—and the Molly Maguires. Half the leaders of the union were Irish-born. The Mollys, composed of Irishmen and favoring tactics of violence, acted as a shadow organization. To gather information against the Mollys, Gowen hired America's foremost private detective, Allan Pinkerton.

At the end of 1874, Gowen declared war on the trade union, inaugurating the famous "Long Strike," which would culminate in the union's defeat and collapse in June 1875. Between mid-June and early September, the Mollys assassinated a policeman, a justice of the peace, a miner, two mine foremen, and a mine superintendent. Two years later, the Molly Maguires were brought to trial. More than fifty men, women, and children were indicted. The star prosecutor at the great showcase trials in Pottsville was none other than Franklin B. Gowen. Twenty Molly Maguires were hanged in all, ten of them on a single day, June 21, 1877, known to the people of the anthracite region as Black Thursday.

experience out of the ethnic ghetto and into mainstream culture, was Finley Peter Dunne of Chicago. He was a product of Irish Chicago, and he turned that experience and knowledge into a regular series of sketches featuring his main character, the bartender Martin Dooley. More than a century after Mr. Dooley first appeared on the pages of the Chicago *Evening Post*, he remains a classic in American literary journalism. Through Mr. Dooley, American society (after a while, Dunne moved to New York and syndicated his column) was given an authentic glimpse of the attitudes and world of the Irish-American urban subculture in the late nineteenth and early twentieth centuries. Dunne wrote entirely in an Irish dialect, requiring more than a little effort to translate and appreciate, and often made reference to obscure topics that no doubt went over the heads of his non-Irish or non-Chicago readers. Nevertheless, his characters exuded an attitude that was unmistakably Irish-American: suspicious of the world outside the parish, grounded in the common sense of the streets, tolerant of no airs, and capable of the blackest sort of humor. Dunne's work was considered satire, and like Swift's, behind the words was a rage for justice, never more obvious than on Christmas of 1897.

> I see in th' pa-aper where some wan says Chris'mas dinners has been provided f'r twinty thousan' poor people, but thirty thousan' more is needed. It isn't a merry Chris'mas

DENNIS SMITH

A SOUL FOR THE CIVIL SERVICE

Dennis Smith is the author of REPORT FROM ENGINE CO. 82; *he was a firefighter for eighteen years in the Bronx.*

In my own eighteen years with the New York City Fire Department, I often wondered why so many of my predecessors were Irish. I once heard it said that the Irish came off the farms in Ireland and were homesick for the rear end of a horse, and that's why they joined the fire departments of America! There is no doubt that the clanging bells and the horses galloping through narrow cobblestone streets offered more excitement than ever could be imagined in the bogside. And I am sure horses had something to do with it, because the Irish are still to this day known as having magical powers with equines, and horses did pull New York's fire engines until 1922. But I believe that the Irish were first taken into the fire departments because of their considerable strength and bravery. And

f'r thim. Nor is it f'r poor Flannigan. 'Tis betther f'r his wife. She died to-day; Father Kelly dhropped in on his way home afther givin' extremunction. His hear-rt was sore with sorrow. Half th' people iv Flannigan's neighborhood has been out iv wurruk f'r a year an' th' sight iv th' sivin fatherless little Doyle childher almost made him cry with pain.

The dialect may be rough on the eyes; the story is even rougher on the heart.

It is hardly a long road from Finley Peter Dunne's Mr. Dooley to the masterful creations of Jimmy Breslin's Queens. Nor is it hard to draw a line from the intensely personal journalism of Nellie Bly to the work of Anna Quindlen. In their own way, they and their Irish-American colleagues have made a contribution to American journalism and letters that is distinctively Irish and utterly popular and accessible. Just as the precinct captain brought democracy into crowded tenements, Irish-American journalists helped bring journalism, with all its quarrels and color, into the neighborhoods, and vice versa. Jimmy Breslin's reaction to winning the Pulitzer Prize for his columns about New York City spoke for his own work and that of his predecessors. Usually, he said, they give Pulitzer Prizes

being natural raconteurs, they must have been most appreciated at the afternoon tea breaks around the firehouse kitchen table.

In the first ten years after New York created a paid fire department, beginning in 1865, five of the twenty firefighters who died in the line of duty were Irish. In the next thirty years, from 1865 to 1905, one hundred firefighters made the supreme sacrifice, and sixty-six of them were Irish. Seventeen of our first twenty-three fire commissioners were Irish, as were thirteen of our first seventeen chiefs of the department. And two of these, Hugh Bonner and John Kenlon, were actually born in Ireland.

I grew up on the East Side of New York, where the neighbors were almost all Irish, where my friends had fathers who were cops or firemen or construction workers, and where my own thoughts about working were molded by bits and pieces of conversations through the years. The first thing I learned was that to be a cop or a fireman meant that you would never be laid off, and that to be a construction worker, even in the high-paying skilled trades, was not quite as good because there were always layoffs when the construction booms ebbed, and, most important, because they did not have the twenty-year pension.

Roman gladiators and soldiers had a twenty-year pension, but they were not expected to live much past forty. New York City firefighters and police were awarded the twenty-year

to columnists who write about cabinet secretaries. Breslin won his for the stories he found on Queens Boulevard, where, as he might say, the people do nothing but experience life in all its absurdities, glories, and horrors. In other American cities, Irish-American journalists interpret the world around them: Jack McKinney of the *Philadelphia Daily News*; David Nyhan and Mike Barnicle of the *Boston Globe*; and Kevin Cullen, also of the *Boston Globe*, who is one of the few reporters stateside covering Northern Ireland on a regular basis; Mary McGrory, the dean of Washington columnists at the *Washington Post*; and Francis X. Clines, the peripatetic *New York Times* reporter.

*

Postwar affluence and suburban assimilation may have brought an end to the Irish urban experience and perhaps contributed to a lost sense of identity and community, but there is no denying that the last four decades of the twentieth century saw Irish Americans armed with college degrees and self-assurance taking leadership roles in American business. It was a trend the bimonthly magazine *Irish America* spotted in the late 1980s, when it introduced a yearly review of the top one hundred Irish-American business executives. (They ranged from Donald Keogh, CEO of Coca-Cola, to Tom Monaghan, CEO of Domino's, to Cathleen Black, president of Hearst Magazines.) And the mid-

---

pension soon after the turn of the century because, it was rightly argued, they were both extremely strenuous and important jobs, and it was necessary to induce the brave-hearted to retire early so that the average age in the departments was kept young and the men physically viable.

*

I remember the day I became a firefighter as clearly as a king remembers his coronation or a cardinal his elevation. It was a day of exuberance. I passed a firehouse on the way to the subway that day. The fire engine had a number on it, but I saw William Carlos Williams's figure five in gold, ecstatic that I would soon be a part of the whining sirens and clanging bells. I felt both reverence and the excitement of a new beginning when I was finally presented the three-inch silver Maltese Cross, which is the firefighter's badge.

The badge to me was the shield of the lower-class diligent, for I was now in a job that was a fulfillment of a goal, a job that I was to grow to love in the same way patriots love America. There was so much good about it; the people were so decent and courageous.

The job would not make me rich, but what it provided made me wealthier than Croesus, for I had at last the "independent feeling in my breast" that would allow me to

1990s saw the emergence of another new magazine called *World of Hibernia*, laden with upscale advertisements and filled with profiles of Irish-American business leaders and other achievers.

Father Andrew Greeley, the sociologist, novelist, and longtime observer of Irish America, has noted that Irish success in America is hardly new. In fact, he argues that the turning point for the Irish in America was not 1960, the year of John Kennedy's election as president, but 1920, when the Irish first began sending their children to college at rates higher than the national average. But it has taken more than a half century for the emergence of what Father Greeley believes to be a new symbol of Irish-American achievement: not the business executive but a class of Ph.D. holders and intellectuals who traffic not in trade but in ideas. Their wealth may be moderate, or even small, compared to the business leaders in *Irish America's* annual roundup, but their influence in mainstream America can, or will be, much greater.

Firefighting was—and remains—both a dangerous and a prideful profession. More to the point, for the Irish immigrants and their offspring it offered a secure job with a pension. At right, Irish-born James Malone, a charter member of the Virginia City Fire Department, about 1870.

plan a future, to continue my education, to get married, to have a family, and to provide. I had made it, and I had it made, for I had become what all in my neighborhood respected, a cop or a fireman.

I spent nearly two decades with the New York City Fire Department, and I know that I will never again feel the thrill or the sense of accomplishment that came with pushing into the whirlwind of smoke in a burning building with those men of Engine 82 and Ladder 31—all neighborhood guys, like me, many with names like McCarthy, Bollon, Cassidy, and O'Meara. The Irish were central to the reputation for bravery in the annals of the

Job security could often be a grim trade-off. Irish-American police officers and firefighters have given their lives countless times, leaving their grieving families to dwell on the tragic ironies of working in such "secure" professions.

department, but there were others, too, with names like Miloslau, Knapp, Coscia, and Rivera. Today, there are more Italians in the department than Irish, and there are more Hispanics and African Americans than ever before. The personality of the department will change according to immigration patterns, and it could be said that the Irish prevailed in numbers and administrative power for about one hundred years. It is time now for other groups to prevail. No one group can ever own the kind of glory that comes with the job, but every group can become a part of it. All you need is a high school diploma and a yearning for security.

That's the way the Irish did it. ❖

With the Irish in America about to put another century between themselves and the canal workers and domestics of the 1800s, it is tempting to suggest that it is time to cast aside old images and celebrate the new. But perhaps it's a little early for that. The 1980s brought a reminder of a past generation's struggles and heartbreak. Beginning in Ronald Reagan's first term, a new wave of Irish immigrants began arriving in America's cities. While jet travel and modern communications have softened many an immigrant's experience, the new Irish brought with them their own sort of grievances. The generation that came of working age in the 1980s had been led to believe that emigration was a part of Ireland's tragic past, expunged from the present and future by a vibrant economy and a well-educated workforce. When that supposedly vibrant Irish economy collapsed, beginning in the mid-1980s, the Irish once again found themselves looking for work across the Atlantic. Their numbers were nothing like those of a century before, but that there were numbers at all suggested that America remained, as ever, the place where the young Irish went to find work.

They came without papers, for there were tight limits on Irish immigration, and they found work on construction sites, in restaurants, and as nannies. Some jobs paid better than others, and some of the young immigrants were better off than others, but it was off-the-books work, with no medical benefits. Many a Saturday-night social was held in the catering halls of Irish America to help pay for some illegal Irish immigrant's medical expenses.

Eventually, the illegal Irish immigrants of the 1980s, many of whom settled in old Irish-American urban neighborhoods and helped revitalize them, organized a campaign to win green cards. Thanks to Irish-American political clout—it still was there—the campaign was a success.

But the ordeal was bitter, and, as so many Irish ordeals seem to do, it produced a ballad. It was called "The Flight of the Earls," and it spoke of a generation of Irish immigrants who "just can't throw away these precious years." They turned their eyes, then, to America, but unlike those who left Ireland in the nineteenth century, they held out hope that emigration was not forever. After all, "those big airplanes go both ways."

Ten years after the first of the new Irish began appearing on the streets of American cities, the Irish newspapers in America carried reports—sporadic, to be sure, but noteworthy all the same—of Irish immigrants in America leaving their adopted land and going back. While Ireland was losing as many as twenty-six thousand people a year to emigration in 1991, by 1996 emigrants and exiles were returning to the place they never stopped thinking of as home.

Reverse migration was something new for the Irish in America, and it remains to be seen how many immigrants decide to pack up and try their luck back home. But it's a fair guess that the vast majority will remain. After all, they still have work to do.

PEGGY NOONAN

AUNT MARY JANE'S NOT-SO-COMMONPLACE BOOK

Peggy Noonan was special assistant to President Ronald Reagan. She is a writer who lives in New Jersey.

Look at this picture. They're beautiful, aren't they? They're young immigrant girls in America, circa 1920 or so. That's Mary Jane on the left—it doesn't quite capture her elegance, but this is the earliest picture we have—and her sister, the sturdy and practical Etta, on the right. Between them is their friend Bridie, about whom we know nothing but her name and the fact that she existed. From the suits and hats I'd guess the picture was taken on an occasion—Easter Sunday, perhaps, and probably in Brooklyn, where Mary Jane and Etta lived, or Manhattan, where they worked. Mary Jane was a lady's maid and Etta was a cook. Bridie was probably a domestic, too.

Mary Jane and Etta Byrne were my great-aunts, the sisters of my maternal grandfather Patrick Byrne. They were all born on a small family farm in the town of Glenties in County Donegal. The story my mother told me long ago is that Patrick was a young man of ambition who didn't want to be a farmer, as his people had always been, but a teacher. He went to the local schools and then went to Scotland, where he received or studied for an advanced degree. But when he came back to Donegal he couldn't find a teaching job, or any other job that required wearing a suit, which is what he wanted to wear. He was bitterly disappointed and decided—this would have been just before 1910 or so—to go to America.

Etta quickly said she'd go, too—things were sleepy in Glenties, a small farming area in the hollow of the hills where family farmers raised sheep and grew potatoes. She wanted more.

Mary Jane didn't want to go—she was happy where she was—but her father decided that she should follow Patrick, and then Etta, and help them out in their new country. (They left behind a brother, the dreamy and silent Jimbo, who would continue the farm, and their sister Ellen, about whom nothing is known in my family except that she, too, was quiet, and loved Jimbo.)

Years later, when I was in college in the seventies, I went back to the home they left, met the neighbors, and was introduced to a bewhiskered old man named P. J. Kennedy, who had been my grandfather's best boyhood friend. Mr. Kennedy told me he was there the day my grandfather walked to the bottom of the lane to wait for the lorry that would take him to the ship. Patrick's father walked along with him, silently, and then looked at his son and said, "Go now, and never come back to hungry Ireland again."

Grandpa came and settled in Brooklyn, and Etta soon followed, and then Mary Jane. Now, Mary Jane was in her late teens or early twenties when she came over; we're not sure because we don't know what year it was. I still have the Ellis Island health card she wore on her coat when she landed in the Port of New York, but the date has been obscured, penciled over. At some point the beautiful Mary Jane began lying about her age, and apparently changing the arrival date helped. However, it looks to me like 1909, and in the family history that would make sense.

The small Byrne clan settled in Brooklyn one by one and looked for jobs. Etta went into Manhattan and became a cook in the great houses of Park Avenue, and Fifth. She was a good cook and had a cook's temperament. Years later when they were retired and living in a little house in Selden, Long Island, I remember Etta and Mary Jane arguing in the kitchen and Etta chasing "Jane Jane" and slapping her with a hand towel and screaming "Whhisssshhtt! Whhisssshhtt!" which I understood to be Irish for "Get away from my stove," and then bursting into great put-upon sobs.

Patrick got a job with Brooklyn's electric utility company, the Edison Company. It required him to wear a suit, his dream; if he'd got a job that required a suit in Donegal, I would be writing this essay about my Irish forebears who didn't go to America. On such small things do fates turn. Patrick was an eligible Brooklyn bachelor from his twenties through his forties. Then he met Mary Dorian, a poor and big-boned immigrant from Clare. He married her, and wisely, for she was sweet, modest, and so slow to take offense that when Etta ragged her for coming from a family so thick and lacking that they sheared the sheep in the parlor, Mary thought her family was being complimented for kindness to animals. Patrick and Mary had four children: my mother Mary Jane, Peggy, Johnny, and Patrick.

And my great-aunt Mary Jane—well, I notice I keep losing her in the narrative, a reflection perhaps of the fact that, in a way, she got lost in the family. She was central to it, surely, and yet never did the kind of dramatic things—insisting on leaving for America, marrying, having children—that made her seem central. She followed Etta into Manhattan and became a lady's maid, again in the great houses of Park, and Fifth. It was a job for which she was both suited and not. Suited because she had a very natural way—she was pretty, delicate featured, willowy, and loved handsome hats and dresses. Now she would be surrounded by all the material things of the rich, furs and stylish clothes and the best perfume and makeup. None of it would be hers but she'd be close to it and learn, by observing, How the Rich Do It, which was something she wanted to know, not out of any apparent ambition to be rich but as a knowledge to have and to share, like a teacher. She loved what she would have called the fine things of the world but didn't aim for them, didn't seem to think they were . . . her fate. When I knew her she gave away all her money in birthday checks and Christmas gifts and twenties shoved in your pocket as you left. But she loved beautiful things and liked being near them.

She was suited to domestic work, in the eyes of society, for she was an Irish immigrant woman and it was the sort of job such women could get: the scut work of the affluent, the cleaning and cooking and shining. Her friends were domestics, too. It was a good, solid job and she considered it an honorable one, as she considered all forms of honest employment to be honorable. And—here is something hard to communicate, for it is at odds with our understanding of the twenties and thirties and forties—being a lady's maid gave her a certain status, even an air of glamour. A lady's maid was a trained professional: she knew how to care for a wardrobe, how to work in a great house, and if she was good at her job she was eminently employable, the known holder of a steady, no-heavy-lifting job, which gave her standing in the neighborhood (and she with a brother who wore a suit to work). As for the glamour, she spent her days in elegant surroundings with a wealthy mistress with whom she had a warm relationship, and on her days off she went to the movies where, in drawing-room comedies and period dramas and Fred-and-Ginger musicals, the lady's maid, a stock character, was as elegant and willowy as (and only a shade less beautiful than) the ladies she served, the characters played by Garbo or Louise Reiner or Billie Dove.

*

When I was a little girl in the fifties and Mary Jane would visit our house on Long Island, I thought she was the most glamorous woman in the world. She didn't dress like everyone else: she wore a fine gray suit with high Joan Crawford shoulders and white gloves and shiny black walking shoes. I thought she was like Roz Russell.

But Mary Jane was not suited for her job in that she was highly sensitive, highly intelligent, and had the soul of a poet. She should have been a teacher, or a writer.

For years Etta and Mary Jane worked hard, long days and six or seven days a week, saved their money—unlike workers today they were not, please note, heavily taxed—and after fifteen or so years in America they bought a little brownstone on a cobblestone street near what would become the Brooklyn Navy Yards. It was to this house that, in the 1930s, Patrick and his family moved when, after many years of successful employment, he lost his job at Edison. We don't know why he lost it—it's shrouded in mystery, my mother was a child and her parents never told—but Patrick had begun to drink heavily when he came to America and I believe the reason he was fired, and never worked steadily again, was alcoholism.

And so when he and his family, including my young mother, hit hard times, it was the cook and the lady's maid who kept the family together. (I have noticed this pattern in more recent immigrants—the women sometimes more quickly get the lay of the land, fit into the new reality, work, flourish; the men are a little more likely to lose discipline, lose heart, in the strangeness of it all.)

Years passed, Etta married, in her forties, a widower named John Conlon, a carpenter. Patrick's children grew up, my mother married my father, a Brooklyn boy name Jimmy Noonan who, just back from World War II, joined the merchant marine. They had three children in three years—this was known at the time as Irish triplets—and to have their fourth, fifth, sixth, and seventh children they moved to a Levittown-style house in Massapequa, Long Island.

Mary Jane now, in the 1950s, went to work for a family in Darien, Connecticut, and after that, in the early 1960s, she retired. This was wonderful because she got to visit us a lot, and it is here that my memories of her become truly vivid. She would come and stay for months at a time, helping my mother and father, making dinner, doing the shopping. She would stay up with us at night and tell us stories about Ireland and share her views of history, which included (a) Eamon De Valera is a great man, (b) the English and the French are rather wicked, (c) especially the English, who tried to stamp out both Ireland's Catholicism and its culture and naturally failed, for God protected us, and (d) Woodrow Wilson's great document of World War I, The Fourteen Points, was a marvel of democratic thinking that, had it prevailed at Versailles, would have created a better world for us all.

*

It was at this time that I, aged eight and ten and twelve, realized Mary Jane was not only interesting and kindhearted and artistic but also deeply eccentric. She loved poetry and loved to recite it, walking around the house declaiming in a lilting and dramatic voice the popular poems of her young womanhood, and this would have been only and completely charming if she'd done it during the day, which she did, but she also did it at night, at 2 A.M. and 4 A.M., which brought a certain Eugene O'Neill–Tennessee Williams quality to it. I would be sound asleep in my room in the dark and suddenly I would be jerked awake to the sound of "In Flanders Fields" being recited in the doorway by a woman in a long white nightgown, her long gray hair loosed from her bun and tumbling around her shoulders. I'd scream. She looked like a ghost, or an angel. She was so dreamy and strange, and now I know she must have been lonely. For her brother had married and was surrounded by children and grandchildren, and Etta had married and, with her husband, bought a little house in unpopulated Selden, Long Island. But Mary Jane was alone. She had never married, though she often told us of her many suitors, which was believable because she was so pretty. But she never said why she'd never chosen one. Perhaps it was like affluence and attainment; perhaps she didn't think it was her fate.

And so in the 1960s, when she was in her seventies, she had only us and, of course, God, for she was religious in the old-fashioned Irish way of worshipping God, loving Him, incorporating Him into her life, and showing that incorporation through the symbols with which she decorated wherever she was—the mass cards tucked in the bedroom mirror, the rosary beads on the headboard of the bed, the crucifix on the wall. So us and God and her poems, that's what she had.

And when she died, living in Selden with the widowed Etta, in 1969, I found that she had something else. In her room in the little house, under the bed, behind boxes and bags, I found a book, a big brown book, a thousand-page ledger with imitation leather covers and a binding worn down to the cardboard. I opened it and showed it to my sisters, and we saw that for a decade of her life she had written down all the poems that she loved, and hoarded newspaper and magazine articles that caught her eye, as well as pictures from the supplements and old letters. But mostly the book contained poetry, written in her hand, page after page, most of it copied from popular poems of the day but some of it, perhaps, original.

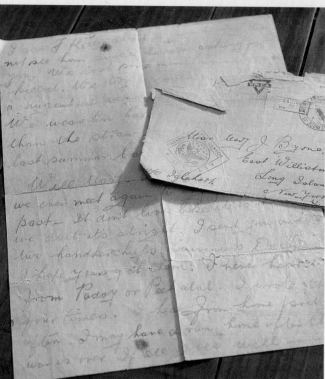

It was her commonplace book. It is on my lap as I write. She kept it, it's clear, wherever she lived and worked, and it is wonderful, a piece of the American immigrant experience, a book that traces the arc of that experience.

There are poems about longing for home:

> *I am Going back to Glenties*
> *Where the harvest fields are brown*
> *And the autumn sunlight lingers*
> *On my little Irish town . . .*
> *'Tis far I am beyond the seas*
> *And the yearning voices call*
> *Will you not come back to Glenties*
> *And your wave washed Donegal....*

Here is another—there's no title on it, and indeed she may have written it:

There's no time like the old time
When you and I were young
When the flowers of April blossomed
And the birds of April sung . . .

Here on the next page is "Before It Is Too Late":

If you have a grey haired mother in the old home far away
Sit down and write the letter you put off day by day.

Don't wait until her tired steps reach [indecipherable] pearly gate
But show her that you think of her before it is too late.

Here are notes she took on something called the language of stamps: "The stamp on the top right hand corner of the envelope means (if) upright: I desire your friendship. Across—Do you love me. Upside down—don't write home again. Crooked—write at once. At the bottom corner on right hand upright it means: your love makes me happy. On the bottom left hand corner—upright: be true to me. Across: fidelity will be rewarded."

Was she ever in love? I don't know; she never said. Maybe these notes were about communicating with people back home.

Further into the book, after the notes on stamps, there is this: "How sublime a thing it is to suffer and be strong. And because she has suffered and been strong and because she has inspired her men to do and dare and to struggle and to achieve and to keep the faith and fight the fight—we honor the Irish women tonight."

Lord, what was that? From a newspaper column or essay? Did she write it herself? Was she writing a toast of some sort?

I was thrilled to find this treasure: a letter she saved from a young man at the front in France. It's stamped "Soldiers Mail, 1918—Passed by Base Censors"—and the letterhead reads, "On Active Service with the American Expeditionary Forces." It is from a cousin I have never heard of.

Well, Mary, we just got back from the front a couple of days ago. I may tell you it's a hot bed, shells dropping all around. No sleep, up all night and very little to eat. . . . We lost some men—wounded and killed. We try to cover ourselves in a dugout to save us from the shrapnel. We wear tin hats, much heavier than the straw hats we used to wear last summer back in New York. Well Mary, I don't know will we ever meet again to enjoy the happy past—It don't look like it to me. If we don't it's alright. I sent you and Etta two handkerchiefs (Souvenirs De France). . . . We are still driving the Germans back. I am writing this letter in the tent in the woods. . . . Write soon. Good-bye. As ever, your cousin, Jos. Dunleavy, 308 Infantry, AEI.

I don't remember hearing of Joe Dunleavy when I was young. I wonder what happened to him. (I just called my mother: "He was her favorite cousin. He was killed in World War I." I read my mother the letter, and she said, "Oh my God." Then she added, "I think she was in love with him. I remember her talking about him. And I think the Dunleavys had another boy who was a priest.")

On the book goes, marked by longing for Ireland, for home, and love for those who fought in the great war, especially, I guess, Jos. Dunleavy of the 308th.

*

By the end of the book, though, the poems and clippings change. They are just as sentimental in style, they are written with the same florid hand, they are copied with the same approval, but now they are no longer about Ireland.

Now they are about America.

A newspaper photo of the Saint Patrick's Day parade being reviewed by, as the caption puts it, Cardinal Farley and the Reviewing Party in front of Saint Patrick's Cathedral.

Here is a clipping from the *New York Times*, April 3, 1921—a picture of Pope Benedict XV "bestowing upon Archbishop Dennis Dougherty of Philadelphia the Red Hat of the Cardinalate."

Here is a poem about an American holiday called "Thanksgiving":

> *There's a charm to your name, Thanksgiving*
> *When the gray goose spreads its wings*
> *From the frost-bound lakes*
> *To the Southern brakes*
> *Where the gulf breeze softly sings.*

She was becoming American. As Robert Frost said at the inauguration of JFK, "The land was ours before we were the land's." Now her land was truly becoming hers; now the poems aren't about loss and longing but about the delights of her new country.

Here, from the back of the book, in one long page of elegant script, she had written out the most famous poem of one Henry Van Dyke, sentimental poet of the day, who was writing here for the immigrant Americans who'd gone back to Europe to fight in the war, and longed to return. It is called "America for Me," and reads in part,

> *'Tis fine to see the old world*
> *and travel up and down*
> *amongst the famous palaces*
> *and cities of renown*
> *To admire the crumbly castles*
> *And the statues of the kings*
> *But now I think I have had enough*
> *of antiquated things.*
> *So it's home again and home again*
> *America for me.*
> *My heart is turning home again, and there I long to be.*

In the land of youth and freedom
beyond the ocean bars
Where the air is full of sunlight
And the flag is full of stars.

I remembered that poem from my childhood. I knew it because it was one she had loved to recite. And I realized as I read, and realize again today, that in the old brown book she had recorded more than popular poems—she had recorded her transit from Irish girl to American girl.

*

Shortly after I found the book, just after Mary Jane's death, I took the Van Dyke poem from the book, framed it, and put it up in the apartments I lived in after college, in Boston and New York. And I took it with me when in 1984 I left New York for Washington, to work, in the White House, for the son of a hard-drinking Irishman named Jack Reagan. Here I put it not in my home but in my office, where it belonged.

One of my first assignments as a speechwriter for the president was to work on his remarks when he landed in Alaska on his return from the European trip in which he had marked the fortieth anniversary of D Day at Point du Hoc. The Alaska stop would be a brief one but there would be a small crowd waiting for the president, and something had to be said. And so, daydreaming in my office, I thought of coming back to America, and Reagan's feelings about America, and of the idea of returning home, of coming back to the place you love. And what would be nicer than my own unknown tip of the hat to Mary Jane Byrne, lady's maid, who'd suffered her wounds and made her long journey and, by the end, found herself in a place she'd come to love.

A few weeks later, when Ronald Reagan returned to U.S. soil from his great trip abroad, he quoted the old words she had long ago recited, and written down: "It's home again and home again, America for me . . . to the blessed land of room enough, beyond the ocean bars, where the air is full of sunlight and the flag is full of stars."

She would have liked that he did that. She would have liked the end of the journey, and knowing the book in which she'd recorded it had traveled so far. ❖

Eugene O'Neill set the table for the dramatic playing out of family tragedy. In *Long Day's Journey into Night*, he told the story of the Tyrone family, the barely disguised O'Neills. Bradford Dillman and Jason Robards played the sons to the parents Florence Eldridge and Frederic March at the Helen Hayes Theater on Broadway in 1956.

CHAPTER 5

THE
PLAYERS

IRISH ONSTAGE

EUGENE O'NEILL WAS enraged when he heard that the producer of his newest play, *The Straw*, was determined to cast a nineteen-year-old actress as the female lead. *The Straw* was based on O'Neill's six-month stay in a tuberculosis sanitarium, where he befriended a sensitive young woman named Kitty McKay, who was dying of the disease. She served as the model for Eileen Carmody, the tragic heroine of *The Straw*, which O'Neill believed at the time to be "far and away the best and truest thing I have done."

Earlier in the year, he had won the acclaim of New York's theater critics for *Beyond the Horizon*, the first of his plays to make it to Broadway. He was not about to take a chance now on an inexperienced actress for the role of Eileen Carmody. "The role is so tremendous," O'Neill said, that only a stage veteran ought to be considered.

Of the young actress proposed to play the sensitive Eileen Carmody, O'Neill simply sneered: "Who is Helen Hayes?"

She may have been young, but Helen Hayes was no newcomer to theater. Besides having been born into a family drama worthy of an O'Neill production, she was a child prodigy, pushed onstage by her mother, the daughter of Famine immigrants who rejected Catholicism and heritage in the pursuit of American glamour and success.

Hayes was born with the century, into a house in Washington, D.C., where the Irish-American experience was both close at hand and far removed. Her beloved Irish immigrant grandmother was a masterful storyteller and she kept young Helen in thrall as she spun bizarre and often gruesome tales even as her fingers worked at some embroidery. Like Eugene O'Neill's grandparents, Ann Hayes and her husband Patrick fled Ireland when the potatoes failed, and their lives and the lives of their children, riven by conflict and awash in the false comfort of alcohol, would sound familiar to the great playwright whose work was so steeped in similar experience.

Like so many other Irish immigrants, Patrick Hayes found a job with the government, which paid for a small house and allowed him the time to indulge in his favorite hobby—Shakespeare. Patrick Hayes hoped one day to translate the Bard's works into Irish, an indication that theatrical blood ran in the Hayes family and that Patrick himself hailed from the Irish-speaking countryside that the Famine destroyed.

Patrick Hayes was also a drinker, and the habit was passed on to some of his children. Drink helped shorten his life—he died before his granddaughter Helen was born—and his tyranny at home drove his children into early marriages to get out of the house. Patrick Hayes's unforgiving demeanor and dark moods, no doubt made all the darker by the accident that left him blind in one eye, sent Ann and the children in search of comfort and status outside the parish and the bitter future that seemed to be theirs. Helen Hayes's mother, Catherine, seemed to have managed some degree of escape in marrying a man named Francis Van Arnum Brown, whose slightly better-off family had come to America in the eighteenth century. They were mighty disapproving of their son's marriage to an Irish "scamp," and indeed the marriage soured, not because of Catherine Hayes's low origins, ironically enough, but because her husband proved to be a little too comfortable with his lot as a meat salesman. Catherine's burning ambition to leave behind the immigrant experience and the embittered world of her father extended to her determination to free herself from an airless and artless middle-class life. Such ambition would be handed down to young Helen Hayes (who took her mother's maiden name professionally) as well.

Old Patrick's enthusiasm for the theater was handed down, too. After her marriage and the birth of Helen, Catherine Hayes Brown harbored dreams of becoming an actress and putting what she saw as the drudgery of domestic life behind her. Her struggles were evident in the deep lines on her face and her red, raw hands. She did, eventually, find her way into small-time show business for a while, but it was through her daughter that her dreams would be realized. Helen would bury the past and find the better life, the glamour and fame for which her mother, the daughter of Famine immigrants, yearned.

If the world of the young Helen Hayes, with its tortured relationships and unspoken tragedies, was not as fearsome as that of the Tyrone family in Long Day's Journey into Night, it was a reasonable facsimile. Later in her career, after O'Neill was dead, Helen Hayes would take the stage in the role of Mary Tyrone in Long Day's Journey, in what became her final appearance on Broadway. As Mary Tyrone, she was playing a character based on O'Neill's mother, a woman who, like Helen herself, once considered convent life. Mary Ellen O'Neill was famously mismatched with O'Neill's actor-father James, the son of a man who left Ireland during the Famine only to return after abandoning his wife and children in Ohio. Both James O'Neill and Catherine Hayes had married up in class, into solidly middle-class families, and both marriages were disasters. In Long Day's Journey, Mary Tyrone eases her pain with drugs (morphine), just as surely as Mary Ellen O'Neill did and just as James O'Neill and Patrick Hayes took to the bottle—fog people, stumbling through mists. Eugene O'Neill did not recognize

Eugene O'Neill, whose father, James, came to America during the Famine as a young boy, contended that his Irishness was the element most of the critics missed. Although early on he did not see the talent of the young Helen Hayes (below), whose upbringing was scarred by the legacy of her impoverished and alcoholic Irish immigrant grandfather, she would win roles in several O'Neill plays, including a star turn as Mary Tyrone, the putative O'Neill mother, in *Long Day's Journey.*

Helen Hayes's name in 1920, but that was all he did not know about her.

Years after O'Neill snubbed Helen Hayes, the actress arranged for a live performance of *The Straw* on her nationally broadcast radio program. As was the custom in radio days, the performance was aired twice, once for the East Coast audience and once for the West. Between shows, Helen Hayes received a telegram from Eugene O'Neill: "It is seldom that a playwright has the privilege of hearing his character realized exactly as he had imagined it. Tonight, you have given me that." The granddaughter of Famine immigrants, now the leading lady of American theater, at last had won the admiration of a grandson of the Famine, now America's greatest playwright.

The Irish found their way in sports, too, earliest and perhaps most memorably in boxing. John L. Sullivan, the Boston strong boy of Famine immigrants, was the last of the bare-knuckle champs. Gene Tunney had movie-star looks combined with fast feet and hands. He bested Jack Dempsey in the famous "long count" fight, and his son ended up as a United States Senator. The Irish were also drawn to baseball. John McGraw, a legendary manager considered the best of all time by expert Bill James, is pictured below with the austere Connie Mack, an Irish American who managed the Philadelphia Phillies for fifty years. Here, they "choose up sides" at the 1933 All Star game after McGraw's retirement.

The Fighting Irish of Notre Dame have, since the 1920s, commanded the loyalties of Irish Americans across the land, however tenuous the connections to leprechauns and things Irish. Although early in the century, a struggling Irish American might be able to escape his day-to-day life by pinning his hopes on becoming an athlete, things have changed. How many Irish remarked upon the Irishness of Frank Winters, who centered for this year's Super Bowl–winning Green Bay Packers?

Irish actors and minstrels found work and a working-class Irish audience at the turn of the century. Vaudeville would become a significant venue for the Irish to advance a stereotypical if entertaining notion of Irishness.

*

For both James O'Neill and Catherine Hayes, theater offered a way out of the Irish immigrant ghetto, a glimpse of a world beyond parish and precinct, and their drive and ambition to escape came at considerable cost to their personal lives and, in O'Neill's case, to the lives of his children. Yet the same economic and psychological insecurities that drove other Irish immigrants and their children into politics and the civil service became, for Eugene O'Neill, Helen Hayes, and other Irish-American artists and athletes, expressions of genius. An astonishing number of Irish-American entertainers were the grandchildren of Famine immigrants, like O'Neill and Helen Hayes. The laughter that Fred Allen reveled in, for example, hid a childhood of torment; the lovable ditziness that Gracie Allen came to epitomize hid her early years in the ethnic ghetto. Who knows how much of the laughter masked fear and anger, and how much the role-playing betrayed a search for acceptance as something other than Irish-American?

Entertainment, the arts, and sports have long been vehicles for those outside the American mainstream. They have allowed individual members of ethnic groups to win adulation and fame, foster-

MICK MOLONEY

OLD AIRS AND NEW: FROM REELS TO *RIVERDANCE*

Mick Moloney is a musician and folklorist and a professor in the Irish Studies program at Villanova University.

The Clancy Brothers and Tommy Makem brought Irish traditional music to a broad American audience in the sixties and seventies.

In 1993, an experimental dance production called *Riverdance* was performed in Dublin on live television during the Eurovision Song Contest, before an estimated audience of 600 million Europeans. The seven-minute piece brought together newly created music with innovative Irish dance routines. The reaction was unprecedented. *Riverdance* mania swept the continent. A general European audience discovered Irish dancing, and public perception of Irish dance within Ireland was transformed, literally, overnight. No longer was it considered stiff and old-fashioned. Now it was sexy and trendy.

An elaborated version of the show was produced and the format expanded to encompass other forms of percussive dance including flamenco, clogging, tap, and Russian folk ballet. The show opened in Dublin and played to capacity audiences for ten weeks. It moved to London and sold out in the West End for five months. It then arrived at Radio City Music Hall in March 1996, playing to capacity audiences of six thousand per night, and returning in late 1996 and 1997 for a nationwide tour. Cloned versions now run simultaneously worldwide. Fortunes have already been made by composers, choreographers, artists, and producers, and international reputations have been won.

When *Riverdance* arrived in the United States it was in a sense coming home. The two principal dancers—Michael Flatley and Jean Butler—were born in America of immigrant Irish parents. Butler was born and raised in Long Island and had been studying Irish dance since she was seven; Flatley was born in Chicago and had been dancing since he was eight.

Riverdance was a public validation of a national culture on the international stage, demonstrating and celebrating the capacity of traditional Irish dance to become cosmopolitan without losing its identity. The traditional dimension came from Ireland; the innovations, from America. *Riverdance* could not have happened without both.

This tension between the old and the new, between the urge to traditionalize and the urge to innovate, has always been at the heart of the story of Irish culture in America.

✳

At the heart of Irish culture—be it the dance, the poetry, or the language itself—is music. And for hundreds of years Irish people have expressed their deepest, most heartfelt concerns through reels, airs, and tunes. They carried this tradition with them to their new home in America—or Amerikay, as it was known in many of the thousands of songs of emigration written in the eighteenth and nineteenth centuries. Much of the music of the Appalachian Mountains was shaped by the songs and tunes brought over by immigrants from Northern Ireland in the latter decades of the eighteenth century. In the mountains of Tennessee, Kentucky, Virginia, West Virginia, and the Carolinas, Irish music came together with English, Scottish, and later African-American music. The music that emerged was known as hillbilly or old-time mountain music and is heard there to this day. The branches that grew from this early cultural influence include bluegrass and country music, both with strong Irish accents.

One Irishman who stood up for his Irishness amidst a kind of vaudevillian fever to be what the audience wanted was the famous Irish tenor John McCormack, whose extraordinary success on the American stage stirred the pride of Irish-American communities. Ed Harrigan and Tony Hart further bridged the gap between vaudeville and legitimate theater. Today, Cherish the Ladies with Joanie Madden (opposite), among many other musical groups, are part of a fresh Irish idiom, mixing rock, folk, and traditional music.

Many of the Irish immigrants who flocked to America in the wake of the Great Hunger in the latter decades of the nineteenth century came from the western counties, which were home to much of the traditional music of Ireland at that time. Hence a lot of traditional musicians ended up in America, and they brought their music with them.

Irish traditional music is a sophisticated, highly evolved art form. It is characteristically played on instruments such as the fiddle, uilleann pipes, wooden flute, tin whistle, accordion, concertina, tenor banjo, and mandolin, often accompanied by guitar, piano, bouzouki, bodhran, or bones. The repertoire is composed of dance music pieces such as jigs, reels, hornpipes, polkas, mazurkas, flings, and waltzes and other instrumental forms such as slow airs, marches, and planxties. Some pieces date from as far back as the sixteenth century, while others are more recent in origin.

In the large American cities, musicians from widely separated villages in Ireland came together, and a rich cross-fertilization of styles and repertoires ensued. These cultural traditions are now as American as they are Irish. New styles and forms developed from a new generation of Irish-American musicians in Boston, Chicago, Philadelphia, and New York. Classic 78 rpm recordings were made of great Irish musicians in America between 1916 and the early 1930s. Musicians such as uilleann piper Patsy Tuohey from Galway, the Flanagan Brothers from Waterford, Dan Sullivan's Shamrock Band from Boston, fiddlers James Morrison, Paddy Killoran, and the incomparable Michael Coleman of

Sligo recorded in the 1920s and 1930s for Victor, Columbia, Decca, and other companies. These recordings made their way back to Ireland, where they had a profound effect on the evolution of the tradition in the home country.

By the 1960s, however, traditional music was inexorably declining as a force in Irish-American social and cultural life, a trend hastened by changing musical tastes and diminishing immigration. The old Irish dance halls, which provided a major social outlet for the music, had long vanished from urban America.

Today, however, young American-born Irish musicians are in the forefront of the Irish music scene in this country, and when the All Ireland dance and music competitions are held each year in Ireland, Americans of Irish ancestry are sure to be among the winners. Virtuoso young musicians are enlivening this venerable tradition all over America, and the future for the music has never been brighter. American-born musicians such as Eileen Ivers, Seamus Egan, and Joannie Madden, leader of Cherish the Ladies, the only all-woman band in traditional Irish music, have achieved major success in the popular music market. New tunes are also being composed daily in America, adding to the great store of music that has been passed down through the centuries.

✳

There has been a similar resurgence in purely Irish singing, owing to the commercial success of the Clancy Brothers and Tommy Makem in New York in the early 1960s. Their style was a classic hybrid, combining an Irish and Scottish song repertoire with a performance style directly derived from the American folk song revival. Their success was instant and meteoric, catapulting them to international stardom and creating overnight a commercial market for a new genre of Irish song culture in America and also back in Ireland. Audiences found their new rhythmic approach to the performing of Irish songs and their novel use of harmonies along with guitar and five-string banjo accompaniment refreshing and captivating. Their legacy can be found in the profusion of Irish groups now performing in Irish bars across America—a milieu in which many Americans hear Irish singing for the first time.

✳

Today there are more places in America where Irish music and dance are performed than in Ireland. One can enjoy them at festivals, events sponsored by cultural and arts organizations, colleges, museums, and historical societies. National Public Radio and PBS bring Irish traditional music weekly to millions of Americans, many of them classical music lovers—a situation that would have seemed impossible twenty years ago. The captains of the ethnopop industry are now eagerly exploiting the "Celtic" market niche, and a steady stream of Irish recordings have reached the top echelons of the world music charts all through the 1990s. Irish rock groups fill the airwaves, and Ireland's most famous rock group, U2, continues to fill the biggest stadiums in the land every time they tour the States. Grammys are handed out annually to Irish musicians and composers. Irish films such as *The Commitments* have achieved cult status among the young. All over America Irish pubs thrive, with live Irish music providing a backdrop to the animated gossip of the crowds who flock to them in record numbers. The country becomes greener with every passing Saint Patrick's Day. In fact, just about everything Irish is *in* America as the millennium approaches.

Which brings us back to the healthy tension between the old and the new. Doing things in a traditional way involves taking responsibility for the future and also being respectful of the past. This is a truly humble act but also a supremely assertive one. ❖

ing hope among their peers and acceptance in the heartland. American popular culture often serves as a barometer of social progress, which is why Jim Thorpe, Jackie Robinson, and Arthur Ashe were famous beyond the parameters of their sports, why Sidney Poitier's courtship of Katharine Houghton in *Guess Who's Coming to Dinner* was a cultural breakthrough, and why gay and lesbian characters in television sitcoms today serve as an indication that another set of barriers has fallen.

The Irish in America used the same tools to dismantle fear and loathing. In fact, in many cases, the Irish used them first. Theater, music, sports, and literature all have served to further Irish ambition, explain the Irish to the larger society, interpret the Irish experience, and, in the case of theater, music, and literature, to critique the very society that stood in judgment, withheld its affection, and, in the end, was forced to abandon the ramparts of nativism and prejudice.

✳

Irish theater was all the rage in pre–Civil War New York, yet Irish-American entertainers themselves remained outsiders. The audiences for legitimate theater were not ready to deal with interpretations of the Irish immigrant experience, but they couldn't get enough of authentic Irish accents, which invariably prompted great bellows of laughter. Shut out of uptown theaters, the Irish found a niche in the music halls and backroom stages that were

George M. Cohan, a real Yankee Doodle Dandy (he wrote the tune, after all), was sunshine to Eugene O'Neill's Irish darkness. Cohan hailed, literally, from an entertaining family. The Four Cohans (pictured in a business card), with the young George as a key player, worked the minstrel circuit.

emerging along New York's Bowery and in similar places in other cities. There, some of the songs of Stephen Collins Foster, descendant of Protestant Irish immigrants, made their debut to crowds of working-class people whose otherwise grim lives were touched, ever so briefly, by music. It was in such venues that the Irish helped found and develop one of their first contributions to popular culture, the minstrel show.

As outsiders, the Irish competed economically, socially, and politically with another despised group, the free blacks of the North. Often the relationship between the two groups was hostile and violent; still, some observers took note of the fact that the Irish and blacks lived in close quarters with each other, and that eventually there could be what one described as a "fusion" between the two groups. Such a development, an anonymous nineteenth-century pundit noted, "would be of infinite service to the Irish. They are a more brutal race and lower in civilization" than blacks.

There is a special poignancy, then, to the legion of Irish actors and singers who blackened their faces with burned cork and acted out roles that often featured the worst aspects of stage Irishness and crude racial stereotypes. Blacks were not allowed onstage, needless to say, and nobody was particularly interested in Paddy's music and stories, so Irish entertainers took on the look—in grotesque stereotype—of blacks, borrowed from their dance and music, and took to the stage playing not Paddy but Sambo.

An Irish American from Ohio named Daniel Emmett founded the first minstrel show in 1842 in New York, and an Irish American named Thomas "Daddy" Rice created the first popular minstrel dance, "Jump Jim Crow." Rice's nickname came from his role as father to the minstrel industry. He was making a meager living playing the part of the eternal Paddy until he came upon the idea of smearing his face in black and dancing. He was a sensation. Soon, advertisements for Emmett's Irish-minstrel troupe featured pictures of African-American men with stereotypical features dressed in an Irish American's stereotypical clothing as they plucked on banjos and scratched away at fiddles. The entertainment Dan Emmett created would enjoy a life so long as to be unseemly; there were versions of it on the radio in the 1940s.

Emmett and Rice were song-and-dance men whose talents were not wanted in the legitimate theater, so they plied their trade along the Bowery, dancing and writing songs that played on black stereotypes to be performed by Irishmen who were being stereotyped uptown. One of Emmett's songs made its way out of the music hall and into American folk memory—"Dixie," the national anthem of the Confederate States of America. There is no indication that Emmett ever set foot on soil south of the Mason-Dixon line, just as Stephen Foster never knew firsthand whether or not the sun really does shine bright on old Kentucky homes.

The industry Daddy Rice brought into the world gave life to the careers of another child of Famine immigrants, Jerry Cohan, who started off as a dancer, then formed his own minstrel show, and finally and most famously, collaborated with his wife, Helen, his daughter, Josie, and his son, George M., to form a vaudeville troupe known as the Four Cohans.

Minstrel shows still were standard fare in American popular entertainment in 1878, when George M. Cohan, in the role of a newborn, took his first bow. Raised in the itinerant world of minstrel-show Irishness, Cohan brought the Irish-American music-

(continued on page 196)

THOMAS FLANAGAN

THE IRISH IN JOHN FORD'S FILMS

Thomas Flanagan is the author of THE YEAR OF THE FRENCH, *which won the National Book Critics Circle Award for Fiction in 1979;* THE TENANTS OF TIME; *and* THE END OF THE HUNT. *All four of his grandparents emigrated from County Fermanagh in the nineteenth century.*

John Ford (1894–1963), nee John Feeny, was born to immigrants from Galway. His films are a blend of Irish themes, Hollywood drama, and an evasive notion of truth. Still, his vision, regardless of setting, reminds the Irish of themselves.

He was born John Feeney into a family of immigrants from the Galway coast and grew up in a fiercely Irish enclave in Portland, Maine, the son of a saloonkeeper and a mother who never learned to read or write English. As the director John Ford, he was the recipient of six Academy Awards, none of which he accepted in person, and he is by now the subject of a critical literature that speaks of him as one of the finest artists ever to have worked in film.

John Ford made specifically "Irish" films, like *The Informer*, based on Liam O'Flaherty's novel about republican intrigue (above, with Ford favorite Victor McLaglen), and *The Quiet Man*, with John Wayne testing Maureen O'Hara (opposite). But his most Irish film might very well be *The Grapes of Wrath*, about poverty and exodus, with Henry Fonda, "wandering on the roads to starve—part of the Irish tradition," said Ford.

He presents us with one of art's perennial mysteries: how someone who was in many ways coarse and sentimental could create works that, while often exhibiting the same traits, are at their frequent best luminous, enchanting, and profound. He was a perfervid American patriot who did not consider himself a first-class citizen until the Irish-American Kennedy had been elected president. An Irishman who knew him said that the great tragedy of his life was that he had not been born in Ireland. He was a dramatist of myths whose truest subject was America itself and the West as it exists in the American imagination. He was a mass of contradictions, some of which derive from his double sense of himself as at once American and Irish.

He grew up in American film, following his brother Francis (who changed the family name) to Hollywood as a teenager, and in 1915 riding—or so he would claim—as one of the sheeted Klansmen in *The Birth of a Nation*. Two years later he was directing two-reelers for Universal, and in 1924 he created one of the masterpieces of the silent screen, *The Iron Horse*. At times it seems to imply that the railroad that linked east and west was built by Irishmen, with Chinese and Italian laborers offering subordinate and comical assistance. The film announces what would be recurring themes and images: America's national destiny and Abraham Lincoln as a spiritual force by whom that destiny is guarded and assured. Lincoln's presence is often invoked in Ford films.

In 1939, the year in which Ford re-created the Western in *Stagecoach*, he made *Young Mr. Lincoln*, with its portentous evocation of a backwoods lawyer who carries greatness within him. In *Cheyenne Autumn* (1964), almost his last film, an engraving of Lincoln looks down reproachfully upon the Secretary of the Interior who is relocating the Indian tribes.

✻

Ford was to claim that an uncle, Michael Connolly, had told him stories of laying track for the Union Pacific. But Ford was a terrible liar, and the most fructifying of his lies were the ones he told about himself. He also said that four of his uncles had fought in the Civil War, one of them at Gettysburg. Ford gives his uncle the lines, "It was horrible. I went six days without drink," which could as easily have been spoken by Victor McLaglen, the eternal sergeant-major in Ford's later U.S. cavalry films. Ford would also have us believe that he punched cattle as he drifted west to Hollywood, and that the gunfight at the O.K. Corral, as he staged it in *My Darling Clementine* (1946), accorded with the facts as given to him by Wyatt Earp. When he visited Galway in 1921, most of his cousins, in one version, were on the run, and he himself was tracked by the Black and Tans. He believed devoutly that certain "traits of character" are Irish, among them the impulse to translate drab reality into myth. This impulse was central to his genius. When he shaped his images of the American West and of Ireland, he truly believed that in some way he was telling the story of his own life and inheritance.

Like Eugene O'Neill, he believed that being Irish carried with it a burden of moods, stances, loyalties, quarrels with the world. Working with the most popular of American cultural forms, he was conscious of a majority culture, from which the Irish, despite their bellicose loyalty to it, stood somewhat apart. And yet, again like O'Neill, he was a deeply American artist. He wanted to be known only as "a man who makes Westerns," which was part of his mask of philistinism, and at the same time an essential truth.

Ford made many kinds of films, of which some of the most famous—*The Informer* (1939) and *The Quiet Man* (1952)—are set in Ireland, but the West is his true setting and subject. Even *The Quiet Man*, so "Irish" in sentiment that it gives off an aroma of Guinness-soaked shamrocks, carries with it a wind from the West in the figure of the quiet man himself, John Wayne, back from America and carrying with him the New World's largeness of frame and spirit. Wayne had recently starred in Ford's cavalry trilogy—*Fort Apache* (1948), *She Wore a Yellow Ribbon* (1949), *Rio Grande* (1950)—and he and Ford, between them, had shaped the quintessential image of a certain kind of American.

And yet, most curiously, the cavalry in these films bears a slight resemblance to historical fact but a large one to Ford's imaginary community. It resembles, in fact, an Irish monastery. Within it, men are closely bonded by rituals, ceremonies, forms of language, and we are kept reminded of how bad the pay is, how poor the food, how strenuous the discipline, how rich the rewards to the spirit. The setting in Monument Valley towers above the troopers, stretching outward to infinity, upward to eternity.

There is an actual Irish character in *Rio Grande*, the County Cavan–born Phillip Sheridan, who had been Wayne's commanding general in the Civil War and now is the army's chief of staff. But this is an exception. In the Ford Westerns, as in fact, the Irish occupy subordinate positions—sergeant-majors rather than officers. In *Fort Apache*, Colonel Thursday (Henry Fonda), a stiff West Point martinet of good New England stock, reminds Sergeant-Major O'Rourke (Ward Bond) that they are separated not only by hierarchy but by class. During the war, O'Rourke had been a major (in the Irish Brigade, of course), but he has reverted to a rank proper to him by nature.

In *The Last Hurrah* (1958), based on Edwin O'Connor's novel about the blarneying and corrupt reign of Boston's mayor James Michael Curley, Ford had to confront directly the conflict between WASP and Celt, native and immigrant. It was a conflict that he had spent his Portland boyhood in the midst of, and he could draw upon early snubs and memories of bigotry. The Protestant establishment is represented by a newspaper editor (John Carradine) and a banker (Basil Rathbone), figures so pinched in spirit and appearance that they seem to have not faces but profiles pressed together. The Irish, by contrast, are open-faced, warm-hearted, easy in manner, witty. Spencer Tracy, "Mayor Skeffington," is a tribal chieftain, shrewd, humane, loyal to his traditions and his people, and surrounded by his gallowglasses, precinct workers ready to do his bidding. But the film never so much as hints that his power is based on graft and corruption, nor does it make clear why he will lose the election, his last hurrah. More than anything, it implies the defeat of traditions by modernity, a defeat that was beginning to weigh upon the aging Ford.

*

Someone has suggested that Ford's most Irish film is *The Grapes of Wrath* (1940); probably not Ford himself, whose wit was not paradoxical. But he did say "the story was similar to the famine in Ireland, when they threw the people off the land and left them wandering on the roads to starve—part of the Irish tradition." And his film carries strong echoes of that central Irish memory.

The opening scene from that film, in which Tom Joad, fresh from prison, and Casy, the questing hedge-preacher, walk into the abandoned Joad farmhouse and then learn of the fate of neighboring farms, bears an uncanny resemblance to folk memories of the abandoned Famine villages of Connaught and Munster. Tom is like the Irish rebel son of such memories, sweet-natured but quick-tempered and capable of murderous rage. And, as the Joad family splinters, the patriarch senile and the father helpless, it is the mother, massive and nurturing, who becomes the source of strength. The Joads, descendants of Ford's cow-punching plainsmen, are the ethnic opposites of the Irish, but the myths echo against each other. The Joad journey across dusty roads in their limping and overburdened truck, sustained by catalog photographs of California sunlight upon lemon trees, resonates against memories of the Irish coffin ships headed across the Atlantic. Across water or desert, the American experience, for two centuries, was a movement westward to a complex and ambiguous destination. In this film, Ford's thematic material, Ireland and the West, touch each other.

The touching may remind us, for a moment, of the Jack Feeney who crossed the continent on the railroad that his uncle may or may not have helped to build, and who, among the orange groves of Hollywood and the stark grandeur of Monument Valley, became John Ford, the director. After he had struck it rich, the master of a medium which he had helped to create, he bought a two-masted, hundred-foot ketch. He painted her green and white and called her the *Araner*. ❖

Fred Allen, born John Sullivan, stormed American radio with his irreverent lampooning of privilege and power. His sharp tongue, unabashed Boston accent, and baggy eyes asked for nothing more than an intelligent response to what seemed obvious to him: The world was pretension, and must be humored. Here, he works with his wife, the hilariously deadpan and wonderfully named Portland Hoffa.

Why not? After all, she was a breadwinner, and her husband was thought (incorrectly, as it turned out) to be nothing without her.

Fred Allen, sadly, has not enjoyed the timelessness of Gracie Allen, whose lovable antics can still be seen in TV reruns. The generation that looks to David Letterman for biting social satire and the one that chuckled at the genial prankstering of Johnny Carson have no idea of the debt their favorite comedians owe to the vaudeville juggler and tormentor of network executives and advertising salespeople.

Irreverent, disdainful of pretense, and suspicious of authority, Fred Allen was the Irish rebel of radio—without seeming to be anything more than a generic American, or a generic Bostonian in any case. For fifteen years, he carried on a conversation with millions of listeners who came to regard him as Will Rogers with a Boston accent, sharing Rogers's folkish dissent but adding a sharper, more pointed twist. He was topical, political, tastefully disdainful of the leaders of the day—and for all those reasons has been lost to contemporary audiences.

Young Fred, or Johnny, as he was known to his family, was born near Harvard University, and his birthplace on Union Street on the Cambridge-Somerville border was about as close as the Irish Catholics of his generation got to the Ivy League. His mother died of pneumonia before Johnny was three years old. Johnny and his brother Bob were reared by their father, John Henry Sullivan, whose efforts Fred Allen would later sum up this way: "My father was a stranger. When I grew older, people often told me how funny he was. At that time he didn't seem funny to me. He squandered most of his fun away from home." John Henry Sullivan was an alcoholic, a whiskey drinker whose sons had to help him stumble home after Sunday-afternoon dinners at the home of John Henry's parents. "We looked like two sardines guiding an unsteady Moby Dick into port," Allen wrote.

But before he became Fred Allen, young Johnny Sullivan obviously learned something from his father—between absences—and his father's brothers. "They had the Irish thing: They could make people laugh," Allen once said in a less embittered moment. And how Fred Allen made people laugh, from the time he performed in vaudeville as the self-proclaimed "World's Worst Juggler" to his years as the tour guide through a remarkable weekly sketch known as "Allen's Alley," where the denizens bore names such as Mrs. Nussbaum, Ajax Cassidy, Senator Claghorn, and Titus Moody, all of whom

(continued on page 201)

JASON ROBARDS

PLAYING O'NEILL

A leading O'Neill scholar has said that Jason Robards's image "has been so indelibly stamped on the plays that at times I am uncertain whether I am writing of the playwright or of his principal actor. In the end, it seems a distinction without a difference." Robards has appeared in six O'Neill plays.

I'm only a bit Irish, mixed with Welsh, English, and Swedish, so I don't know exactly why the plays of Eugene O'Neill had such resonance with me. But I fell right into him.

I came from a family that closely paralleled O'Neill's, and that could have something to do with it. His father was an actor, as was mine. My father had given up his greatest talent for the Hollywood scene, and O'Neill's spent his energy playing a crass Count of Monte Cristo all over the country. His mother was vacant, there and not there, as was mine, and I understood that. I had a younger brother, too, like O'Neill. I was at sea, seven years in the navy, in peacetime and in wartime, and I grew up on the water, in California. In O'Neill, there is a love of water; he knows its power. He came to be a manic swimmer.

All these things may have drawn me to his work, but it's not for me to say how, if at all, these parallels, whether consciously or unconsciously, affected my acting. I'm not one of those actors who call on that sort of thing anyway. I learn the lines and get through it and if you know it well, good things start to happen.

I was fortunate to work with the great director of O'Neill plays, José Quintero, who seemed to have a reading on O'Neill, as I did. We saw the work as almost laid out for us. At first we erased O'Neill's stage directions, yet we ended up following them to the last letter. We both seemed to intuitively follow where he was going, without lots of analysis. With O'Neill, if the casting is right, you have it.

It was many years ago when I first encountered O'Neill's work. I was at the American Academy of Dramatic Arts in New York, and they needed people to fill the seats in previews at the Martin Beck Theater. So a friend and I went. It was *The Iceman Cometh*, and we were bored. But the thing that struck me was that James Barton, who played the role of Hickey, had a face that was the mask of death, a look befitting the character and a look I will never forget. It wasn't until ten years later on my way to a radio job in New York that a friend told me that Quintero was doing a revival of *Iceman* in Greenwich Village, and the image of Barton's face jumped to mind. My friend told me, "You have to read for Hickey," and I went to read that day. I got the part, and I did *Iceman* for six months and the play ran for two years.

I've done *Iceman* twice now, thirty-two years apart. I've done *Hughie*, the premier; *Long Day's Journey into Night* three times, playing the father twice and Jamie once, in the U.S. premiere; *Ah, Wilderness*; *A Touch of the Poet*, in my opinion his best play; and the play I adored, *A Moon for the Misbegotten*, with Colleen Dewhurst.

*

O'Neill worked out a lot of things in his plays about hope and despair and a loss of confidence. I think it all had to do with loss, a great ache and yearning, and his trying to understand and explain his feelings about women and men and their relationships. It made for great drama, and it was all true.

There is danger in O'Neill, and that's what makes the work true. I dropped into the O'Neill despair. I dropped into it in *Long Day's Journey*. I didn't know why I was in such despair, and the only thing that saved me was that I kept working. Then, during *Moon for the Misbegotten*, after a period when I had not been drinking for a long time, I went back to the bottle again as soon as I got into that part of Jamie. In a funny way, O'Neill got me back into it but he also showed me the way out. One day, halfway through our eighteen-month run, I barely made it to the matinee. As I stood there on the boards, I realized that O'Neill had given Jamie a choice: love or death. And though it is clear in the play that the character chooses death, I said to myself, No, I'm not going to do that. I could see it was so important just to live. I chose to love.

I had some great times, make no mistake about it. But if you can't handle it, you have to stop. I was forty-nine. O'Neill stopped in his forties, too.

*

O'Neill's people came over during the Famine. That was such an awful time. He refers to it in *Moon*—"the praties they grow so small." Surely, all these terrible memories and episodes must have been cooking in his mind. You lose a mother, to whatever it might be—death or drugs or a distancing—and it gets connected with other things you've lost—a country or a culture or, for many of the Irish, even a language. And you tend to keep losing, or doing things in a way that will make sure you do lose even the things you tell yourself you most want.

After a bout with TB in his early twenties, O'Neill determined to become a great dramatist, and his output was incredible, more than seventy plays. And there are some we didn't even see. He tore up almost all of the Cycle, nine plays to be called A Tale of Possessors Self-Dispossessed, a history of the Irish in America. Those plays could have been the Henrys of Shakespeare. *A Touch of the Poet* is the only one that survives intact from this cycle. The plays were about an Irish family coming here in the eighteenth century and how they managed over a period of 150 years. The last play of the Cycle ends with a family that has a son who becomes president of the United States. When they tore these works up, Mrs. O'Neill supposedly said it was like "tearing up babies."

To play O'Neill is to plumb the depths of the Irish tragedy and to share in its poetry as well. To play O'Neill is to be an honorary Irishman. ❖

The quintessential O'Neill player, Jason Robards, in *Moon for the Misbegotten* with Colleen Dewhurst. About O'Neill as a dramatist, Robards says, "I fell right into him."

Was Walt Disney the first Irish American to receive an Oscar? Could be. In 1930 he was awarded the Academy's prize for best short subject. Many more were to follow. The Irish connection of the Disney family, lurking in some films like *Darby O'Gill and the Little People*, wasn't thoroughly pursued until Walt's nephew Roy began to research the family tree, and found relatives in County Carlow.

acted out their assigned stereotypes with the affectionate humor of a bygone era, when identities were not so easily bruised and social commentators not so thoroughly intimidated.

Ethnic humor, it has been noted, began disappearing from Irish stage acts when the eternal Paddy gave way to the creations of George M. Cohan, and Cohan in turn witnessed the rise of the Hollywood Irish, where ethnicity received the airbrush treatment. In presenting the Irish in any one of several stereotypes—the hard-hearted gangster (Jimmy Cagney), the wise priest (Pat O'Brien, Spencer Tracy, and Bing Crosby), the feisty colleen (Maureen O'Hara), to name just three assigned roles—Hollywood embraced a safe ethnicity, but for the most part told stories that Father Francis Duffy, chaplain of the Irish-dominated Fighting 69th, seemed to prefer. "We are just plain human," Father Duffy said of the men who served in the famous regiment. And Hollywood and popular culture seemed content to leave it at that. Distinctly Irish movies—that is, Hollywood's idea of acceptably Irish movies—were full of affable blarney that spoke to sentiment, not reality.

✶

The Academy Awards and motion pictures with sound were but two years old when the statuette was presented for the first time to an Irish-American entertainer. Walt Disney won the first of his several special awards in 1930. The following year, Helen Hayes won the award for best actress for her role in *The Sin of Madelon Claudet*. The Irish were about to make their presence, and their talents, known to Hollywood in, yes, dramatic fashion. In the years between 1935 and 1945, the bulk of Hollywood's golden era, Irish Americans dominated the Academy Awards. Walter Brennan and John Ford both won three awards, and Spencer Tracy won two. It was also during these years that James Cagney and Bing Crosby won their only Academy Awards.

Having been such a force in vaudeville and the stage, it was not surprising to see the Irish take to the screen from the moment the film industry was born. The tradition of Irish-American movies, those that receive new life and a new audience every year on or around March 17, started in the silent era with the early work of John Ford, Leo McCarey, and Hal Roach; prospered during the golden age; and continues with the directorial success in the 1990s of Irish immigrants Jim Sheridan and Terry George, and the Irish-American son of a New York City police officer, Edward Burns.

Jimmy Cagney at twenty-one years of age in *Public Enemy*. Cagney, a Yorkville New Yorker, assumed the mantel of America's tough guy, a rough Irish kid who, it turns out, could act, not to mention dance. He won an Oscar for his portrayal of fellow Irishman George M. Cohan in *Yankee Doodle Dandy*.

Another tradition started in those bygone days of the silent film: the offended audience. One of the first Irish films in America, *The Callahans and the Murphys*, was set in an urban tenement and focused on two quarreling families. As Joseph M. Curran noted in his book *Hibernian Green on the Silver Screen*, critics were amused to find scenes of Irish brawling, with the *New York Times* noting that such a treatment of the Irish was "nothing if not orthodox." More than a decade after Irish groups staged mass protests over performances of J. M. Synge's *Playboy of the Western World* (the notion of an Irishwoman wearing a "shift" was the principal transgression), *The Callahans and the Murphys* met with a similar reception. Performances were canceled in some cities, while the studio, MGM, gamely pointed out that the film couldn't be all that bad, as an Irish American (Eddie Mannix) was its director.

The protests continued, and Curran notes that a lesson was learned. Irish movies in the future steered clear of dangerous stereotypes, although those of a less threatening nature (genial priest, genial cop, feisty bonny colleen) were deemed suitable for general audiences.

Thanks in large part to a fine stable of Irish talent assembled at Warner Brothers, the 1930s and 1940s saw a proliferation of Irish movies and stars and directors, all of whom added texture to the emerging story of the Irish in America, as told by the Irish in America. American film, mostly through the efforts of John Ford, also tried its hand at Irish history in such films as *The Informer*, *Parnell*, *The Plough and the Stars*, and *Beloved Enemy*. These Irish-American films explored Ireland's struggle for freedom at a time when the Irish in Ireland were living with the legacy of their brutal Civil War in 1922–23, which produced a chilling effect on discussion of what had happened and why.

It would not be until 1996 that the Irish would tell the dramatic story of their lost leader, Michael Collins, in the film of the same name. Perhaps not surprisingly, it was a Warner Brothers release, and it came exactly sixty years after Samuel Goldwyn's *Beloved Enemy* featured a Michael Collins–like character as its hero. In a bit of revisionism that any student of Irish history might appreciate, Goldwyn quickly realized that audiences didn't like the ending—when the Collins character is assassinated, as he was in real life—so he substituted a happier ending, with Collins taking a bullet and not only surviving, but having the presence of mind to toss off a witticism to his girlfriend.

(continued on page 207)

EAMONN WALL

THE IRISH VOICE IN AMERICAN FICTION

Eamonn Wall's fiction has appeared in the anthology IRELAND IN EXILE: IRISH WRITERS ABROAD. *He teaches English at Creighton University in Nebraska.*

Modern Irish-American fiction begins with that remarkable Chicagoan Finley Peter Dunne. He was the first writer to make the Irish immigrant experience a central issue in his writings, and the first to truly succeed in making the concerns of the Irish—socially and politically—part of the realpolitik of American fiction and public life. Dunne's finest creation, Mr. Martin Dooley of Archery Road, Chicago, is one the funniest, most humane, and remarkable figures in American fiction, and there is no livelier or more diverse stage in the world of literature than the saloon he presides over. For the first time in Irish-American fiction, place is celebrated without reservation. The small streets and houses where the Irish dwell and parade, though unremarkable in many respects, are described in such detail and with such reverence that they become important, beautiful, and central to American life. Furthermore, in *Mr. Dooley in Peace and War* (1898) and *Mr. Dooley in the Hearts of His Countrymen* (1899), as well as in other volumes, Dunne celebrates the gifts of the Irish—intelligence, range of interest, loyalty to Ireland and the United States and to families in both countries, and their quite inimitable gift to turn the raw material of language into sparkling conversation.

Though Dunne provided Irish-American writers with a language and a voice, not all modern writers have chosen to follow his lead. The reasons for this are quite complex, though a difficulty that Irish-American writers have faced is one of audience. F. Scott Fitzgerald, one of the most identifiable Irish-American names in modern American writing, was certainly aware of the limitations of writing only about Irish Americanness. Only in his first novel, *This Side of Paradise* (1920), through his protagonist Amory Blaine, and in his final novel, *The Last Tycoon* (1941), through Irish Pat Brady, father of the narrator Cecilia Brady, does he allow Irish Americans to become significant players in his fiction. Another well-known writer who grew up Irish-American is John O'Hara. The author of such novels as *Appointment in Samarra* (1934) and *Butterfield 8* (1935), O'Hara reveals a mixture of ambivalence and hostility to his ethnic background. As many commentators have pointed out, O'Hara preferred to caricature Irish Americans rather than confront his own past.

One writer who did not ignore Finley Peter Dunne's influence is his fellow Chicagoan James T. Farrell, who in *Studs Lonigan* (1935) captured the essence of the Irish-American experience. This long work is a classic realist novel that has suffered somewhat in the eyes of critics because it was published at a time when modernism was all the rage. Still, his work, unlike Dunne's, remains in print.

In recent times the dominant figure in Irish-American fiction has been William Kennedy, who has found a wide audience of readers extending far beyond Irish America and the English-speaking world. His best-known novels are his Albany trilogy: *Legs* (1975), *Billy Phelan's Greatest Game* (1978), and *Ironweed* (1983), which was awarded the Pulitzer Prize and made into a successful film. In their celebration of ordinary life, these novels recall the work of Dunne and Farrell, but they also, in the range of their influence, take Irish-American writing in a new

Young Colum McCann, Irish born but now a New Yorker, is making his mark with extremely well-reviewed novels and short stories about Ireland and America.

Mary Gordon, who is mixed Irish- and Jewish-American, has written insightful novels, stories, and nonfiction about her heritage and what it means to be Irish.

direction. Kennedy has been profoundly influenced by modern Irish writing—by the more traditional and familiar storytellers such as Frank O'Connor, and by the more avant-garde work of James Joyce, from whom he has learned how to accommodate such techniques as multiple narration and stream of consciousness. In *Ironweed* in particular, the use of such techniques provides the work with sparkling originality, and allows Kennedy's down-and-out characters to articulate their deepest thoughts, feelings, and visions. Although their location is Albany and their heroes are Irish-American, for the most part Kennedy's novels, because of the sophisticated techniques he employs, have found a wide international readership.

Two remarkable Irish-American women writers have made their mark since the 1970s, Elizabeth Cullinan and Mary Gordon. In Cullinan's *House of Gold* (1970), family and

William Kennedy, who was raised in Troy, New York, continues to chart the Irish-American experience—and aesthetic—in his novels. His latest, *The Flaming Corsage*, details the courting of a beautiful Dutch-American beauty by a son of Ireland in nineteenth-century Albany.

relatives have gathered to await the death and then to wake Julia Devlin, a strong and devout matriarch who in life exercised tight control over her family. Her children, gathered round her bedside close to the local Catholic church in the Bronx, understand that they have found it impossible in their own lives to break free of their mother's influence. Under the holy pictures in the apartment, they come to realize the limits of both religion and Irish America: To remain faithful to their upbringing and to the place their mother has created for them has entailed forgoing many of the pleasures and freedoms that America has to offer. One senses in *House of Gold* the conflict between two worlds—the old, puritanical, and gloomy Irish-American one and the modern American one, which offers excitement and prosperity.

Mary Gordon offers a more ambivalent view of the Irish-American experience. She has been attacked by some commentators for exhibiting some of the same self-hatred and hostility to Irish Americans that is evident in the work of O'Hara, but such criticisms often pale in the face of her

Michael Stephens has employed experimental techniques in his own family storytelling. Raised in Brooklyn, Stephens's *Brooklyn Book of the Dead* and *Season at Coole* owes as much to the Irish tradition of Joyce and Flann O'Brien as to any American tradition.

artistry. In her remarkable first novel, *Final Payments* (1978), Gordon explores the movement of Irish Americans from the confines of a strict, church-based world to an exciting but difficult secular one. Isabel Moore, who has given up her youth to take care of her ill and house-bound father, shows little remorse at his death and quickly decides to sell the family house in Queens. While taking care of her father, she was devoted to him, but now that he has passed away, she quickly decides to make up for lost time. With great haste, she heads for her friend Eleanor's apartment in Manhattan, acquires a new wardrobe, contraception, and a job, and has affairs with two married men, one of whom is the husband of another childhood friend, Liz. Gordon shows in *Final Payments*, and in her other works, that slavish loyalty to family and church is destructive, an issue that resonates long and loud in many an Irish-American home.

Will Irish-American fiction survive or die? Many commentators have noted that the move away from the city neighborhoods to the suburbs represents the end of the line for the Irish as a distinct ethnic group. The historian Lawrence J. McCaffrey believes that the Irish have assimilated: They have become better educated, secured comfortable standards of living, and bought houses in the suburbs where they look and act like everybody else. The Catholic Church, the parish hall, and the Democratic Party no longer play central roles in their lives. Their old apartments in the city have been taken over by new immigrants from other places. Their immigrant energy has evaporated. Moving to suburbia, away from the tightly knit world of city block and neighborhood, involves buying into the suburban ethos and leads to assimilation. In suburbia, sense of place dissolves.

Active in the dissolution of place are two fine novelists who have taken a measure of how hard it is to reestablish what was lost. The first, Michael Stephens, in his most recent novel, *The Brooklyn Book of the Dead* (1994), chronicles the return of the Coole siblings to Brooklyn for their father's wake. In his will, Coole had stipulated that he be waked in Brooklyn, where he had been happy, and not on Long Island, where he had moved his family in the flight to suburbia after World War II. The second, Thomas McGonigle, in his *Going to Patchogue* (1992), details a return as well, that of a forty-year-old man to Patchogue, Long Island, where he grew up. He hopes in some small way to recapture the past and his place in it, but this is not possible. Fittingly, these tales are told in a fractured postmodernist style that owes more to Joyce, Celine, Thomas Bernhard, and Flann O'Brien than to James T. Farrell or any other Irish-American writer. Though less well-known than Gordon and Kennedy, Stevens and McGonigle are Irish-American writers of daring originality and honesty, and they are full of promise.

A very recent development that bodes well for Irish-American fiction has been the arrival in America of a new generation of Irish-born writers, who have begun to publish important work dealing with both life in Ireland and the immigrant experience. Perhaps the two most remarkable novels to appear to date from this group are Emer Martin's *Breakfast in Babylon* (1995), a sparkling novel of poverty, petty crime, drugs, and love; and Colum McCann's *Songdogs* (1995), a widely praised first novel that follows, with beautiful lyricism, the journey of a photographer across North America. These young writers possess double visions—Irish and American, local and international. It is likely in the future that more young novelists will come to the United States from Ireland and will enrich the writing here. And the same is going on in reverse: It is a cross-pollination of the best kind that will challenge anthologists of "Irish" and "American" literature in the years to come. ❖

The early years of motion pictures with sound also saw the emergence of two memorable Irish characters, one as a type, the other as an individual. James Cagney, the red-haired son of the streets of New York, burst upon the film industry at the age of twenty-one in his unforgettable lead role in *Public Enemy*. Though he would later display an astonishing versatility and win his only Oscar playing song-and-dance man George M. Cohan, it was Cagney's movie debut that defined his image, and that of a distinctly Irish-American type. So definitive was Cagney's portrayal as an Irish tough guy that no less an authority than Daniel Patrick Moynihan described it as a "quintessential" urban Irishman: "Fists cocked, chin out, back straight, bouncing along on his heels." The miracle of James Cagney in the 1930s is that he managed to personify the notion of the menacing urban Irishman, an image that had frightened or repulsed America for nearly a century, while exuding a magnetism and charm that were also particularly urban Irish-American. That he did so was a tribute to his magnificent talent, but it was also a sign of changed times.

The second memorable Irish character born of Hollywood managed to be both obviously Irish and unforgettably American. Katie "Scarlett" O'Hara remains America's most famous fictional female, and while some might argue that Vivien

The Kellys, Grace and Gene, though unrelated, helped transform popular notions of Irish ways: Grace, the daughter of a well-to-do Philadelphia merchant, was a dignified embodiment of female beauty; Gene was not only the quintessential song-and-dance man, but he carried with him a sense of class and refinement that appealed to both men and women.

Leigh (an Englishwoman!) played her as a Southern belle and a symbol of the Confederacy's lost cause, there's no denying Scarlett's Irish Catholic roots. Her father, Gerard O'Hara, is an immigrant who leads the family in prayer at night and who, in one of the film's dramatic scenes, reminds his daughter that "land is the only thing that matters, the only thing that lasts." To which Scarlett complains, in the impatient tones of many a first-generation American, that her father "talks like an Irishman." The actor who played Gerard O'Hara, Thomas Mitchell, certainly did talk like an Irishman; he was an Irish immigrant who won an Academy Award not for playing Katie Scarlett's father but for his role in John Ford's *Stagecoach*, which was released the same year as *Gone with the Wind*, 1939. Another Irish American, Barbara O'Neil, played Scarlett's mother, the gentle Ellen O'Hara.

Within a little more than a decade, another pair of actors would serve to represent not simply Irish-American assimilation in Hollywood but also an acknowledgment of Irish America's complexities. In Grace Kelly and Gene Kelly, the public could behold two Irish Americans whose style and background were startling contrasts to the sort of Irish characters made famous by Cagney (and others). Grace Kelly, the daughter of a prosperous Philadelphia merchant, was no longer the feisty colleen, a role that saw its finest and loveliest expression in Maureen O'Hara's portrayal of Mary Kate Danaher in that Saint Patrick's Day classic, *The Quiet Man*. Grace Kelly was high society; Gene Kelly was elegance and panache. That both were Irish mattered little. The very notion of Irishness, abetted by the silver screen's larger-than-life image-making, had expanded at last beyond its traditional stereotypes. As Gene Kelly danced and sang obliviously in the rain, he became an indelible image of Hollywood itself.

Such an evolution of the Irish character, from minstrelsy through "stage-Irish" stereotypes to the urbane suavities of Gene Kelly, marked a nearly total assimilation of what was distinctively Irish, at least in Hollywood terms. The quarter century or so following John Kennedy's election—an event that seemed to put an end, at last, to the Irish-American struggle for acceptance—was accompanied by a dwindling of Hollywood's interest in Irish America and in Ireland itself. But the mid-1980s saw the rise of two Irish-American immigrants, Jim Sheridan (who has since returned to Ireland) and Terry George, as major directors. In such films as *In the Name of the Father* and *Some Mother's Son*, they have explored the conflict in Northern Ireland in ways that were unthinkable a generation ago. At the same time, Edward Burns catapulted onto the Hollywood scene with his study of modern Irish America in the suburbs, *The Brothers McMullen*. In Burns's work, a new generation of Irish Americans, far removed from the days of Jimmy Cagney, are coming to terms with the questions of identity that seem eternal in the American immigrant experience, no matter how far removed. Romantic relationships with Jews, the loss of community in the suburbs—such themes are at the core of Burns's work and are central to the Irish-American experience on the eve of a new century.

✻

Of course, the story of Irish America has not been confined to movie theaters and playhouses. Novelist John O'Hara occupies a large and problematical place in the pantheon of Irish-American mythmakers. The sometimes heated debate that surrounds O'Hara's reputation is not so much about the authenticity of his heritage, for he was as green as they come, but about his choice of subject mat-

(continued on page 213)

DENIS LEARY

ON BEING BORN IRISH-AMERICAN: A GLOSSARY

Denis Leary, an award-winning (and highly irreverent) comic actor, whose parents immigrated to Worcester, Massachusetts, from Ireland in the 1950s, says he can next be seen in MY RIGHT FOOT, the story of a working-class Irish American who lives his life in a wheelchair due to sheer, unadulterated laziness.

Denis Leary: an Irish-American comic, son of Irish immigrants, who spent his youth surrounded by plenty of paneling.

Being born Irish in America has become a privilege most of us take for granted. The days when NO IRISH NEED APPLY signs hung from every other jobfront are so distant that they shock our sun-protection-factor-55-covered ears upon retelling. We grew up in the shadow of Jack Kennedy and The Duke, drinking Guinness out of gas-powered cans while watching U2 perform live at Giants Stadium. We're cops, firemen, athletes, doctors, lawyers, bagmen, senators, presidents, and heads of state. Okay, so we still haven't had our own pope. But look at the bright side: neither have the French.

What follows is my own glossary of terms for those precious few who may still have trouble understanding what it means to be an Irish American. Sit back, crack open a can of Dinty Moore beef stew, suck it down in two quick huge gulps, and fall asleep. When you wake up in four hours' time with cottonmouth and lower gastrointestinal pain, read on.

BREAD, IRISH

Fine Irish delicacy made from equal parts butter, limestone, and lead. See "Paperweights."

CABBAGE, CORNED BEEF &

Only eaten on Saint Patrick's Day. Probably with green potatoes and milk. Why? Never mind why. Just shut up and eat and then wait in your room until your father comes home and after he's through with you I'll bet beans against baseball bats you'll think twice before you put a cherry bomb in Sister Agnes Catherine's desk again.

CIVILIZATION, HOW THE IRISH SAVED

I remember my father saying that John Lennon, though born and raised in England, was actually of Irish descent. This stems from the age-old Irish-American desire to make all things Irish. For instance, Robert De Niro—that Italian-American acting icon—is actually half-Irish. On his mother's side. Ditto Marlon Brando. Not to mention Al Pacino. And Woody Allen. And Abraham Lincoln and Elvis and Jesus and Mother Teresa. That's the rumor I'm starting, anyway.

CLINTON, BILL

Big, loud, brazen, short-tempered, stubborn, overweight, and underread guy. And he claims he's only *half* Irish?

DAY, SAINT PATRICK'S

A holiday based on the work of an Irish holy man whose main miracle was chasing the snakes out of Ireland. The facts? There *were* no snakes. The country had been on a century-long bender born of British oppression, they all had the D.T.'s and *thought* they saw snakes. Patrick came in, made seven thousand kegs' worth of coffee, and five hours later the sober, snake-free masses declared him a hero, a real saint. Of course, facts can be painful. I mean, how do you explain to a New York City full of 12 million green-faced, green-beer-swilling, green-bagel-chomping Irishmen (not to mention the green-for-a-day-so-I-don't-get-the-crap-beat-out-of-me Puerto Rican, Chinese, and Pakistani party participants) that Saint Patrick was a fraud? Answer? You don't. You eat the green bagel, you drink the green beer, you sing "Danny Boy" in a holding cell with seventy-five other guys till six in the morning and then you go home. God would've wanted it that way. *See* "Cabbage, Corned Beef &;" "Fighting, Fist"; "Guinness"; "Ireland, Kathy."

DIVORCE

What you get after two years of marriage to Mary Feeney—the sultry redhead from down the block—after realizing you also married her alcoholic old man Billy, who's got the gout; her Vietnam vet brother Whitey, who's paralyzed from the neck up; and sixty-seven other blood relatives who range in condition from slightly retarded to clinically insane.

FIGHTING, FIST

Invented by the Gaels as a way of settling family disagreements and handed down thereafter from generation to generation. Immortalized by John Wayne and Victor McLaglen in *The Quiet Man*. Organized as a sport when several Irish Canadians put on skates and pretended to chase a small black scone around a frozen pond in between beating the ever-loving daylights out of each other.

GAB, GIFT OF

Supposedly given to the precious few by birth, allowing them to con their way out of any situation in which the truth would get them hurt or dead or both.

GAELIC

What your Irish-born parents, uncles, and aunts speak after fifty fingers of whiskey. Several English phrases may still sneak out, such as "fookin' hell," "fookin' Brit basterds," and "where's my fookin' teeth?" *See* "Guinness."

GUILT

What you feel from the moment you wake up in the morning until your sex-crazed, booze-addled, Christ-killing, sin-committing skull hits the pillow at night. *See* "Guinness"; "Ireland, Kathy."

GUINNESS

What tastes like God's nectar on the soft green plot of olde Ireland tastes like flat Coke with a chocolate Yoo-Hoo mixer here in the States. But that doesn't stop every third-, fifth-, and fifteenth-generation pink Irish mick from downing seventy-seven pints of the gooey mess in fake Irish bar after fake Irish bar until—of course—their blood alcohol levels reach the heights of the Empire State Building and they feel the need to vomit.

IRELAND, KATHY

Irish? Yes. American? Yes. Is she up on her Irish history? Who cares?! Just put her in a kelly green bikini on the beaches of Saint Barth's and that's all you really need to know about why God created the Emerald Isle. In fact, I'd like to be in Ireland right now!

JOYCE, JAMES

Better known as Jimmy. Lives on Second Avenue with his parents. Drives a purple Nova and dated your sister for half an hour in tenth grade. Sits in Breen's Tavern drinking piss-warm Harp and rants about the British government while putting away two packs of Parliaments, unaware of the irony involved. Doesn't know anybody named Ulyssess and at Tommy Finnegan's wake drank seventeen pints of ice-cold Guinness before puking on the coffin.

NOVENAS

What your mother says fourteen of after she hears about your divorce from Mary Feeney.

PANELING

The Irish-American opiate. A symbol of success for the working and middle classes (and easy to clean: you don't). Paneling, and plenty of it. The living room, the den, the bedroom, the bathroom, the kitchen. Ceilings and walls. Even the car: a station wagon with the fake wood paneling on the side. Nobody has ever taken credit for inventing paneling, but I'm pretty sure it was a short, heavyset Italian guy who walked away from Sullivan's Bar & Grill one night, after a heated discussion of Italian vs. Irish literature, with several bruises on his face and a desire for revenge on his mind.

PAPERWEIGHTS

Irish bread, video copies of *Far and Away*, scones, the Clancy Brothers boxed set, Ronald Reagan's autobiography, every bottle of Irish Mist ever manufactured, etc.

SPRING, IRISH

Look, I've been to Ireland. I grew up in America around Irish people. And I've never smelled anything even remotely resembling the odor of this green-and-white-striped concoction. You want a soap that smells Irish? Pour half a glass of Jameson and a pint of Guinness in a stopped-up sink, add a dash of milk and a slice of cheese, and then dip your face in it for forty-five seconds. *That's* what being Irish really smells like.

U2

Your little sister wanted Bono when she was thirteen. You thought in five or seven years' time she'd get over it. Unfortunately, during that half decade your old Uncle Aeneas (pronounced "Anus," much to your entire Irish-American family's chagrin) has come to see the band as the Irish version of the Beatles. And your sister—now twenty-eight—still wants Bono. And your Aunt Eileen considers U2 *and* the chick from the Cranberries to be far superior role models than Sinéad O'Connor, who's the one Irish rock icon you'd pay your little sister to sleep with just so you could meet her. Such is life. And Catholicism. (You know Jesus will get all the accolades, but the guy you really wanna have a beer with is Judas. No such luck.) ❖

ter. Pal Joey, of his "Pal Joey" stories, clearly was not the sort of character O'Hara admired or found worthwhile. The characters in his best-known novels—*Appointment in Samarra, Butterfield 8, A Rage to Live*—and several others are a far cry from the world of Pal Joey, or, for that matter, James T. Farrell's Studs Lonigan. The writer and diplomat William V. Shannon, among others, criticized O'Hara for his obsession with the culture and society of affluent, Protestant America, the very social group whose rejection and snubs O'Hara suffered in eternal hope of acceptance.

O'Hara is a natural counterpoint to F. Scott Fitzgerald, who achieved greater fame and respect. Both were born outside the borders of the typical Irish Catholic experience in America. O'Hara was born in Pottsville, Pennsylvania, in 1905, the Irish Catholic son of a successful doctor who died young, depriving O'Hara of his dream of attending Yale University. Fitzgerald was born in 1896 in Saint Paul, Minnesota, to a well-off merchant family. Whereas O'Hara missed his chance to attend Yale and thus receive his admission slip into that bigger, better world outside the parish and precinct, Fitzgerald got his, attending Princeton and mixing it up with the American aristocracy that soon would provide him with the raw material for his fiction.

Both authors shed their Catholicism at an early age as they reshaped

KILKELLY

Kilkelly, Ireland 18 and 60, my dear and loving son John,
Your good friend the schoolmaster, Pat McNamara, was so good to write
Your brothers have all gone to find work in England, the house is so empty and sad
The crop of potatoes is sorely infected, a third to a half of them bad
And your sister Bridgett and Patrick O'Donnell are going to be married in June
Your mother says not to work on the railroad; be sure to come home soon

Kilkelly, Ireland 18 and 70, my dear and loving son John
Hello to your missus and to your four children and may they grow healthy and strong
Michael has got in a wee bit of trouble, I guess that he never will learn
Because of the dampness there's no turf to speak of and now we have nothing to burn
Bridgett is happy and name a child for her although she's got six of her own
You say you found work but you don't say what kind or when you'll be coming home.

Kilkelly, Ireland 18 and 80, my dear sons Michael and John
I'm sorry to give you the very sad news that our dear old mother has gone
We buried her down at the church in Kilkelly, your brothers and Bridgett were there
You don't have to worry she died very quickly, remember her in your prayers
And it's so good to hear that Michael's returning with money he's sure to find land
For the crops have been poor and the people are selling, any price they can

Kilkelly, Ireland 18 and 90, my dear and loving son John
I suppose that I must be close on 80 but it's 30 years since you've gone
Because of all that money you sent me I'm still living out on my own
Michael has built himself a fine house and Bridgett's daughters are grown
Thank you for sending your family picture, they're lovely young women and men
You say you might come for a visit, what joy to see you again

Kilkelly, Ireland 18 and 92, my dear brother John
I'm sorry I didn't write sooner to tell you that Father has passed on
He was living with Bridgett, she says he was cheerful and healthy right down to the end
Why you should have seen him with the grandchildren, and Pat McNamara your friend
We buried him along side of Mother down at the Kilkelly church-yard
He was a strong and feisty old man considering his life was so hard
And it's funny the way he kept talking about you and called for you at the end
Oh why don't you think about coming to visit, we'd love to see you again.

—PETER JONES AND STEVE JONES

John O'Hara (right) and F. Scott Fitzgerald, cutting the rug with Zelda and Scottie: two Irish-American novelists from opposite sides of the tracks, whose works reflected their Irish heritage in ambiguous and different ways. Where O'Hara self-loathed and forgave, Fitzgerald self-aggrandized and did not.

themselves into something more comfortable, something less threatening to literary and social elites. Fitzgerald for the most part ignored his Irish roots and won critical acclaim. O'Hara tried to deracinate his prose in the way that Fred Allen deracinated his name, but failed nevertheless to win the plaudits accorded Fitzgerald, and O'Hara's extraordinarily productive career, ending with his death in 1970, has yet to win the respect he wanted.

Neither Fitzgerald nor O'Hara lived the typical Irish-American experience of their time. In that sense, they were outside the world James T. Farrell lived in and wrote about, just as they began life outside the Protestant Anglo-American culture they wished to chronicle. O'Hara's Irish characters, when he tried to create them, were, in essence, Pal Joeys—hustlers and small-timers—not particularly admirable in dress or manners.

Fitzgerald's novels were distinctly non-Irish, too, but he can't help himself—his view of the Jazz Age's hedonistic rich rompers is clearly and conspicuously Irish Catholic. The excesses of his characters repulse him, and those who aspire to their circles inevitably suffer or are disillusioned once they shed, or believe they have shed, their status as outsiders.

O'Hara's defenders dismiss the often made observation that his fiction was charged with the resentments of an eternal outsider, forced to bear the slights of the elites who welcomed Fitzgerald. His supporters argue that O'Hara's fiction was much broader, and, in fact, his short stories set in the fictional town of Gibbsville, Pennsylvania, are grounded in social and cultural observation of a group far from the literary and cultural centers of America.

If O'Hara did, in fact, shake his fist at those who denied him respect and acceptance, what of it? What would be more Irish Catholic? As William V. Shannon noted of O'Hara's prose: "One hears speaking through his work the inarticulate, half-strangled, half-conscious rage and resentment of every Irish man and Irish woman who was ever turned down for a job in an old-line Protestant law firm, ever snubbed for the 'sin' of having gone to the wrong college, ever left out of a fashionable party, ever patronized for wearing slightly wrong clothes."

Of Irish-American writers who consciously wrote about the world they knew, some are more affectionate, or at least less angry, than others. James T. Farrell; Jimmy Breslin, author of several Irish-American novels set in Queens; Anna Quindlen, the columnist-turned-author; and Mary Gordon offer pictures of Irish America that are either disturbing, openly hostile, or decidedly ambiguous. Suffice it to say that none of the latter three (Farrell died in 1979) will ever lead a Saint Patrick's Day parade, although Breslin at least seems a great deal more comfortable with tradition and heritage than his female counterparts. Quindlen, in *Object Lessons*, describes an Irish Catholic family that is "well enough off not to be anxious about much except the slow, inexorable encroachment of those who were not their kind." This lack of economic anxiety is a rather new theme in Irish-American letters and one that apparently deserves closer study. The suggestion that even in the suburbs, where Quindlen's novel takes place, the Irish fear "those who were not their kind" is a rather old accusation, a variation on a theme struck since Farrell recorded the movement of the Irish from Bridgeport to more affluent neighborhoods in Chicago. It, too, is an echo of the complaint heard in the middle of the nineteenth century, when the Famine Irish, spurned for their poverty and religion, huddled together inside the parish walls for protection from a hostile world. America in the late twentieth century isn't nearly as hostile anymore, but in the eyes of some observers, the Irish apparently haven't learned to live with those "others," although the question of whether "others" wish to live with the Irish often goes unasked, as does a corollary question: Are the Irish unique in their supposed fear of outsiders? A brief survey of American history would seem to provide the answer.

Complex, even baroque, are the sentences, plots, and characters of Irish America's foremost historical novelist, Thomas Flanagan. A generation of Irish-American readers has learned about the history of its ancestral homeland from his trilogy, *The Year of the French*, *The Tenants of Time*, and *The End of the Hunt*. The novels are a tour de force of scholarship and writing. Flanagan has achieved something remarkable in the field of Irish-American literature, for it has been this American professor who has helped bring alive the history not of the New World but of the old. Like the Aussie writer Thomas Kenneally, whose historical novel *Confederates* ranks as one of the finest novels of the American Civil War, Flanagan brought to the history of another country a fresh set of eyes as well as a masterful pen. Flanagan's art serves as a reminder that history is too important, and has affected too many lives, to be left to historians, archives, and the biographies of famous men and women. History, as experienced by Hugh McMahon (*The Tenants of Time*) and Janice Nugent (*The End of the Hunt*) is intensely personal: the brute force of power and politics bringing itself to bear on solitary individuals, whose courage, cowardice, and, most often, confusion is the stuff of glorious storytelling, even if it often is beneath the notice of conventional history.

While Flanagan's novels are classics, it is James T. Farrell's fiction that remains the standard text of the pre–World War II Irish-American immigrant experience, though time has not been kind to his reputation. Farrell's Irish-American Chicago resonates with truth, perhaps, as Father Andrew Greeley noted, only one version of truth, but truth nevertheless. Farrell foresaw what eventually became the mass movement of Irish America out of the old neighborhoods, and saw as its impetus the coming of American blacks. The role of the Irish in the eternal American struggle of race is a common theme in Irish-American literature. In Jimmy Breslin's *World Without End, Amen*, an Irish-American cop who supports George Wallace's presidential campaign in 1968 discovers that everything he has said about American blacks is being said about Catholics in Northern Ireland. Though harsh in its depictions of Irish-American civil service life, Breslin's book, published at the height of civil rights marches on both sides of the Atlantic, made a disturbing but valid point about attitudes, class, and the eternal burdens of poverty.

In their fiction, Farrell, Breslin, and other Irish-American writers have argued (though not in these words) that if the potato fungus forced the Irish to board coffin ships, then the coming of "others"—as in blacks—to Northern cities encouraged them to hire moving vans and head for the suburban tracts of postwar America. To be sure, the story of relations between the Irish and blacks, so filled with conflict, competition, and (less-known) collaboration, is made for a novelist's eyes and ears. From the draft riots of 1863 (a period brilliantly evoked in Peter Quinn's novel, *Banished Children of Eve*) to the battle over busing in South Boston in the 1970s, blacks and the Irish have found their fates intertwined, to neither group's satisfaction.

*

(continued on page 221)

MALACHY McCOURT

ACTING IRISH: TO BE OR NOT TO BE

Malachy McCourt is an actor and writer living in New York City.

According to legends circulating in the Irish community, 'twas ourselves who discovered America. First, there came Saint Brendan and his monks in their currachs—those cowhide-covered boats still used by Irish fishermen. If you can't credit that legend, here is our fallback position: When C. Columbus was on his way to India, didn't the poor man make a stop at the city of Galway in the western part of the Emerald Isle to pick up a drop of water, some turnips, and a bit of Irish bacon, and in the course of his peregrinations around that ancient city having a pint of stout here and a pint of stout there, didn't he run into that very rare being, a loquacious Irishman, a man named William Erris or Ayers? William, in the course of conversation, said that he had done a bit of traveling on the heaving seas and had seen things, as Captain Boyle said to Joxer in *Juno and the Paycock*, "that no mortal man should speak about that knows his catechism."

This spate of verbiage so impressed Christy C. that he hired our man on the spot, room and board provided and a reasonable salary, to be the navigator for the three *Santas*, indeed the whole expedition. Of course, William had no intention of going anywhere near India, as he knew well that they, the Indians, would never be prepared to receive the millions of Irish who would immigrate in later years to America, so of course he steered them to this continent.

'Tis said W. Erris or Ayers, was the first man ashore and great actor that he was, he temporarily convinced the Boss that this was the home of the Hindu. And that's how the first Irish actor came to America, and they've been applauding us ever since—at least a small fraction of us.

*

It's strange business being an Irish actor in the United States. Despite the long list of Irish playwrights from Congreve, Sheridan, Wilde, and Shaw to Yeats, O'Casey, and Beckett to Carroll, Friel, and Behan, it is the exception rather than the rule to find the Irish actor in the Irish part. Though he be white-complected and appears to be Caucasian as well as fluent in the tongue of the oppressor, as soon as the mouth is opened to expel the words, there is a collective shake of the casting folks' noggins because the accent is not American.

Out in La La Land, Hollywood, I was once sent to audition for the role of a priest in a television show. The description of this man in the casting breakdown sheet was as follows: He is a prison chaplain, late fifties, gray-haired, heavyset, ruddy complexion, blue-eyed Irish, going by the name of Father O'Hara. I went to the place of audition and was going over the "sides" (which is the term used for a script excerpt), when a voice said, "Is there a Malachee Makort heah?" I raised my head and observed a female, who might have been verging on her fourteenth year, so I raised a forefinger to indicate that I was present. She told me to follow her, which I did, and we proceeded down a corridor, and into a room went this diminutive lass, followed by me. I was gawking around furtively to see if there was a responsible adult present when the diminutive one informed me that I would be reading for her, that she was Mindy (I believe all casting directors are called Mindy in Hollywood). As good an actor as I am, it was

Malachy McCourt playing the colorful Irish-American machine politician George Washington Plunkitt.

hard to conceal my astonishment that this mere child was going to judge my professional capabilities. However, not for me to judge, so we began the reading, she going first, with me responding.

I was startled by a series of yelps from Mindy, to wit: WHAT WHAT WHAT IS THIS?
What is what? sez I, thinking that a rat had entered the room, she was so exercised.
What is this dialect you're using?
That is not a dialect, sez I, that is an accent.
What's the difference? bleated Mindy.
An accent denotes a national origin, and a dialect denotes a specific region of that nationality.
Well, whatever it is, it won't do.
The script says O'Hara is Irish, sez I.
Not your kind of Irish, sez she.
It would appear, sez I, that we are on different wavelengths.
Mindy agreed and I left rather rapidly lest I commit casticide (i.e., murder of a casting director).

There was a time when that great exponent of Beckett's works, Jack MacGowran, much beloved by The Samuel himself, was in New York City and he was experiencing a bit of financial difficulty, as happens to all

Malachy, it seems, hearing the confession of the widow Frank McCourt, in their play, *A Couple of Blackguards.* Such a story as theirs, via Frank's memoir *Angela's Ashes,* has enraptured hundreds of thousands of readers.

actors from time to time. Though a smallish man, Jack had a powerful, deep, and distinctive voice—a trained voice, so that every word he spoke was understood. There was still the hint of his native Dublin in it, which added to his charm. Anyway, someone, an agent perhaps, said Jack should do commercials for the money that was in it. So off he went full of good cheer to audition for a voice-over, the character in the commercial being a Martian. The ubiquitous THEY gave him the script, the usual minute of dialogue. Jack got behind the microphone and gave it his powerful all, only to be informed by a male Mindy that that was not the way Martians spoke. A stunned MacGowran asked politely, "How is it you know what a bloody Martian sounds like?" No response being forthcoming, Jack stalked out and never attempted a commercial again.

✳

Historically the good and the not-so-good Irish have made their mark here. They founded the first newspaper, they printed the Declaration of Independence, they invented the submarine, they found the Comstock Lode, and a half a dozen signers of the Declaration were Irish-born. And weren't they gunmen, sheriffs, brothelkeepers, slave traders, priests, pariahs, railroad builders, Custer's cavalrymen, way out of proportion to the general population? But in film, onstage, and in television, if an Irish accent is heard, it's usually one of the "shure and begorrah" brigade speaking. People here in these Unidos Estados have been brainwashed by the Brits into thinking that all Irishwomen are husband- and priest-ridden, fit only for domestic service, and that all the male micks are shiftless, good-for-nothing abusers of alcohol and each other.

The truth is, we are like any other oppressed race—it's impressed on us that, as subhumans, we're in bondage because our oppressors are superior to us in every way. Thus the dimmest nitwit Brit considers himself superior to the most brilliant Irisher, by birth and by virtue of force of arms. And we bought it, every ounce of it. We groveled and fawned and tugged the forelock and imitated them, because we thought that's the way to get on. Because we learned to despise ourselves, we wanted desperately to become someone else. So with all our hearts, minds, souls, brains, and spirits, we did become someone else, thus laying the foundations of a nation that has produced not good, but great, actors. You eventually become the things you hate the most, as AE (George Russell), another Irisher, said. Becoming someone else is the essence of the art of acting, so in the secret recesses of my own mind, there are times I doubt my talents as an actor simply because I don't really want to be anyone but myself.

I once opened a saloon in New York and called it Himself, knowing full well that that appellation would be applied only to me. All my life I craved attention and love and admiration, and the older people would say, He should be an actor, he should, but there was no acting place for me in the stratified Anglophilic arena of Limerick's upper crust. No place for a guttersnipe who wanted to be an actor so that he could be someone else. The other way of becoming someone else was through drink, the drug, and the death.

*

But, I must say, America has let me become the actor. I went to work on a soap opera called *Ryan's Hope* and had an eight-year run, followed by two years on *Search for Tomorrow*, and, more recently, *One Life to Live*, to which I appear to be returning for a "command performance"! And all along I've been working in theater in O' Casey and Brian Friel and the work of other stalwarts of the Irish stage who have made such an impact on the world of theater.

*

The main qualification for being a veteran actor is to live long enough. And having done that, I've been blessed with some great roles: the Da in *Da*, Father Farley in *Mass Appeal*, my time at the soaps, not to mention playing Honey Fitz on a miniseries about JFK. In other professions—the civil service, the army, the law, law enforcement, business—if a person does a job reasonably well, he gets promoted consistently onward and upward. But the actor, the poor, benighted thespian, works a bit, becomes unemployed, and it is off we go again auditioning to prove to someone with impaired eyesight, hearing, and sensibilities that I am qualified, yes I speak English, yes I can move and remember lines at the same time, yes I can act, yes, yes, for crissakes yes, I am an actor, that's what I do for a living, and if I couldn't do it I wouldn't have the temerity to come in here and strut my stuff. Whose life is it anyway? As an actor, be assured it is not yours.

So now I am writing a memoir, *A Monk Swimming*, wherein I am the producer, the director, the casting director, the manager, the agent, the agent's receptionist, and I am the star, costar, supporting cast, and crew, and I'm not likely to turn myself down for any or all parts.

Places please, then, lights to half, houselights out, stage lights out, onstage Malachy, lights up. Speak the speech, I pray thee, for they await the Word. ❖

The transformation of Irish America from an urban people to suburban homeowners has been under way for nearly a century. What began as a trickle out of Bridgeport and out of Farrell's fictional parish of Saint Patrick's became a flood in the 1950s and 1960s, transforming old Irish neighborhoods in a matter of years. The process has encouraged Irish writers to ponder what the Irish in America have given up in exchange for long-sought acceptance and hard-won security. While the newly middle-class Irish saw no reason to look back at the tenements they left behind, for all they saw there was poverty, those who could afford to speculate about the trade-off, and the reasons for the new Irish diaspora, did so. What was sacrificed when parents began sending their children in greater numbers to Harvard rather than Holy Cross, or the state universities rather than Fordham, Villanova, and Notre Dame? What happened to the spirit of shared values when Irish Americans decided that suburban school districts were preferable to the parish schools of old? What has intermarriage, not simply between Irish and Italians or Irish and Germans, but between Irish Catholics and Jews and Irish Catholics and Protestants, done to "the old ways"? Suburbanization and the rise to levels of affluence and assimilation unthinkable even eighty years ago have transformed the Irish in America. But while Irish America produced a body of literature documenting one immigrant's experience in the teeming cities of pre-World War II America, it has yet to produce a chronicler of the staid and stay-at-home passions of the suburb or of middle America, a literature of unspoken Irishness. A few, novelists Michael Stephens and Tom McGonigle, for example, have made postmodern pastiches out of the disorientation of posturban Irish-American life in novels owing more to James Joyce and Dublin "paralysis" than to James T. Farrell. But as yet, there is no John Cheever of Irish-American suburban storytelling.

Unless, of course, it is Edward Burns.

MARY HIGGINS CLARK

AND GIVE ME YESTERDAY

Mary Higgins Clark is the author of, most recently, PRETEND YOU DON'T SEE HER.

In the autumn when the trees become streaked with red and gold and the evenings take on the warming chill that promises winter, I inevitably dream the same dream. I am walking alone through the old neighborhood. It is early autumn there as well, and the trees are heavily laden with the russet leaves they will soon relinquish. There is no one else around, but I experience no sense of loneliness. Lights begin to shine from behind curtained windows, the brick and stucco semidetached houses are tranquil, and I am aware how dearly I love this Pelham Parkway section of the Bronx.

I walk past the winding fields and meadows where my brothers and I used to go sleighriding: Joe, the older, sets the pace on his Flexible Flyer, little Johnny is clinging to my back as we follow Joe's sled through the twists and turns of the steep drop we have dubbed Suicide Hill. Jacoby Hospital and the Albert Einstein Medical Center cover those acres now, but in my dream they do not yet exist.

I walk slowly down Pinchot Place, to Narragansett Avenue, and pause in front of the house where the Clarks live. Once again I am sixteen and hoping the door will open and I may just happen to run in to Warren Clark, the twenty-five-year-old who is the subject of my secret dreams. But he is not there and I hurry along the next block to Tenbroeck Avenue and open the door of my own home.

Everyone is around the table, my parents and brothers, aunts and uncles, cousins and courtesy cousins, the close neighbors and friends who have become extended family. There's a kettle whistling, a teapot waiting, and everyone is settled in for a good gabfest. I take my place among them as the latest happenings are discussed, the old stories retold. Sometimes there are bursts of laughter; other moments brighten with unshed tears at the memory of this one or that one who had such a terrible time. But after a tragedy is recalled, someone is bound to say, "Of course, it was God's will."

*

I am often asked where I get my ideas for the books and stories I write, for the characters in them. It's a hard question to answer. Why in the maze of event and remembrance does one situation haunt the heart, press at the mind, invade the dreams until finally, often reluctantly, as I write, I say, "Your time has come. I will tell your tale."

I can speak for no other author. We are indeed all islands, repositories of our own memory and experience, nature and nurture. But I do know that whatever writing success I have enjoyed is keyed, like a kite to string, to hand, to the fact that my genes and sense of self, spirit, and intellect have been formed and identified by my Emerald Isle ancestry.

I have often said in rueful truth that when the mythological godmothers passed my cradle, most of them rushed on to a more interesting appointment. I can't sing on key, I dance with the grace of a battleship being tugged into harbor, my daughters remind me that their Girl Scout merit patches were pinned to their sashes, not sewn, and the hems on their school uniforms were Scotch-taped. But at least one godmother lingered beside me. "I bequeath you," she whispered, "the need to write, the heart hunger to record. I will you remembrance. Listen to the people around you. The Irish are natural storytellers, blessed in abundance with tales of wit and woe."

At age seven I was given the usual leather-bound five-year diary. I began to record in it. The first entry doesn't show much promise: "Nothing much happened today." But before too long the pages began filling, until now a trunkful of diaries record the years. Fortunately for me, the Irish linger around the dinner table for a good talk, and as long as children don't fidget, they're welcome to stay. The stories filled my ears with tales of tender love matches, of bad bargains made at the altar and endured for a lifetime, of irony and humor and survival.

And that was the key: faith and optimism. In the time of trouble, heaven was stormed with prayer. But when tragedy occurred, faith took over: "God's will be done." Triumph from tragedy. I learned it around the dining-room table. If you're down today, surely you'll be up tomorrow. On the other hand, when things are going well, don't take it for granted. Like as not, there's trouble brewing. My mother would get a "feeling" about this one or that one, and as day follows night you can be sure that the subject of her attention was in for a rough time. Yet when she endured her own darkest hours, the deaths of my father and brother, she never lost the buoyant hope that everything would eventually right itself.

It was that sense of persistent hope that kept me at writing for the six years that I received rejection slips. My first short story was sent out forty times before a magazine in the Midwest bought it for one hundred dollars. During those years, Mother cheerfully minded my babies to give me a couple of hours a day to write. "You'll make it," she assured me. But when the first checks began to come in, she urged me to bank them all. "You never know when you'll run out of ideas, and I don't want you taxing your brain too much." She had already passed on when I had my first big commercial success, but my aunts, her sisters, were thrilled to hear the news, to rejoice with me, to urge me to put some money by, you never know what will happen.

*

I have been asked why so often I write about children. "And they're always in danger," someone joked. "Is it that you really hate kids?" Of course, the opposite is true. The Irish love their children with a fierce passion, and the greatest of tragedies is to lose a child. When I write about children in danger, I am expressing the fears that I have carried over to adulthood. At age five, I was taken to the funeral of a thirteen-year-old cousin. She'd been in the hospital with that ailment known in the old days as Saint Vitus's Dance. The usual prescription was six weeks of bed rest, but Kathleen was a clinic patient. Her mother, May, was told of a marvelous new cure, a series of injections that would have her up and about in only a week. Trustingly, May signed the necessary permission forms. The first injection was administered, and a few hours later Kathleen was dead. I can still hear the heartbroken protests of her mother, "I want Kathleen, I want Kathleen," as the coffin was lowered. With head shakes and sighs, that story was recalled at our dining-room table. "If May had been able to afford a private doctor, they'd never have experimented on the poor child." The urge to get ahead, to somehow always be sure that my own children would have private doctors, became sealed on my soul in those discussions.

*

Whatever name I have made as a writer has been in the suspense field. Writing suspense is challenging and satisfying. I write about very nice people whose lives are invaded by evil. I grew up among very nice people whose lives were invaded by the human condition, with its peaks and valleys. From them I learned that it is not always how we *act* but how we *react* that is the measure of our worth. Someday I want to take a year off from suspense writing and tell the tale of my Irish heritage. I already have the title of that book in mind: *And Give Me Yesterday.* The title comes from a poem that begins, "Lord, put back Thy universe and give me yesterday."

I do not wish yesterday back, only the fullness of its memory, a memory that guides and strengthens me always. Because of it, I have my own concept of heaven. If it pleases the dear Lord and I have been admitted through the gates, I will be assigned my permanent place. A door will open onto a large dining room, and everyone I loved who had gone before me will be around the table. A kettle will be whistling and a cozy waiting to keep the teapot warm. Someone will say with great satisfaction that now we do have time for a grand talk, and the storytelling will begin. ❖

Little Mary Higgins of the Bronx (center, bottom row) remembers fondly her yesterdays. Opposite, in veil (far left) and center, squinting into unknown tomorrows.

CHAPTER 6

THE
NEWIRISH

KEEPING A
CULTURE ALIVE

IN HIS BOOK *The Inheritance,* writer Samuel Freedman traces the true stories of three twentieth-century Catholic families, one of which is Irish-American, the Garretts. The movement of these families and millions like them from the Democratic Party of Roosevelt, Truman, and Kennedy to the Republican Party of Richard Nixon and Ronald Reagan is one of the most important political developments of the postwar years. The Garrett family, whose saga of early death, backbreaking labor, and unstinting effort was common at the turn of the century, lived for a time in the Manhattan Irish ghetto called San Juan Hill in the days when less than 1 percent of Irish-American children finished high school. The Garretts were trailblazers of sorts, but for the wrong reasons—they left the urban ghetto during the Depression because they were so poor they couldn't afford the city rents. They moved instead to an ethnic enclave in the Westchester County town of Ossining, where the Irish lived in ramshackle cabins, traveled on unpaved roads, fed their families potatoes fried in lard, and sent their children to a one-room schoolhouse. The town's wealthy residents referred to the Irish as "those people."

FDR's Works Progress Administration helped lift the Garretts out of poverty, a development that turned the family away from Father Coughlin's increasingly rabid, red-baiting, anti-Semitic radio sermons. Eventually, the Irish overthrew the town's Republican machine, led by a charismatic candidate who invited his constituents to "shake the hand that shook the hand of Al Smith." The New

The soaring Michael Flatley, star of *Riverdance* and *Lord of the Dance:* The traditions of Irish dance and the innovations of a Chicago-born Irish American have raised Irish arts to unprecedented heights.

Deal and World War II left the Garretts intact, better off, and loyal Democrats, but when a grandson of the original Garretts, Tim Carey, went off to college in the 1960s despite having been given only vocational training in secondary school—that was deemed enough for "those people"—everything changed. Carey was appalled by overprivileged antiwar protesters, by race-based formulas that put him at a disadvantage despite his own family's hardships, and by the social chaos he saw unfolding all around him.

Carey came under the wing of a Republican millionaire named Lew Lehrman, a man with conservative ideas and a vision who took the time to listen to this bright kid with a community college degree and a blue-collar background. The social and economic chasm between the two men could be measured in light years, but Lehrman didn't hold himself above those of less-privileged backgrounds. By 1994, Tim Carey, grandson of an Irish immigrant who preached the gospel according to Franklin Roosevelt, was a top Republican lawyer and among the leaders in a revolution that in New York State overthrew Mario Cuomo, the last New Dealer.

The story of the Garrett family, repeated millions of times over, is the story of Irish America in the thirty years since the election of John Kennedy. For even while Kennedy was taking the oath of office as the first Irish Catholic president, the Irish were leaving the old neighborhoods, the ancestral parishes, the transported villages, and moving to suburbia. Just over a century after they left behind the stricken land of Ireland for the cities of America, the children of the Famine packed their belongings into station wagons and set out for places like Nassau and Suffolk Counties on Long Island, where great fields of potatoes now sprouted thousands of facsimiles of the new American dream—home ownership, convenient shopping malls, backyard barbecues, a piece of equity in the very system the Irish had challenged and changed.

The Irish urban neighborhood disappeared with astonishing speed, rather like the transformation of the west of Ireland in the 1840s, when it changed almost overnight from an overcrowded region of villages into a fearsome ghost town. In the late 1950s, the South Bronx still was the sort of community that had nurtured its legendary political boss, Ed Flynn, a place where the borough's Irish political leaders still trooped off to mass at Saint Jerome's. The South Side of Chicago still retained its Irish presence—why, it was home to the last of the great Irish bosses, Richard Daly. But by the end of the 1960s, the South Bronx was synonymous with urban decay, and the South Side of Chicago was not far behind. Meanwhile, a thousand Levittowns served as a symbol of the American Century's affluence and, for the Irish, a prized token of long-sought acceptance. The three-bedroom Cape Cod and two-car garage—often paid for with a civil-service salary—was visible evidence of the new place accorded the Irish in American society.

And it was a new journey. The struggle for acceptance, the self-segregation into ethnic ghettos, the obsession with economic security, became remnants of a world that existed only in bittersweet memory. As the Irish reached the pinnacle of political power at the zenith of the American Century, their lives were changing in ways that were almost as dramatic as the dispersal of their ancestors from Ireland to America. It was as though Irish Americans sensed that the century-long struggle was over, and that a new chapter in the narrative was about to begin.

Indeed, as this second Irish diaspora continued, their once formidable hyphen seemed on the

A promise fulfilled: John Kennedy, grandson of Famine immigrants, delivers his Inaugural Address in 1961. His brief presidency marked the end of one chapter in the Irish-American narrative, and the beginning of another.

verge of disappearing into the proverbial melting pot. Likewise, the Kennedys themselves became less distinctly Irish and more generically rich and famous. The family's princes and princesses took exotic spouses from other cultures and backgrounds. Scandal seeped through oak study doors. Just as theater critics saw the Tyrone family saga in *Long Day's Journey into Night* as a generic, though dark, tale about the human condition, the tragedies and triumphs of the Kennedy family became a genuine American fable. Joseph Kennedy Sr. 's dream had been realized—the man who once asked what it would take to be thought of as simply American got his answer posthumously. It took the triumph of power and the humanizing quality of tragedy, and finally an astonishing change in culture that blended the rich, the powerful, and the wealthy of all creeds, colors, and nationalities into an entirely new class that knows nothing of identity, geography, ethnicity, or even morality: the Great American Celebrity Class. As charter members of this group, by the 1980s the Kennedys finally had been stripped of ethnicity and accorded the transnational identity of celebrity.

They were not alone. The children of Irish-American success, from Mia Farrow (daughter of Maureen O'Sullivan) to Maureen Reagan (daughter of Ronald Reagan) to George Clooney (nephew of Rosemary Clooney), rarely are described or thought of as Irish-American. When surveys of successful, influential, and powerful Americans produced such names as Joan Gantz Cooney, founder of the Children's Television Workshop; Thomas Murphy, former chief executive officer of media giant Capital Cities/ABC; Daniel Tully, chairman of Merrill Lynch; and Mary Higgins Clark, author of best-sellers (whose $36 million book contract was a milestone of its own), few thought their ethnicity was worth mentioning or celebrating. For several years in the 1980s, three of the nine members of the Supreme Court had distinctly Irish-American names: William Brennan, Sandra Day O'Connor (the first woman), and Anthony Kennedy. Nobody, including the Irish, seemed to notice. For a time it seemed as though there really was a melting pot, and that Irish America had been broken down and then recast as something else, something not as threatening, not as foreign. Something American.

Entertainers, of course, always have had a way of transforming themselves into something other than Irish American. Edna Rae Gillooly became Ellen Burstyn. Carroll O'Connor, whose uncle published an Irish newspaper in New York, became television's everyday American male, successor to roles played by Jackie Gleason and Art Carney. Irene Dunne never played an Irish-American woman; her most famous role was as a Norwegian in *I Remember Mama*. On stage, screen, radio, and television and in print Irish Americans could adopt new identities, transforming themselves, through their art, into something unhyphenated, something simply human.

If actors and actresses and writers could hide behind new identities, the rich could likewise transcend the ethnic ghetto with manners and money. The Kennedys could go to the finishing school of Harvard. For the bulk of Irish America, however, the road to assimilation was a concrete gash through the old neighborhood that took them to vast tracts of look-alike homes, where identity was subsumed by a culture of conformity and middle-class respectability.

*

It is safe to say that politics is no longer important in the way it once was for the Irish. If they remain

(continued on page 236)

HELENA MULKERNS

THE NEW IRISH CHIC: THE IRISH ARTS SCENE

Helena Mulkerns is an Irish-born writer living in New York City.

Although nobody could refer to the already established Irish-American community as the "old Irish," the term "New Irish" did seem the obvious one for the streams of us who made our way over here from the early to mid-eighties onward. We needed to distinguish ourselves from the established community, especially from an artistic point of view. We often arrived reluctantly, and illegally, with an unspoken sense of disillusionment that we were here at all, all of which made us determined to succeed here without forgoing or compromising our own cultural identity.

We undoubtedly took on America with the same old dreams that fired immigrants for centuries, but we were also the first generation to be so demographically varied. Architects, actors, artists, writers, lawyers, musicians, and engineers arrived in droves, university degrees at the ready, complementing immigrants with more traditional professions—carpenter, accountant, barman. This has produced a community that includes a healthy mix of both artists and patrons which, fifteen years after the first New Irish arrivals, is just now finding its feet.

This strong New Irish sense of identity is in part related to the fact of being the wetbacks in the New World while being dismissed as "the ones who got away" in our homeland. But it also has a lot to do with the blossoming of Irish arts in a general sense. Since the late eighties, a stronger image of Ireland has emerged, one that has saved the new immigrant from conforming to the old "tears in my beer" stereotype that prevailed of yore. It simply is not possible for Ireland to fade into a sentimental memory these days, because its culture has become a vibrant, respected international force, just a short plane ride away. In film, music, letters, theater, poetry, and fine art, the strength and originality of a culture long suppressed by the colonial process and the influence of the Roman Catholic Church has finally emerged through a powerful metamorphosis in the international arena. Ireland has finally established a postcolonial identity, which has inspired the New Irish community with the confidence to create their own output in America, in almost every art form there is.

New Irish artists do reflect, as with any exiled group, the loneliness of exile and separation from home and family, but they also—importantly—embrace and absorb the influence of the new, and do so with an increasingly balanced confidence. This duality of the new immigrant can be seen particularly well in literature, a medium that has traditionally shunned the theme of immigration. In 1993, writer and publisher Dermot Bolger edited *Ireland in Exile*, which was in effect Ireland's first self-avowed immigrant anthology. The stories and poems from U.S.-based writers and poets Eamonn Wall, Aidan Hynes, Sara Berkeley, and Colum McCann helped give a voice to the New Irish. In his review of *Ireland in Exile*, Frank McCourt suggested that the silence previously observed in Irish literature on the subject of immigration was now broken.

In film, the New Irish experience is perhaps best depicted in Myles Connell's 1992 short, *In Uncle Robert's*

Footsteps, a poignant, funny take on the coming-to-America theme, while *Fishing the Sloe-Black River* (1995), based on Colum McCann's book of the same name, delivered a moving allegory about parents left at home in youthless Irish towns.

In theater, works such as Tony Kavanagh's *Down the Flats* and Janet Noble's *Away Alone*, both written and first performed in the United States, have explored the immigration theme with great success. Both plays enjoyed several popular runs in New York and Los Angeles. Irish theater groups generally have been a particularly vibrant and busy part of the New Irish arts community, from coast to coast. In New York alone, the Irish Repertory Theater, the Irish Arts Center, Dædalus Theatre Company, the Irish Bronx Theater, Macalla, and other smaller companies are finding new and expanded audiences for the influx of New Irish talent.

While theater necessitates a venue, it is interesting to note that as the Irish moved into different neighborhoods in America, their respective cultural focus points have not, as was the tradition with previous generations, been tied strictly to a parish or to official "centers," but have gravitated more toward strictly unofficial cultural spots, such as cafés or bars. This may not be completely without precedent, but it is one of the primary ways in which the New Irish are forming contacts and building up arts networks across the country, whether in Boston, Philadelphia, Los Angeles, or New Orleans. In New York, there simply would be no New Irish arts scene without venues like Sin-é Café, Tramps, Paddy Reilly's, Anseo, Rocky Sullivan's, An Béal Bocht in the Bronx, and others.

Sin-é Café on Saint Mark's Place in New York's East Village was a critical catalyst for the New Irish community in downtown Manhattan and the New York area. As it became a showcase for many breaking acts visiting from Ireland, Sin-é's glamour

Roddy Doyle, author of the Dublin Trilogy (*The Commitments, The Snapper,* and *The Van*), reads from his work at Rocky Sullivan's, an Irish saloon and literary hangout on Lexington Avenue in Manhattan.

grew, especially when people like Bono or Sinéad O'Connor would drop by unannounced. At the other end of New York City, deep in the Bronx, the café An Béal Bocht has provided a similar focus point for the arts. There, live music can be heard several nights a week, and literary readings are frequent. Paddy Reilly's bar became the mecca for much New Irish music, fostering not only Black 47 but outfits such as Paddy-A-Go-Go and musicians such as Seamus Egan, John Doyle, Eileen Ivers, and Joanie Madden. Tramps, an eclectic blues establishment on Twenty-first Street, opened its doors to young Irish bands, featuring acts as diverse as Shane McGowan, the Saw Doctors, and Eleanor McEvoy.

In a more classical vein, Ireland House in Greenwich Village opened in 1992 with a view to "creating a bridge between two worlds, old and new." The impressive premises, financed by Lewis L. and Loretta Brennan Glucksman, has played host to such writers as John Banville, Nuala Ní Dhomhnaill, Roddy Doyle, Eavan Boland, John Montague, Paul Muldoon, Eoin MacNamee, and many others. It also provides classes in the Irish language, hosts a film festival, and runs special lecture series.

Elsewhere across the United States, similar developments have been taking place. While fledgling theater groups, writers, or musicians can be found in most cities working on their own agendas or playing local venues, frequently New Irish arts activities are galvanized by an arts group into some kind of large annual event, which provides a platform for younger artists and a focal point for further artistic developments. Such is the case on the West Coast, for example, with the annual Celtic Arts Festival in San Francisco. This is organized by the Irish Arts Foundation, which was founded in 1985 "to foster top quality art and culture from Ireland." In 1990, they kicked off the big festival, which takes in the whole range of Irish arts from music to theater, readings, crafts, and fine art, and packs a large convention center. New Irish and Irish artists in all fields are featured, with big names heading the bill from both sides of the Atlantic.

On the East Coast, Boston's New Irish scene is hopping, centered around a whole cluster of venues that have sprung up over the last few years. As with other cities, music and theater are often very much part of a bar-restaurant's agenda. Festival-wise, since 1994, Pedro Smyth and John Flaherty of The Druid in Cambridge have presented the Cambridge Celtic Music and Arts Festival each October, which offers, as in San Francisco, a varied selection of music, theater, readings, fine arts, and crafts. In 1996, they drew more than twelve thousand people to the event. Philadelphia's nascent community boasts its own traditional Irish music festival each September, as well as an annual festival of Irish film organized by John Buckley, who is currently planning for a larger festival of Irish arts to celebrate the millennium.

The artistic bonding that is vital for the Irish culture in America is coming slowly, with the younger Irish realizing the power and potential of support from the established Irish Americans, who are, on the other hand, beginning to accept the "New Ireland." With Irish Oscars, a coveted Booker Prize, the Nobel Prize for poetry, the Pulitzer for biography, and so on, there is an awakened sense of identity for Irish Americans. As the New Irish arts scene reinforces and renews this new cultural identity, its activities are not only worthy of examination but support. ❖

The faces of Bono, Sinéad O'Connor, and Van Morrison are as recognizable as any figures in popular music; Delores Riordan (far lower right), of the Cranberries, may soon be. And such perfomers as the virtuoso fiddlers Kevin Burke (below) and Eileen Ivers (bottom panel) keep close proximity to the traditional sources of Irish music. Global popular culture has helped transform old ideas of identity—U2 is as accessible in America as it is in Ireland.

somewhat overrepresented in the field, it is a cultural time lag that very likely will disappear in a few years. The Irish, after all, saw politics as the most accessible means to an end, not necessarily as an end itself. And the end is, indeed, near.

Politics has broken down barriers to new professions, places the Irish rarely saw fifty years ago. Even in medicine, in the past hardly an Irish domain, the Irish are making their mark: One of the nation's most prominent psychiatrists is Dr. Paul McHugh of Johns Hopkins University, and New York's Dr. Kevin Cahill, president-general of the American Irish Historical Society, is a leading expert on tropical diseases.

The suburbs, the sense of accomplishment, and the fading of once conspicuous Irish institutions like the clubhouse and the precinct would seem to have ratified the end of Irish America's hyphenated experience. In his essay on the Irish in *Beyond the Melting Pot*, Daniel Patrick Moynihan, writing in the 1960s, noted that once proud Irish institutions were falling into disrepair, among them the prestigious American Irish Historical Society on Fifth Avenue in New York. Moynihan, who would one day be honored by that very society at a grand reception in the Waldorf-Astoria, saw in the 1960s only a shell, with an unused library and a collection of Irish-American trophies nobody wanted to see anymore.

However, as early as 1980, the sociologist and author Father Andrew Greeley was combing through his data on Irish Catholics and discovering trends that led him to a bold prediction: There soon would be, he wrote, an explosion of Irish-American culture, led by a new intelligentsia that supposedly had been scrubbed clean of ethnicity. "There almost certainly will be a return to higher levels of self-conscious Irish identification," Father Greeley wrote in 1981.

Such a notion ran counter to prevailing notions of what Irish America had become—a group content to display its heritage once a year, a domesticated, Americanized, home-owning constituency that gladly left behind the traditions of an old world for the promise of a new world. Gone were the resentments handed down through generations like heirlooms. Those who remained anything more than once-a-year Irish Americans were like the Famine victims left behind in County Mayo. Time and circumstance had left them behind, prisoners of a culture that no longer existed. It was one thing to root for Notre Dame every Saturday in the fall and wear a green tie on Saint Patrick's Day. It was quite another to, say, patronize a local Irish theater group, attend a lecture on Irish history sponsored by some dusty old society, or buy a CD featuring some obscure traditional music group. Such activities were reserved for the "professional Irishmen."

Some fifteen years after Father Greeley predicted an Irish resurgence, news outlets across the country were proclaiming, seemingly out of nowhere, that Irish America was in the midst of a surprising and inexplicable (or so it seemed to some observers) resurgence in literature, the performing arts, movies, dance, song—nearly every aspect of American life save politics, which success and affluence had rendered almost superfluous, at least as a stepping stone.

✻

In 1997, the best-seller list of the *New York Times* reflected the growing Irish chic: A memoir by retired schoolteacher Frank McCourt zoomed to the top of the list and seemed destined to stay there forever. *Angela's Ashes* told the story of an Irish childhood, a story made bearable only because we know that, in the end, young Frank turned out all right. Its success demonstrated the power of storytelling and superb writing—qualitites that some book lovers feared were disappearing from American culture.

McCourt's book was but one manifestation of a cultural phenomenon that seemed to take everyone save Father Greeley by surprise. *Riverdance* and *Lord of the Dance* have been spectacular, indeed astounding, successes. In a lovely irony, two Irish Americans, Jean Butler and Michael Flatley, created the craze in Irish step-dancing, an art form that had been relegated, in Ireland as well as in America, to demure festivals and obscure competitions.

Something, it is clear, is going on. Irish movies are all the rage, often touching on subjects that seemed off-limits for years—miscarriages of justice in Northern Ireland and Ireland's freedom struggle in the early twentieth century. Terry George, an immigrant from Northern Ireland who spent years developing his craft in the Irish-American subculture, has emerged as a recognized Hollywood director and screenwriter, and Edward Burns brought the Irish-American suburban experience to the screen. Thomas Cahill, who was in charge of religious books at the publishing house of Doubleday, wrote a few hundred pages about Saint Patrick, Saint Bridget, and the monks who copied great Western masterpieces during the Dark Ages. He called the book *How the Irish Saved Civilization*. It was on the paperback best-seller list for more than a year.

An Irish-American woman, Anna Quindlen, became the voice of a generation of American feminists; she was succeeded on the op-ed page of the *New York Times* by another Irish-American woman, Maureen Dowd, who sets the standard for a new generation of political writers. Both women have inspired an industry of imitators, not unlike their older, male counterparts such as Jimmy Breslin and the *Boston Globe's* Mike Barnacle. Irish-American journalism itself has spawned an old-fashioned newspaper war between the two New York–based, nationally circulated Irish weeklies, the *Irish Voice*, founded during the early years of the Irish resurgence, and an older but revitalized *Irish Echo*. The magazine rack offered two new titles: *Irish America* magazine and *World of Hibernia*, a quarterly with *Vanity Fair*–style slickness and an overlay of material achievement.

Meanwhile, traditional Irish music—which generations ago helped spawn the distinctly American form known as bluegrass—is enjoying

THE FIFTH PROVINCE

Meeting in a cafe, we shun the cliche of a pub.
Your sometime Jackeen accent is decaffed
like our coffee, insisting you're still a Dub.
You kid about being half & halfed.
The people populating your dreams are now
American, though the country they're set in
is always the Ireland within a soft Dublin.

In the country of sleep the voiceless citizens
trapped in my regime of dreams are Irish,
but they're all the unlikely green denizens
of an island that's as mysterious
as the volcano, bird or sheep islands
that Brendan with his homesick crew,
bound for the Promised Land, bumped into.

Last night I combed sleep's shore for its name.
A familiar adze-crowned man appeared
waving his crook's question mark, nursing a flame
on a hill and impatiently declaring in weird
pidgin Irish that the fifth province is
not Meath or the Hy Brasil of the mind.
It is this island where all exiles naturally land.

—GREG DELANTY

Seamus Heaney: A Derryman, lately of Dublin, of Oxford, and of Cambridge, Massachusetts, won the Nobel Prize for Literature in 1996. "Sheer, bloody genius," he says, accounts for the recent popularity of things Irish.

such a surge of interest. The music for *Riverdance*, filled with jigs and reels, won a Grammy in 1997, edging out the music for the cultural elite's favorite play, *Rent*. Groups such as Cherish the Ladies, an all-female traditional group featuring the renowned flutist Joannie Madden, appear regularly on public television and in concerts across America.

How to explain how Irish dancing became glamorous, how tales of Saint Patrick and the McCourt family (rarely discussed in the same sentence) became must-reads across America, how Irish-American women in music, film, and journalism became role models for a generation? Seamus Heaney, the Irish Nobel laureate who periodically teaches at Harvard University, supplied the answer. "Sheer, bloody genius!" he told a reporter.

No doubt. But clearly the Irish seized upon a movement that in part owes its roots to, well, *Roots*, Alex Haley's epic drama of an African-American family. Haley's book and the television miniseries that followed inspired a generation of Americans of all backgrounds and ethnicities to ask questions that they had never asked before, to seek answers that they never thought mattered. When, in the late 1980s and early 1990s, academics and politicians began talking about cultural pluralism and multiculturalism, the Irish were well positioned to take them at their word. Dozens of colleges and universities, from Loyola University in Chicago to Stonehill College in Massachusetts to the University of California at Los Angeles to the University of Notre Dame, offer Irish studies programs or courses in Irish studies. In the early 1990s, New York University established an Irish studies program based

(continued on page 242)

TERRY GEORGE

CRICKET IT AIN'T: AN IRISHMAN'S APPRECIATION OF BASEBALL

Terry George is a filmmaker from Northern Ireland who now lives in New York. His latest film is SOME MOTHER'S SON.

Until I came to America I was not a great fan of spectator sports. This was probably because I grew up in Belfast, where my choices were extremely limited. Watching soccer was dangerous, tribal, and sectarian, while Gaelic football and hurling branded you a nationalist in the eyes of the forces of law and order.

Rugby was for the Protestant middle classes. And then there was cricket. Well, cricket was for people with lily-white clothes and who had lily-white clothes friends in Belfast.

When I first came to America I associated the sight of a man hurling a small leather ball and another trying to hit it with that boring, snobbish, polite, lily-white game called cricket, the only sport in the world where the players break for tea. So I was, you might say, not favorably disposed to the game of baseball.

My first encounter with baseball took place in a New York bar. It was a warm summer afternoon. A friend was late, so I watched the afternoon broadcast to combat the loneliness that overcomes a solo drinker. Baseball seemed slow like cricket. It seemed to go on forever, like cricket. But there were small clues that something was different here. The players wore outlandishly colored clothes. Very American. In the tradition of those American tourists with their black-and-white-checked polyester pants and barn-door-size Bermuda shorts. My attention was captured. The guy with the bat swung it dangerously; the other guy threw the ball with the passion of a bogside rioter. And when they were waiting for the next terrifying exchange, both men looked as though they had taken to chewing a spare ball to exercise their jaws. Then the thrower spat! The batter spat! And the man behind him in the blazer and chest plate lifted up his mask and he spat! God Almighty, this wasn't cricket.

By the end of the game I was completely baffled. The batter's objective was obvious: to hit the ball out of the field. But what was the thrower aiming at? Why did all these numbers keep flashing on to the screen? And why was the drunk next to me talking like a nuclear physicist? "Well, eh, Mattingly has forty RBIs and he's batting three-oh-five, but today he's oh for four."

A few weeks later I got the chance to go to a game at Shea Stadium. On the subway ride to the stadium I conjured up memories of my other brushes with spectator sports. There was the soccer memory, where I was sandwiched somewhere in the middle of ten thousand screaming savages hell-bent on killing a crowd of equal size at the other end of the pitch. In the middle of this lunacy, a soccer game was in progress. My enjoyment of the game was somewhat tempered when the warriors around me began chanting "We're going to kick your f***** heads in." Then there was my Gaelic football memory, where I stood, freezing, at the edge of a wind-swept, rain-lashed cow field in the middle of rural Ireland as thirty brave men in shorts and T-shirts slid through cow pats and mud pools for the glory of their town or village.

It was a warm summer night when we reached Shea, so there was little chance of Gaelic football–induced pneumonia. But as the crowds poured from the subway I began to get that old soccer hooligan phobia, and the awesome size of Shea Stadium did nothing to alleviate it. We climbed to the third tier, where I was confronted by a strange and wonderful sight.

There were seats. Seats everywhere. Better still, people were sitting in them; ordinary people, not skinhead armies but groups of friends, couples, even families with young kids kitted out in their team colors. An attendant showed me to the seat. He wiped it!

That night Shea seemed to buzz with good-humored expectation. It felt like some sort of giant outdoor cinema before a good movie.

Vendors passed by selling food, soft drinks, and beer. Beer! Are they crazy? I thought. Okay, the atmosphere was very laid-back, but this was really pushing it. Selling beer at a soccer match was the equivalent of burning the Stars and Stripes at West Point.

As the sun set, my friend Johnny Hamill and I sipped our plastic containers of Bud as he explained the rudiments of the game while the loudspeakers belted out Springsteen's "Born in the USA." "The pitcher has to get the ball past the batter, but it must be inside the strike zone," he explained. "Who decides if it's in?" I asked. "The umpire." "But there's no proof," I said. "The ball doesn't knock anything down. It doesn't stay in any net."

"The umpire decides," Hamill declared matter-of-factly. What an awful job, I thought. Could you imagine a referee having to make such a call in a soccer match? "Sorry, England, that ball was just wide of the imaginary goal area." You could bury the remains of the poor man in a cigarette box.

✻

As the game progressed and the lights of Queens twinkled in the distance, I learned about double plays, earned run averages, about stealing a base. I watched Mookie Wilson hit a home run into the stands, watched the ball disappear into a forest of outstretched arms. In the middle of the seventh inning we all stood up and sang, not about illegitimate referees and the sexual preferences of their parents but about peanuts and Cracker Jack and taking me out to the ballpark. Sure I saw a couple of drunks get obstreperous, but I'd seen worse on a Sunday morning in my native town when the bars were supposed to be closed.

Johnny Hamill explained how his father, Billy, a Belfast émigré, had grown to love baseball. Irish immigration and baseball grew up together, he said. The history of the game was woven with great Irish names; John McGraw, Connie Mack, the accursed Walter O'Malley who took the Dodgers from Brooklyn.

The Mets won in the ninth and as I watched the fans—couples, families, friends—leave the stadium, I realized that baseball was not about tribal warfare or about sport as penance; it was about entertainment. People went to a ball game to enjoy themselves. I had certainly enjoyed myself.

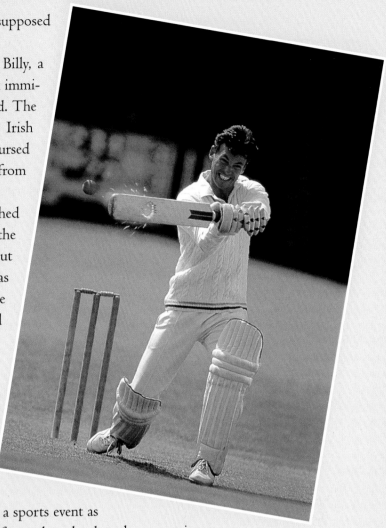

*

As I began to follow the game, I learned more about hit-and-run, curve balls, and balks. Back then I liked the Mets because they were underdogs and the Irish always side with the underdog. In 1986, the Mets took me through a World Series that was as exciting a sports event as I ever saw. I was a complete convert. I looked forward to the day when some ignorant Irish visitor would make the mistake of mentioning baseball and cricket in the same breath.

Recently, my brother-in-law arrived on a visit. We stopped in my neighborhood bar for a celebration drink. The Yankee game on the TV caught his eye. The moment when I could prove I was truly American had finally arrived. He turned away from the game, looking puzzled, and said to me: "Can you believe the Yanks signed Strawberry?" My jaw almost hit the bar. "CNN," he declared. "Cable TV. We get it all back in Dundalk. Can we get tickets?"

Take me out to the ballgame—in Dundalk? Never! ❖

in the newly created Glucksman Ireland House, named for patrons who represented the new stage of the American immigrant experience—Loretta Brennan Glucksman, an Irish American, and her banker-husband, Louis Glucksman, the descendant of Jewish immigrants. And the headquarters of the American Irish Historical Society has been restored, in appearance as well as in vitality.

✻

Far from the parish walls of yore, years removed from the protective embrace of machine politicians, the Irish have done what few would have expected thirty years ago—they have rediscovered their story. Some have argued that, as in Ireland itself, the secularization of society and the diminishing hold of the Church have helped inspire the Irish-American cultural renaissance. Blessed with so much of what America promised, what past generations dreamed about and strived for, the Irish no longer defer to their traditional protectors and authority figures—politicians and clergy. The experience has been liberating, though not without pitfalls, for who can deny that the parish and the precinct were more orderly, or at least seemed that way, in the cities that once were so conspicuously Irish.

The spurt of creativity is a sign, too, that traditional Irish insecurity—culturally, economically, and otherwise—has given way to a more creative spirit. You don't, after all, set out to become a champion Irish dancer if you are obsessed with security of any sort, and yet that is exactly what Jean Butler and Michael Flatley did, and what countless other musicians, artists, writers, actors, and others are doing, 150 years after the first Famine immigrants began arriving on American shores. And you don't enter the cockpits of American capitalism, whether in a law firm in Los Angeles or Chicago, or a brokerage house in Boston or New York, believing that you are set for life, that the clock has begun ticking toward that fine day when you're eligible for your pension.

Very much a part of this new Irish scene are the true new Irish, the immigrants of the 1980s who came to these shores without papers (as the Famine immigrants did) but were determined to carve out a life that seemed beyond their reach in Ireland. Though measured in thousands rather than millions, these young Irish immediately established themselves as something new and quite different from the most immediate immigrant wave of the 1950s. These new Irish were well-educated and worldly, many of them eager to embrace their cultural roots (many young Irish have Gaelicized their names) even as they moved away from the overweening influence of the Church. Their music was rock and roll, but often with a distinctly Irish tone. Some of these new Irish aggressively challenged mainstream Irish-American ideas of identity and culture. Gay and lesbian organizations demanded, unsuccessfully, to be included in Saint Patrick's Day parades in New York and Boston.

The adolescents that Father Greeley rightly predicted would rediscover their Irish roots are adults now, old enough to have children of their own. The cultural resurgence found a voice in the fiction of novelist Michael Collins and an artistic expression in the feet of Michael Flatley—both products of Father Greeley's Chicago. They and millions of their peers have no memory of John Kennedy's election. They were born after the migration to suburbia, after the collapse of the machine and the transformation of the parish. The old world of the urban ghetto, populated with ward heelers and cops and monsignors, welded together by a sense of grievance, a distrust of "others" (whether they be of a different race, a different religion, or, on occasion, a different county) and an ever pre-

(continued on page 247)

GREG DELANTY

THE POETRY OF IMMIGRATION

Greg Delanty, born in County Cork, is the author of AMERICAN WAKE, SOUTHWARDS, *and other books of poems. He lives in Vermont.*

The late Brian Coffey, seen with his wife, Bridget, and Irish President Mary Robinson, in 1991. Coffey was perhaps the earliest Irish poet to come to America and reflect significantly upon the immigration experience.

Yet we must leave America,
bitter necessity no monopoly
of Irish soil.
It was pain once to come,
it is pain now to go.
—FROM "MISSOURI SEQUENCE"

Since emigration is such a profound part of the Irish historical psyche, it is no wonder that occasionally it has been a topic of poetry, especially contemporary poetry. The late Sean Dunne and Thomas McCarthy (both born in Ireland in the 1950s) used emigration as a theme to write about ways of life and events in present-day Ireland, including the reality that many must still leave in order to find work and live sustainable lives. In "Refugees at Cobh," Dunne notes the irony of seeing foreigners dock in the port where thousands of his own people left the country. "So strange," he writes, "to see emigrants to Ireland / Huddled near posters telling us to leave / The broken farms for New York streets." In "Letter from Ireland," Dunne explains how such constant "going" evokes a "country dying." Likewise, Thomas McCarthy equates emigration with death.

Today, many Irish poets live and work in the United States, and several of them speak to their immigrant status in their poems. Among them, Gerard Donovan (left), who teaches on Long Island; and Eamonn Wall, who calls Nebraska home. Eavan Boland (opposite), perhaps the most prominent woman Irish poet, lives in a suburb of Dublin, and writes of her own immigration from the city-centered, male-dominated Irish poetic tradition toward a new territory in her remarkable memoir, *Object Lessons: The Life of the Woman and the Poet in Our Time.*

In "November in Boston," the speaker is overcome by feelings of displacement though he visits a city with a legendary Irish presence. As he crosses streets named "Lismore" and "Waterford," he remarks how "special" he is made to feel, as if he were "resurrected" from an "island grave." The poem evidences a feeling of loneliness in an environment of long-established familiarity.

Inasmuch as such work bears witness to those who actually left Ireland, what is even more curious is the virtual absence, until recently, of poetry written by the Irish who actually immigrated. Although Eavan Boland, John Montague, Eamon Grennan, and Derek Mahon have written poems that explore the experience of displacement, they tend to be from the point of view of someone who has stayed in Ireland rather than moved from the country; that is, they tend to be about *emigration*—the going from somewhere, rather than *immigration*—a coming to somewhere. Such poets have not perceived themselves as *immigrants*.

In contrast, Brian Coffey is perhaps the first Irish poet who adopted the perspective of someone who has arrived in America. After a stint in London, where he worked as a teacher, Coffey moved to Saint Louis in 1947, where he taught philosophy until 1952. This period is evoked in a lengthy poem called "Missouri Sequence" in which the poet, among other things, compares and contrasts life in the United States with life in Ireland. Dividing the poem into four parts, one for each season, Coffey explores how his children grow American rather than Irish, how life revolves around a river rather than an ocean, how German and Bohemian accents are heard along with Irish "bloss," how the climate makes dramatic shifts rather than remaining more stable.

Amid scenes describing day-to-day life in Saint Louis, Coffey also gives voice to the more complex nature of an immigrant's existence. The speaker notes that, having left Ireland, Ireland becomes a place of dreams, "the fictive form of heaven on earth." Notions of what it means to "come" and "go" also become more ambiguous. The speaker even worries about where he will die. Unlike Boland, Dunne, McCarthy, and others,

Coffey describes the act of leaving as well as the impact of settling somewhere else, the effect of which seems profound and life altering.

The hiring of full-time writers in American universities has enabled more Irish poets to follow Coffey's lead and take up residence in the United States. I teach at Saint Michael's College in Vermont, and there is no lack of fellow Irish poets stateside: Eamonn Wall is at Creighton University; Gerard Donovan is at Suffolk Community College in New York; Nuala Archer is at Cleveland State. We have been allowed to get inside American life rather than to view it as an outsider looking in.

Unlike in Coffey's generation, Irish poets are, for the first time, well represented among the body of Irish citizenry that has left Ireland. As a result the immigrant experience is being articulated in firsthand accounts and by more than a single voice, which lends it a diverse quality. Because we are often at the mercy of academic openings, wherever they may be, we are not finding ourselves working the same turf and the same Irish enclaves but are collectively finding all of America.

Despite the changes since Coffey's generation, there are also similarities that give unity to Irish poetry of immigration. For instance, there is the tension provoked by the simultaneous pain of memory and the desire to re-create life in Ireland. Though distance is often evoked through loss, there is a timelessness to memory that makes it remarkably alive. Coffey wrote of the cemetery near his home in Saint Louis "filled with Irish graves" and of a local priest who speaks as he did the day he left Cork. Such details impart the way that change unnerves us, but within a context of permanence.

In the same way, Gerard Donovan's "Letter from America" worries about the time that is passing but in a space that remains the same because of the act of recollection. He writes:

> *You are probably sitting on the porch,*
> *watching the wind strip the cherry tree down*
> *to a shock of bright pink against the house,*
> *like a child's face sleeping.*
> *It's a time when fall still insists:*
> *the air is damp and restless,*
> *it strips the vision clean. You may be slumped in dream,*
> *with a newspaper thrown on your lap,*
> *full of the afternoon, the relentless*
> *slant away of absent children's steps.*
> *That cloud, hanging to each side,*
> *is raining somewhere else.*
> *All of us have left home now.*

In addition to feelings of loss and longing, perhaps the most confounding emotion that one experiences as an immigrant is the sensation that is provoked by the labeling that comes from leaving one's indigenous culture. Throughout history, the act of naming has functioned as a means to position people amid particular social hierarchies. The modern-day ability, however, to occasionally travel back to one's homeland has made one's "place" a complex and transitory state. In fact, we are literally labeled one thing by the people we left—*emigrant*—and another by the people we joined—*immigrant*. For the Irish, such a state of transient existence might be called the "fifth province," that lost province in Ireland—not Muenster, not Leinster, not Ulster, not Connaught—whose actual whereabouts are a mystery.

Living in a perpetual condition of flux, caused by an inability to be one thing or another with any certainty, also creates a desire to be free from being called anything. Nuala Archer's poem "The Lost Glove Is Happy" intimates the constrictions of labels as well as the liberation experienced when they are cast off. The poem is framed around a pair of lost gloves "worn in Ireland. / Gloves that kept my fingers / warm walking the bitter cold / coastline of Bull Island / with Howth and her necklace / of lights in the background." In the midst of a journey to her mother in Lubbock, Texas, the speaker realizes she has left her gloves behind her in the airport terminal. She then explains why she does not regret the loss:

> *[. . .] My mother had me*
> *fly to Lubbock and on the way*
> *I lost my rabbit-*
> *fur-lined gloves. When I got*
> *there, when I arrived, when*
> *I reached desolation, my mother*
> *alone, in the middle of crazy*
> *cottonfields, my mother in*
> *desolation, I reached her,*
> *I travelled to her,*
> *to desolation, and in desolation*
> *we were as lost as any*
> *two mismatched gloves and*
> *for a few moments we relaxed, lost*
> *and strangely happy,*
> *in the Lubbock Mall, without*
> *labels, stripped to our bones.*

Archer not only frees the speaker from labels, but because she is traveling to Texas, a location seldom associated with Ireland, she also figures her life as something that becomes unfettered by the mythology of being an Irish "immigrant" or "emigrant." Instead, the speaker is liberated to be herself—perhaps an enviable position that all immigrants long to experience. ❖

sent fear that the world would, in fact, break your heart—these are relics of an unknowable age.

Their parents were the most assimilated, most mainstream generation of Irish Americans, raised in the shadow of the twilight struggle with Communism and the aftermath of the Anglo-American victory in the epic struggle of the Second World War. In their formative years, consumerism replaced tradition; conformity suppressed differences, and newly blazed career paths offered a glimpse of the life their ancestors had wished for so many years ago. When a new round of troubles broke out in British-ruled Northern Ireland in the 1960s, only the holdouts, those left behind when the new emigrants set out in station wagons for a new world, seemed to notice, or, indeed, seemed to think it was any of their business.

Their children, however, are growing up in a society that has instructed them to embrace what makes them different, to proclaim their separateness and to wear their hyphens on their sleeves. In late twentieth-century America, it is not only acceptable to proclaim Irish roots, it is downright cool. And it just might be that these young people, raised in a self-consciously multicultural America, have more in common with their contemporaries from Ireland than they do with their native-born parents, who sought the seemingly homogenous refuge of suburbia and who were raised on a cold-war diet of pure Americanism. These young Irish immigrants and Irish-American suburbanites grew up listening to the same music (thanks to the global marketplace of pop culture), share many of the same cultural milestones, and have come to adulthood in a world where seemingly everything that came before has been relegated to the culturally prehistoric. On the eve of the new millennium, of a new chapter in the centuries-old narrative, the Irish in America and in Ireland have been described, tellingly, as post-Catholic. They may fulfill their Sunday obligation in greater numbers than Italian Catholics, Scottish Presbyterians, and Anglo-American Episcopalians, and they still may be more likely to send their children to parish schools (though their enthusiasm has waned as their property taxes have gone up), but clearly the Church that was for some a cultural rock and for others a creative millstone no longer serves as the focal point of identity, however much it still offers spiritual nourishment.

Religious differences among the Irish are, of course, a holdover of Ireland's colonial past. It is the conqueror's construct, so powerful

THE FAMINE ROAD, 1847–1997

Long agonies of the road
stumbled down, shades
of emigrants stain
the asphalt with their blood.

Between the weeds
where people've come
for years now, one
like yourself treads

and sees his shoes
wrapped in rope.
The tangled slope
is brutal, the news

from home silent
as a grave. Inside
the marcher his days
unformed lie in

fallow, still awaiting word
that love has won,
the world become
safe for hunger's urge.

—MICHAEL COFFEY

The many shades of green: Different aspects of the Irish-American experience are evident in a culture that operates at several levels of assimilation. While gay Irish men and women declare their sexual politics at a St. Patrick's Day parade, an older generation catches a last turn on the dance floor at a Cork Association Dance in Queens; a group of mostly Buddhist students besport the St. Patrick's colors at a school in lower Manhattan, while young Irish ladies freshen up for the annual New York Rose of Tralee event; and Irish pubs can be found cheek-by-jowl with Chinese restaurants wherever Americans gather.

THE IRISH IN AMERICA

that it leaped across the Atlantic and served to divide the Irish in America, too. Like any other institution, whether the urban machine to which the working classes and the poor flocked, or the corporations that saw in human sweat and misery an easy road to untold riches, the American Catholic Church, so undeniably Irish, had and has its flaws. Since the time of the Famine, however, it served—by request—not only as Irish America's spiritual home but as a badge of identity, a shelter during a storm of hostility. The Church educated, it nursed, it baptized and buried; it looked after the young and old, the poor in spirit and the poor in possessions; it defended the rights of working people to organize and agitate for their share of American prosperity. The Church's mistakes may have been many, its flaws may have embittered those whom it failed, but for the great mass of Irish Americans, the Catholic Church has done everything asked of it.

Affluence, assimilation, intermarriage, and secularization have frayed the bonds of old. For the young Irish, John Kennedy is an icon of pop culture, not politics, and Al Smith, Dagger John Hughes, and Mother Jones are but black-and-white pictures in a dusty textbook—if that. They would find it impossible to believe that during a long summer's week in New York in 1924, the Ku Klux Klan's contingent at the Democratic National Convention blocked Smith's first attempt to win his party's presidential nomination because he was Irish and Catholic.

The new Irish do not need the kind of Church the old Irish embraced; that Church, after all, was an immigrant Church, with a mission to serve the poor. While there are many poor Irish Americans still, the story of the Irish 150 years after the Famine is one of material success, of power quietly accumulated and influence broadly dispersed. But the institution that sped them on their way has transformed itself, too, and may well be Irish America's most enduring legacy to the immigrants and poor who now live in the old neighborhoods. In cities from east to west and many in between, the Catholic school system, that symbol of aggressive Irish Catholic separatism, serves a new generation of the urban poor. They are not Irish and indeed many are not even Catholic—the Saint Patrick's School on Manhattan's Lower East Side, once filled with the children and grandchildren of the Famine, now is filled with Asian students, 80 percent of whom are Buddhist. But the spirit and function of this once conspicuously Irish institution remain the same. And, in many cases, the Irish influence remains, as vital and important as ever: In late 1996, the Cristo Rey Jesuit High School opened in a predominantly Mexican and overwhelmingly poor neighborhood in Chicago, the Pilsen/Little Village. Cristo Rey is the first new Catholic high school in that city since the early 1960s. The school's president is a Jesuit priest named John Foley. Its principal is a Benedictine nun named Judith Murphy.

The parish walls are gone, and Irish America is scattered in suburbia. But the institution that so defined the Irish-American experience has not fled the place where it was born.

*

On the evening of March 17, 1994, more than four hundred Irish Americans assembled in the East Wing of the White House for what was, amazingly, the first-ever Saint Patrick's Day celebration in the Executive Mansion. Some hours before, the prime minister of the Irish Republic, Albert Reynolds, had presented President Bill Clinton with a bowl of shamrocks. Unlike the party, that ges-

ROY AND PATTY DISNEY
REPLANTING OUR ROOTS:
COOLMAIN CASTLE, COUNTY CORK

Roy Disney is vice-chairman of the Walt Disney Co.; Patty, his wife, is her own self entirely.

Since we came to an awareness of our Irishness from two entirely different directions, we thought a dialogue between us was the best way to explain how we came to be part-time Irish residents and full-time Irish Americans:

ROY: I was more or less halfway through my life before I began to be aware of my Irish heritage, although it didn't exactly come as a blinding revelation at that point—more like a slowly growing glimmer of recognition.

The subject of ethnic background, in my childhood at least, was sort of a nonsubject. As far as I knew, I was an American, like everyone else, and on those occasions when someone asked about our lineage, my mother always said something like, "Oh, well, we're mostly English and German, and a little French," which was fine with me. To my recollection, my dad never mentioned the subject at all, and it wasn't until many years later that I think I finally figured out why he didn't.

A couple of things happened when I was in my twenties that began to change my perceptions: in 1954, my uncle Walt was at work on a film called *Darby O'Gill and the Little People*, a film about as deliberately—and affectionately—Irish as it could be (except that much of it was shot in Burbank), and in 1955 I married Patty Dailey, who began my conversion.

PATTY: I didn't really even think about converting Roy. I was just more comfortable with my Irish roots. One reason was my father and his close friends, who talked about it a lot and taught me Irish songs and told Irish jokes. Also, many years later, I realized the influence the Irish priests and nuns had over me in my Catholic school education. My mother only spoke of her English and French New Orleans background.

ROY: Sometime in the sixties, the archivist at Disney put together a large and quite complex family tree for Walt and my dad, tracing their father's and mother's families back through some fifteen generations, all the way to the middle of the sixteenth century. Among other forebears, it turned out that I had an ancestor named Adam Loftus, who became first provost of Trinity College in 1609. And there was a George Moore, Lord of Drogheda, in 1712. And quite a few other names, all connected to Ireland.

But they were all British and Protestant, as Patty was quick to point out. Interlopers, basically, in her view.

PATTY: I didn't say interlopers. I think I said "persons of the Other Persuasion." As far as my family tree goes,

The Disneys at their Coolmain Castle in County Cork: Discovering the Irish within.

I found quite a few Irish on my mother's side, some with spelling changes, as in O'Keefe changed to Kiefe. My father was John William Dailey (although everyone called him Pete). He had dark hair, blue blue eyes, and was Irish to the bone, but I know only his parents' names and have no idea how or when—or why—they came to America. Dad used to say, "Don't ask. You don't want to know. Our people were probably just a bunch of horse thieves, and that's how they ended up here."

ROY: Then in 1981, Patty's brother, Peter Dailey, was appointed ambassador to Dublin, and naturally, we went to visit—our first trip to Ireland. We spent a week in Dublin, and another driving around the West. And fell in love. And even more, in some mysterious way, felt immediately at home. I particularly remember a misty day, driving past a forest on the shore of one of the Lakes of Killarney, stopping the car on a sudden impulse, and wandering through the ferns beneath the trees, completely convinced not only that little people existed but that this was the place we'd find them. We didn't, of course, but I still think we were awfully close that day.

PATTY: He was converted.

ROY: Whatever. Anyway, not long after that, we were in London and I was plugging one of our films on BBC radio. The interviewer, quite out of the blue, played a tape for me of an interview she'd done with Walt some years before in which he talked at some length about his Irish ancestry, and it rang a bell. Of course . . . all those movies—*Darby O'Gill*, *The Fighting Prince of Donegal*, *The Gnome-mobile*. Hmmmm . . . Maybe there was Irish in my family after all. Funny my dad never talked about it, though.

It came to me then why he hadn't. He came, after all, from a generation during which the American

Irish were very, very low on the social scale. Remember all those IRISH NEED NOT APPLY signs in old photos? It was probably just more convenient not to be Irish.

At any rate, no doubt it was easier not to be Irish if your name was Disney. Pretty hard to do with the name Dailey.

PATTY: Anyway, one thing after another happened. Our children were all grown up and married with families of their own, our parents were gone, so we said to each other, Why not? Why not find our own "Laughing Place"? So we decided to rent a large home somewhere in Ireland to spend the holidays with our children and grandchildren. Instead we bought a lovely old place with meadows that run down to the beautiful sea, which never looks the same.

And in the course of exploring this endlessly fascinating island, we found, out on the Sheep's Head Penninsula, a monument to the clan O'Daley.

ROY: In County Carlow there's an old graveyard with Disney gravestones dating back to 1712.

PATTY: We love the country and the lovely people here. We are mindful of our Irish roots but also mindful that we are not natives here, only guests. My brother pointed out once that many American Irish who visit here become very possessive of this country and its culture, quite forgetting that this is a European country, after all.

ROY: It's a very important thing to remember, we believe. It's really easy to come to this "Ireland of the Welcomes," and feel as if you're coming home. We don't know another country in the world where you're made to feel so at home. The temptation is to suddenly become "more Irish than the Irish," and worse, to leap to the conclusion that you know all about this country and its people and its very long and complex history. But you have only to follow the course of the peace process in the north for a while to begin to understand how much you don't know and, more important, to begin to realize that this is a history that you never participated in. It's sobering.

PATTY: In a way, also, we returning Irish Americans feel a little guilty. Guilty because our ancestors for one reason or another didn't stick it out and we wonder why. We will never know the answer to that.

I never cease to wonder how this lovely, rich, and rare land can seem so peaceful to the eye and ear and have such a tragic and bloody past. It's just one of the many contradictions here that we'll probably never really understand.

ROY: In our beautiful seaside meadow (a sugar-beet field when we purchased the property), we've planted literally thousands of hardwood trees, of types that once grew in abundance all over this island—oak, beech, ash, and elm. They will never mature in our lifetimes, or our children's, but we like to think of them as a kind of tribute to our ancestors, a replanting of our own roots back here, if you will, and we hope that one day our grandchildren and their grandchildren will benefit from their beauty. ❖

A rare photo of billionaire Irish-American Charles Feeney, who secretly gave away most of his nearly $4 billion fortune to help fund hospitals, universities and other groups. He reported his generosity only when forced to amidst negotiations for the sale of his string of duty-free airport shops.

ture was by no means precedent-shattering, for Irish prime ministers have been showering American presidents with Saint Patrick's Day shamrocks for years—it is a sign of the mutual affection between the two countries that Ireland's head of government annually spends Saint Patrick's Day not in Ireland's capital but in America's.

The White House celebration brought together Irish Americans from an assortment of walks of life, displaying the breathtaking diversity of a community that now claims 44 million members, half of them Protestant. The traditional professions of politics, journalism, and literature were well represented, but even within these fields, the richness and complexity of the new Irish-American experience was clear. Among the guests was Congressman Peter King, a conservative Republican from the suburbs of Long Island and one of America's staunchest supporters of a united Irish Republic.

It was the new Irish, however, who made the glittering affair a symbol of Irish-American achievement. Mutual of America's Bill Flynn and billionaire philanthrophist Charles Feeney, in the midst of trying to broker a peace process in war-torn Northern Ireland, represented a combination of Irish-American success and an attachment to Ireland that remained unbroken by affluence and assimilation. Other well-tailored men and women, their faces known only to corporate boards, brushed against Hollywood stars such as Paul Newman and Joanne Woodward. Don Keough, former CEO of Coca-Cola, later told journalist Conor O'Clery that as he surveyed the gathering of power and influence on this Saint Patrick's Day in the White House, he felt as though the Irish finally had arrived.

That, of course, was exactly how another generation felt in 1960 when John Kennedy was elected president. Then, the success and achievement was consciously Irish, celebrated as a group vindication. This time, the celebration and sense of arrival was understated, which made it a much more powerful statement of the new Irish place in America. There was no need to shout.

*

Three years after the White House party and the hopes, later dashed, that gunfire and explosions were part of Ireland's past, marchers in the biggest nonmilitary parade in the Western world paused for a moment as church bells chimed. The Saint Patrick's Day parade in New York on March 17, 1997, stopped in its tracks at noon to commemorate, in silence, the victims of the Irish Famine.

A century and a half after Black '47, the Irish in America had not forgotten. Assimilation had tempted them; new attitudes, which would have startled their grandparents, assured them of a place at the nation's tables of power and affluence. Why, so representative of America had the Irish become that Ross Perot in 1996 delivered without a scintilla of irony a line that long-dead generations would

Presidents Kennedy, Reagan, and Clinton made triumphant returns to Ireland, where each could claim ancestry. Over time, American interest in the resolution of the bloody conflict in Northern Ireland has increased.

have been delighted to hear. Complaining about the preponderance of Asians who had given money to the Clinton reelection campaign, Perot asked: "Wouldn't you like to have someone named O'Reilly out there hard at work for you?"

America late in the twentieth-century offered the Irish every reason to forget all that had come before. The last barriers had fallen; no center of power seemed beyond their reach. The road, it would have seemed, had reached its end. Instead, millions of Irish Americans were marking the 150th anniversary of the Famine with monuments, moments of silence, lectures, and an astonishing cultural revival and strong personal pride.

The hunger, it seems, has never really gone away.

TERRY GOLWAY

THE BRAIDED CORD: FAMILY TALES

Katie's arrival was not unexpected; still, her father found it remarkable that on such an occasion he would be reading Russell Baker's *Growing Up*, filled with characters who lived lives that today seem impossibly remote and distant. The book clearly was an appropriate selection for such an occasion as Katie's birth, but her father had come upon it completely by accident. Or was there, perhaps, an unseen hand at work? For surely there must be such an entity, with practiced fingers working feverishly while we mortals play our assigned roles in drama and tragedy, believing credulously that so much of life is coincidence and happenstance. Oh, yes, there is a hidden hand all right. For mere chance and coincidence, however powerful, could not have presented so precious a gift as Katie and, not long afterward, her brother Conor.

So as this tiny girl's childhood began, her father was immersed in Mr. Baker's youthful memories of a grandmother who held court nightly on a front porch, a mother who chased chickens in the backyard, and aunts and uncles who, with silent desperation, sought to wriggle free of the Great Depression's chokehold on their dreams. It is a world that we have relegated to the unimaginable and long-gone past, like tales of the Plymouth colony's travails, of the building of the Pyramids, or of Moses engaged in conversation with a burning bush.

Yet how distant could that time be, for Mr. Baker is with us still, charming us with his prose on the op-ed page of the *New York Times* and speaking to us about literature from the set of *Masterpiece Theater*. He is alive, he is vital, and his mother once chased chickens in a rural Virginia backyard.

"We all come from the past, and children ought to know what it was that went into their making, to know that life is a braided cord of humanity stretching up from time long ago, and that it cannot be defined from the span of a single journey from diaper to shroud," Mr. Baker wrote as he set out to explain to his own children, and to a million or so readers, how it was once upon a time.

For Katie and Conor, the braided cord begins in New York and stretches eastward across the Atlantic, where it becomes entwined with the tortured history of Ireland, which produced most of their ancestors, quite a few of whom could tell stories as rife with improbabilities as Mr. Baker's Virginia. Such accounts would blend almost seamlessly into tales of a New York that no longer exists, places of vanished villages and parishes where the music of Ireland mixed with the grit of urban America, where life was simpler and a good deal shorter. Such stories one day will seem to Katie and Conor as fantastic as Mr. Baker's stories about his back porch.

"Children rarely want to know who their parents were before they were parents, and when age finally stirs their curiosity, there is no parent left to tell them," Mr. Baker wrote. The same lack of interest, no doubt, applies to the lives of grandparents. In ten years, Katie and Conor will shrug their shoulders when they hear that their mother's Irish immigrant father landed in Normandy on D day. But fifty years from now, when leaders unborn celebrate the invasion's one hundredth anniversary, children will gather round Katie and Conor and gape in astonishment as they regale them with vague stories about their D day grandfather, a sailor whose landing craft ran aground after unloading a cargo of soldiers in the early morning hours of June 6, 1944.

From green card to assimilation and beyond: Neil Duggan, native of Ireland, with his daughter Eileen, born in the South Bronx, and his grandchildren Katie and Conor Golway, born in suburban New Jersey.

By then, they will understand what Thomas Flanagan meant when he wrote that we are all tenants of time.

Katie and Conor were born in the best of health, with blinking machines checking their pulse rate and a doctor observing every move they made while still awash in a churning sea of amniotic fluid. Timothy Duggan, their great-grandfather, the D day veteran's father, worked on the *Titanic* and could not have imagined a world of blinking machines in delivery rooms, for his head was bent against the harsh winds that were an Irishman's lot in the early twentieth century. Tim was a casual laborer born in County Galway who journeyed to the County Cork port of Cobh—at the time called, imperiously, Queenstown—in search of work. His journey then took him to the shipyards of Belfast, where the world's largest passenger ship was taking shape. So intense was the demand for labor in Belfast that even a Roman Catholic like Timothy Duggan could find work, however grudgingly dispensed, in that bastion of Protestant loyalism.

During his first day on the job, in the bowels of a great work-in-progress, he found himself reminded where he stood in the cultural pecking order. The exact words are lost to family history, but their meaning remains fresh in family legend. Politely put, it was suggested that a Catholic such as Timothy Duggan ought to think twice before reporting for work the following morning. He was quick to conclude that he was in some danger, and he hightailed it out of Belfast and returned home to Cobh, where his children, including the future D day sailor, were born.

More than fifty years later, Katie and Conor's mother found the old Duggan homestead—a drafty, two-story stone structure with a few small windows and a billowing chimney blowing smoke that curled toward the steeple of Saint Coleman's Cathedral. It was there, in a back room of a tiny house, with no doctors in attendance, that Katie and Conor's grandfather entered the world.

Eventually, Timothy Duggan made the journey that so many others had chosen, crossing the Atlantic in search of work. He left his wife, Ellen, and children behind in Cobh, thinking he would return to them and Ireland. But one day one of those children died, and Ellen buried her son Denis and packed up her children and left behind the land that held her child's grave. She never returned.

The immigrant family settled in the Yorkville section of Manhattan, living in a railroad flat with a tub in the kitchen, and in the evenings, Timothy Duggan scanned the obituary columns of his favorite newspapers, searching for news of newly deceased natives of County Cork. When destiny provided a corpse, Timothy would put on his only suit and march off to the wake. Nobody in the parish village made his or her last journey alone.

Such a world! There were no chickens in the backyard, but there was a tub in the kitchen. Katie and Conor will hear such stories soon and dismiss them as adult exaggeration, until the day comes when they reflect on the braided cord.

*

Oh, you can be sure they will hear these stories, and more. They will hear of a great-grandfather who sold Christmas trees in a saloon's parking lot on Staten Island to earn holiday pocket money, and another's mysterious young adulthood in an Ireland that was fighting for its freedom in 1920. They will hear tales of their grandmother and her sister walking miles from their apartment in Brooklyn to the shrine called Ebbets Field, saving the dime it would have cost to take the subway. They will hear about summer nights spent on fire escapes while the Third Avenue El rolled by, of twenty-five-cent picture shows in the Bronx, of bread lines forming on the streets of Manhattan, of machine-gun nests built on the shores of Staten Island to ward off a Nazi invasion. They will know, too, that their great-grandmothers grew up in a world where women could not vote and were consigned to the home regardless of ambition and talent.

Such stories will sound as distant and as unknowable as some tale from the Wild West. And yet, what lessons they teach, and what virtues they celebrate.

They will know of the secret held back from the second and third generations of another wave of Irish immigrants, the long-hidden story of the Famine, with its insights into those who wield power and those who have power inflicted upon them. They will learn, too, that as long as children are hungry someplace in the world, the Famine is a story without an ending.

Just as important, though, they will hear a story they may find to be as implausible as any of these, about a beautiful July day on which the two people they know best—two children of firefighters whose comfort and achievement were the product of generations of labor and sacrifice—were impossibly young-looking and dressed in the black and white of sacred tradition. On that day, they danced to a song called "What a Wonderful World," and they believed that nothing could be truly so wonderful as that glorious day.

A few years later, this young couple discovered how wrong they could be. The day arrived—it was June 22, 1994—when they both heard a cry as sweet as any human ear has ever heard. And they heard it again, just as sweet the second time, on November 1, 1995. Suddenly all was changed; there were two new and tiny braids on the cord, and the world was even more wonderful.

(Not long after they were born, Katherine Duggan Golway and Conor Duggan Golway were registered in the foreign births records of the Republic of Ireland. Seventy years after their maternal grandfather left Cobh, they became dual citizens of the Irish Republic and the United States of America.) ❖

MAEVE BINCHY

THE VIEW FROM DUBLIN

Maeve Binchy, a best-selling novelist, also writes a weekly column in the IRISH TIMES.
She lives in Dublin.

Ireland's president, Mary Robinson, kept a light shining in an upper window of her residence, a
beacon to remind those who have left Ireland to come home.

We were always ambiguous about emigrants in the 1950s. For one thing, they sent us
parcels and we both loved and hated those.

We loved the notion of plaid skirts and frilly blouses. But they often didn't fit. Our American
cousins were leaner than we were. And their "shorts" were a funny length, "neither one thing nor the
other," we who had never heard of Bermudas called them.

And though it was nice to have things that people at school didn't have, it was awful to have things that someone else had worn, and everyone knew they were from America because we just didn't have bright colors like that at home.

And I suppose we were envious of emigrants who had done well. Not a very attractive trait but it was there.

I remember we said, "When you think he didn't have a brain in his head and look at him now."

Or, "Would you look at the style of that one after four years in Boston, and her family came from half a door."

It was a begrudging wish that we too had gone, or that we had done as well somehow back home.

*

A full and generous acceptance of the risk taken, the loss and loneliness endured, and the sheer hard work put in, was never bubbling near the surface. We wanted to justify our position of having stayed where we were. It was hard to admit that we might have been better, more independently courageous people had we crossed the Atlantic like so many before us.

But then I speak as someone who didn't come from a long family of emigrants. My people were grocers and, later, lawyers. They found work among the slowly developing middle classes in Ireland. We were not dependent on an elder brother to take us out to Chicago, an uncle to make us a home in Seattle, a sister and her husband who needed someone to mind the little nephews and nieces in Maryland.

Many of my friends were in this category, though, and for them the whole emigrant story was a different one. They were part of it, it was a dream to share, and when they talked they made the rest of us restless.

*

I hated to hear of the girl who would go to her aunt and uncle who had no children in Virginia. She would go to a school where there were both boys and girls, unheard of for fifteen-year-olds in Irish towns. She would go to summer camp and learn skills. She would be all by herself and not have to share her toys and clothes with sisters and brothers like we all had to do. We were full of jealous rage and could scarcely bear to wish her bon voyage.

And since we were still very poor as a country in the fifties, it would be hard to expect us to rejoice at the wealth of the Returned Yanks, as the Irish who had gone to seek their fortune in the States were always disparagingly called. We mocked them when they said "swell" or "I guess . . . " Yet they didn't mock us for holding on to phrases they had outgrown. When they told us of six-lane highways, we didn't want to hear. It sounded as if they were belittling the lanes and borees of the country where they had grown up.

When they talked about the noise and the work ethic and the people from so many different lands we were not sensitive enough to listen for what might be loneliness, a trace of homesickness in the tone. Instead, we saw the proof that they had been right to go and we had been fools to stay.

But to my mind a lot of attitudes changed in the 1960s. It wasn't just our pop music and our hair-styles. Irish people started to travel more; the country was opened up to television and to less-rigid censorship. We actually could *see* what the rest of the world was doing. We didn't have to just sit in wonder and listen to the emigrants' tales.

And shortly after that we began to see ourselves not just as an island off an island off a land-mass but as part of Europe. I believe that the great peace between the jealous stay-at-home Irish and the often homesick Irish emigrant began once we Irish at home realized that we were Europeans.

We have taken to being European much more eagerly than have our neighbors in Britain. We embraced kilometers at once on the signposts; grams and kilograms in the supermarket; liters in the bar, the drink shops, the gas stations.

The competitive costs of air travel meant that our young people could travel and come back again. With the laws of the European Union, young Irish people have become accustomed to working down the road in German, Italian, or Greek cities as once they moved around their own small island. No longer is there a wake with people crying and saying good-bye when an Irish boy or girl leaves home. Everyone knows they will be back before you notice they are gone!

And now the very prosperity of Ireland means that we can admire and love the emigrant as the emigrant should always have been loved and admired. The emigrant is no longer a threat to us as a pointer to how we could have lived our own lives had we only been courageous enough.

Now we know that those people who go are going because they want to, not because their land cannot support them. We know they will bring something of us to the places they settle, not any more a series of grudges. Today, our young men and women don't arrive in America weighed down with a history that turned them into wanderers.

And because we can stay or we can go, the two choices each have their dignity.

Today, we can love the emigrant to America's shores and with generous hearts wish them further success, as it will reflect well on those they left behind but will come home regularly to see.

BIBLIOGRAPHY AND RECOMMENDED READING

✻

The published sources on the histories of Ireland and America and the exploits of those who immigrated are immense; the literature includes everything from broad surveys of the histories of the people to finely detailed disquisitions on the potato and on Irish musical traditions and their impact on bluegrass, not to mention the numerous novels, memoirs, and books of poems that attest, in varying degrees, to the experience of immigration.

What follows is meant as a guide to further reading as well as a bibliography of sources referred to directly or indirectly in this book.

CHAPTER 1: THE GREAT FAMINE

A good starting point for readers interested in details about the Famine and its aftermath is the monumental *Ireland Since the Famine* by F. S. L. Lyons (Oxford University Press, 1971). Also see *Ireland: A History* by Robert Kee (Weidenfeld & Nicholson, 1980), *The Famine Ships* by Edward Laxton (Bloomsbury, 1996), *Emigrants and Exiles* by Kerby Miller (Oxford University Press, 1985), *The End of Hidden Ireland* by Robert Scally (Oxford University Press, 1995), *The Great Hunger: Ireland 1845–1849* by Cecil Woodham-Smith (Penguin, 1962), and *Why Ireland Starved* by Joel Mokyr (Routledge, Chapman and Hall, 1985). A recent anthology of personal reflections on the legacy of the Famine is *Irish Hunger*, edited by Tom Hayden (Roberts Rhinehart, 1997), with contributions by Eavan Boland, Seamus Heaney, Gabriel Byrne, Terry Golway, Mary Robinson, and many others. Also see *This Great Calamity* by Christine Kineally (Gill & Macmillan, 1995). For an interesting fictional look at the rigors of crossing over during the Famine, see Andrea Barrett's National Book Award–winning novel *Ship Fever* (W.W. Norton & Co., 1996), set on Gross Isle in 1847.

Some general works that attempt to deal with various aspects of Irish-American interrelationships include *America and Ireland, 1776–1976*, edited by D. N. Doyle and O. D. Edwards (Greenwood, 1980) and *Irish Americans* by Marjorie R. Fallows (Prentice Hall, 1979). A fine statistical and analytical analysis can be found in *The Irish Americans* by Andrew Greeley (Warner, 1981). Also see *The Book of Irish America* by William D. Griffin (Times Books, 1990), *The Irish in America* by Carl Wittke (LSU Press, 1956), and *The Irish Diaspora in America* by Lawrence McCaffery (Catholic University Press, 1984).

CHAPTER 2: THE PARISH

Studies of the role of the Catholic Church in Irish America are for the most part anecdotal or regional. Significant works include *What Parish Are You From?* by Eileen McMahon (University Press of Kentucky, 1995), *The Life and Times of John England* (The America Press, 1927), "Going to the Ladies' Fair: Irish Catholics in New York City, 1870–1900," in *The New York Irish*, edited by Ronald H. Bayor and Timothy J. Meagher (Johns Hopkins University Press, 1996), *Eloquent Indian: The Life of James Bouchard* by John Bernard McGloin, S.J. (Stanford, 1949), *Old St. Peter's: The Mother Church of Catholic New York, 1785–1935* by Leo Raymond Ryan (U.S. Catholic Historical Society, 1935), *At the Crossroads: Old Saint Patrick's and the Chicago Irish*, edited by Ellen Skerrett (Loyola Press, 1997), *The Annals of San Francisco* by Frank Soul et al. (Lewis Osborne, 1966). Also see *Catholics in America*, edited by Robert Trisco (National Conference of Catholic Bishops, 1976), *The Life of Archbishop John Ireland* by James M. Moynihan (Harper & Brothers, 1953), *Father Coughlin and the New Deal* by Charles J. Tully (Syracuse University Press, 1965). For a portrait of the University of Notre Dame see *Domers: A Year at Notre Dame* by Kevin Coyne (Viking, 1995).

CHAPTER 3: THE PRECINCT

Politics are rife in the history of the Irish in America, and the literature is extensive, and includes studies of Irish nationalism, a movement that has often been afoot both in America and in Ireland. See *Irish-American Nationalism, 1870–90* by Thomas N. Brown (Greenwood, 1980), *Paddy and the Republic* by Dale T. Knobel (Wesleyan, 1986), *America and the Fight for Irish Freedom* by Charles Callan Tansill (Devin-Adair, 1957), *Recollections of an Irish Rebel* by John Devoy (Irish University Press, 1969) and the forthcoming *Irish Rebel: John Devoy and America's Fight for Ireland's Freedom* by Terry Golway (St. Martin's Press, 1998).

There are several memoirs and biographies by or about major Irish American politicians or political figures, including *I'd Do It Again: A Record of All My Uproarious Years* by James Michael Curley (Prentice Hall, 1957) and *The Rascal King: The Life and Times of James Michael Curley* by Jack Beatty (Addison-Wesley, 1992); also see *The Last Hurrah* by Edwin O'Connor (Little, Brown, 1956), a novel based on the life of Curley. For more on Tammany Hall see *Plunkitt of Tammany Hall* by William Riordan, with a new introduction by Peter Quinn (Signet, 1995), and *The Tiger: The Rise and Fall of Tammany Hall* by Oliver E. Allen (Addison-Wesley, 1993). For views of some prominent Irish-American political figures see *Boss* by Mike Royko (Dutton, 1971), a study of Chicago's Richard Daley; *Kennedy* by Theodore C. Sorensen (Harper & Row, 1965), a definitive work in the aftermath of Camelot by a Kennedy insider, and *The Founding Father: The Story of Joseph P. Kennedy* by Richard J. Whalen (New American Library, 1964). There are several books on Ronald Reagan and his administration, but for an insider's look see *What I Saw at the Revolution* by Peggy Noonan (Ivy Books, 1991).

A biography of the first Irish Catholic to run for president is *Al Smith, American* by Frank Graham (G.P. Putnam's and Sons, 1945). And there is Smith's own version in *Up to Now: An Autobiography* (Doubleday, 1929). A good general study of "machine politics" is *From the Ward to the White House* by George Reedy (Scribners, 1991). Also see *Beyond the Ballot Box* by Dennis P. Ryan (University of Massachusetts Press, 1983). Another study that dwells at length on the political evolution of the Irish in America is *Beyond the Melting Pot: The Negroes, Puerto Ricans, Jews, Italians & Irish of New York City* by Nathan Glazer and Daniel Patrick Moynihan (MIT Press, 1970). The classic overview of the Irish in America is *The American Irish: A Political and Social Portrait* by William V. Shannon (Macmilllan, 1966).

Portraits of various cities also cover in some detail the role of Irish Americans in local politics; these include *Boston's Immigrants* by Oscar Handlin (Atheneum, 1968), *South Boston* by Thomas H. O'Connor (Northeastern, 1988), and *The Irish in Philadelphia* by Dennis Clark (Temple University Press, 1973). For the role of the Irish in New York City during the Civil War see *The New York City Draft Riots* by Iver Bernstein (Oxford University Press, 1990). An interesting and entertaining novel set during this period is *Banished Children of Eve* by Peter Quinn (Viking, 1994).

CHAPTER 4: THE WORK

Erin's Daughters in America by Hasia R. Diner (Johns Hopkins University Press, 1983) is the central study of Irish women's immigration to America, with particular focus on the employment they found here. For a look at the Irish in organized labor, one should sample *Mike Quill* by Shirley Quill (Devin-Adair, 1985); *The Butte Irish* by David M. Emmons (University of Illinois Press, 1990), the definitive study of the Irish in the mines of Montana; *Mother Jones Speaks*, edited by Philip Foner (Pathfinder Press, 1983); *Union Pacific* by Garry Hogg (Walker and Co., 1967), a study of the building of the transcontinental railroad; and *Lament for the Molly Maguires* by Arthur H. Lewis (Harcourt, Brace and World, 1964).

For insight into professions with an Irish flavor see *Firefighters* by Dennis Smith (Doubleday, 1988) and *The New York City Cops* by Gerald Astor (Scribner's, 1971). And for a look at the life of civil rights activism on the part of at least one Irish American, see the autobiography *Counsel for the Defense* by Paul O'Dwyer (Simon & Schuster, 1979).

CHAPTER 5: THE PLAYERS

There are some major works on Irish America in entertainment and the arts. Among them are *The Big Book of American Irish Culture*, edited by Bob Callahan (Penguin, 1987), *The Irish Voice in America* by Charles Fanning (The University Press of Kentucky, 1990), *Irish American Fiction: Essays in Criticism* by Daniel J. Casey and Robert E. Rhodes (AMS, 1979), *Hibernian Green on the Silver Screen* by Joseph M. Curran (Greenwood, 1989), and *Irish Minstrels and Musicians: The Story of Irish Music* by Francis O'Neill (Mercier Press, 1987, available in the U.S. from Dufour Editions).

The major biography of Eugene O'Neill is the two-volume *O'Neill* by Louis Sheaffer (AMS Press, 1988, reprint edition); O'Neill's plays are available in *Complete Plays*, 3 vols. (Library of America, 1988), and individual plays are available from a variety of publishers.

There are many works of fiction relevant to the Irish-American experience. The works of Finley

Peter Dunne can best be sampled in *Mr. Dooley & the Chicago Irish: The Autobiography of a Nineteenth-Century Ethnic Group*, edited by Charles Fanning (Books Demand, 1976, reprint). Also see *Studs Lonigan: A Trilogy Comprising Young Lonigan, The Manhood of Studs Lonigan, and Judgment Day* by James T. Farrell (Prairie State Books, 1993). Much of John O'Hara's work remains in print; see *Appointment in Sumarra* (Random House, 1982), *Butterfield 8* (Random House, 1994), and *Gibbsville, PA* (Carroll & Graf, 1992). The works of F. Scott Fitzgerald are widely available from a variety of publishers.

Other novels include *The Year of the French* (Holt, 1987), *The Tenants of Time* (Warner, 1989), and *The End of the Hunt* (Warner, 1995), all by Thomas Flanagan; *The Other Side* (Viking, 1989) and *Final Payments* (Random House, 1978) by Mary Gordon; *House of Gold* by Elizabeth Cullinan (Houghton Mifflin, 1970), William Kennedy's three Albany novels—*Legs, Billy Phelan's Greatest Game*, and *Ironweed* are available together in *The Albany Trilogy* (Penguin, 1996). *Object Lessons* by Anna Quindlen (Random House, 1991) provides a modern look at some Irish-American themes in a New York setting. There are many novels by Jimmy Breslin that explore both local and international issues of growing up Irish American; one that focuses on Irish-American workers in New York City is *Table Money* (Penguin, 1986). Tom Kelly's recent novel *The Payback* (Knopf, 1997) explores the trials and tribulations of a young Irish-American working in the subway tunnels of New York City.

Books by younger Irish immigrants include *Breakfast in Babylon* by Emer Martin (Wolfhound Press, 1995), *Fishing the Sloe-Black River: Stories* (Henry Holt & Company, 1995), and *Songdogs* (Henry Holt & Company, 1994) by Colum McCann. For works in a decidedly experimental vein, see *Going to Patchogue* by Thomas McGonigle (Dalkey Archive, 1992) and *The Brooklyn Book of the Dead* by Michael Stephens (Dalkey Archive, 1994). Also, see Stephens's collection of essays, *Green Dreams: Essays Under the Influence of the Irish* (University of Georgia Press, 1994).

CHAPTER 6: THE NEW IRISH

In recent years, Irishness has been given a new coat of paint, as it were. Several books have contributed to this, including *The Inheritance: How Three Families & America Moved from Roosevelt to Reagan and Beyond* by Samuel G. Freedman (Simon & Schuster, 1996), *How the Irish Saved Civilization* by Thomas Cahill (Doubleday, 1996), and *Angela's Ashes* by Frank McCourt (Scribner's, 1997).

For an interesting look at the Irish issues in the White House, see *Daring Diplomacy* by Conor O'Clery (Roberts Rhinehart, 1997, a behind the scenes view of the Clinton Administration's decision to give a visa to The Sinn Fein's Gerry Adams). For a more apolitical take on the Irish and America, see *Sweet Liberty: Travels in Irish America* by Joseph O'Connor (Roberts Rhinehart, 1996), a rollicking tour of Irish America written by Sinéad O'Connor's journalist brother. A weighty look at a chapter in American political ideology is *Not Without Honor* by Richard Powers (Free Press, 1996), a study of Catholics heavily involved in the cold war against Communism. Also see *Irish America and the Ulster Conflict* by Andrew J. Wilson (Catholic University of America Press, 1995) and *Dissent from Irish America* by John P. McCarthy (University of America Press, 1993), a Fordham University professor's criticism of Irish-American support for the IRA.

For poetic explorations of the Irish immigrant experience, see *Poems and Versions 1929–1990* by Brian Coffey (Dedalus, 1991), *Cast in the Fire* (Colin Smythe Ltd., 1986), *Southwards* (LSU, 1992),

American Wake (Blackstaff Press Ltd., 1995), and *The Hellbox* (Oxford University Press, 1998) by Greg Delanty. Also see Gerard Donovan's *Kings and Bicycles* (Salmon, 1996), Nuala Archer's *From a Mobile Home* (Poolbeg Press Ltd., 1995), Eamonn Wall's *Dyckmann 200th St.* (Poolbeg Press Ltd., 1995), Thomas McCarthy's *The Sorrow Garden* (Anvil Books, 1981), and *Against the Storm* (Dolmen Press Ltd., 1985) and *The Sheltered Nest* (Gallery, 1992) by Sean Dunne. There is also the anthology *The Next Parish Over*, edited by Patricia Monaghan (New Rivers Press, 1993) and *Ireland in Exile*, edited by Dermot Bolger (New Island Books, 1993).

P H O T O   C R E D I T S

*

Page I, 248 (top, left), Martha Cooper, Viesti Associates, Inc.; ii, 56, 94, 109, 110, 118, 120 (left), 121 (top), 128, 159, 182 (bottom, left), 201, 229, 255 (center), UPI/Corbis-Bettmann; 1, 17, 138 (bottom), collection of Immigrant City Archives, Lawrence, MA; 2, Charles Staniland, *The Emigrant Ship.* Bradford Art Galleries and Museums/The Bridgeman Art Library, London; 5 (top), National Archives of Ireland; (bottom), Holt Studios International (N. Cattlin)/Photo Researchers, Inc.; 6 (top, bottom), Rodney Charman; (center), Culver Pictures, Inc.; 10, Famine Museum/The Irish Picture Library, Dublin; 12, 30, 75, 80 (bottom), 100, 150, Library of Congress; 15, National Library of Ireland; 16 (top), National Museum of Ireland, courtesy of The Allen Library, Christian Brothers, North Richmond Street, Dublin; (bottom), National Library of Ireland; 18, 99, 101, 103, 138, 157 (top), 182 (top, left), (bottom, right), 187 (right), 189 (right), Culver Pictures, Inc; 19, courtesy of the Bostonian Society; 23, Strokestown Famine Museum; 24, Mary Evans Picture Library; 25, 40, Hulton Getty Picture Collection Limited; 26, John F. Kennedy Library; 27, Eric Antoniou/Corbis-LGI Collection; 33, courtesy the Shaeffer-O'Neill Collection, Connecticut College; 34, photographed by Will Brown/Free Library of Philadelphia; 35, Ulster Historical Foundation; 36, American Stock/Archive Photos; 37, Kelly/Mooney Photography/Corbis Media; 39, 46, Collection of the New-York Historical Society; 43, *Mullen's Alley,* c. 1890. Jacob Riis Collection, #113/Museum of the City of New York; 44, 53 (left), 111, 114, 121 (bottom), 155, 162 (bottom, left), 196, Brown Brothers; 49, Archives of the Archdiocese of Chicago; 51, Ron Anton Rocz; 53 (right), Avery Architectural and Fine Arts Library, Columbia University; 54, Erin Jaeb; 55, 96–97, 113, 119 (top), 162 (top, left), 202, 214 (top), Archive Photos; 59, The Everett Collection; 60, Sisters of Mercy Archives, Chicago; 62, Franciscan Sisters, Little Falls, MN; 70, Mercy Health Center, Oklahoma City; 73, Archives Center of the National Museum of American History, Smithsonian Institution. Photo, Mark Gulezian/Quicksilver; 77, The Library Company of Philadelphia; 78 (left), Chuck Pelley/Tony Stone Images; (center), L.K. Dunn/University of Notre Dame; (right), P. Finger/Villanova University; 80 (top) Anne S. K. Brown Military Collection, Brown University Library; 82–83, 149, Rick Woods; 86, Liz Keating, Old St. Patrick's Church, Chicago; 89, Courtesy Charney Hospital Foundation; 90, Edmund Nagele/FPG International; 92, James Higgins; 98, Daughters of the Republic of Texas Library; 119 (bottom), 214 (bottom), Corbis-